Europe's Coming of Age

To Christos and Panos

EUROPE'S COMING OF AGE

Loukas Tsoukalis

polity

The right of Loukas Tsoukalis to be identified as Author of this Work has been asserted in accordance with the UK Copyright, Designs and Patents Act 1988.

First published in 2023 by Polity Press

Polity Press
65 Bridge Street
Cambridge CB2 1UR, UK

Polity Press
111 River Street
Hoboken, NJ 07030, USA

ISBN-13: 978-1-5095-5455-3

A catalogue record for this book is available from the British Library.

Library of Congress Control Number: 2022935244

Typeset in 11.5 on 14pt Adobe Garamond
by Fakenham Prepress Solutions, Fakenham, Norfolk NR21 8NL
Printed and bound in the UK by CPI Group (UK) Ltd, Croydon

The publisher has used its best endeavours to ensure that the URLs for external websites referred to in this book are correct and active at the time of going to press. However, the publisher has no responsibility for the websites and can make no guarantee that a site will remain live or that the content is or will remain appropriate.

Every effort has been made to trace all copyright holders, but if any have been overlooked the publisher will be pleased to include any necessary credits in any subsequent reprint or edition.

For further information on Polity, visit our website:
politybooks.com

Contents

Acknowledgements

I owe so much to so many people for their work and ideas they generously shared with me, their feedback and criticism, their support and encouragement over the years. During my long European journey, I came across people from different countries and backgrounds, from ivory-tower intellectuals and senior politicians to journalists, businesspeople and others from all walks of life, who made me richer in knowledge and experience – hopefully also more open-minded. The list is indeed very long and I do apologize for not naming them here. I have done so in my earlier work.

The book contains ideas that have been tried out with many audiences and transformed in the process. I have also had the good luck to teach many bright students from all over the world who have taught me back. Let me only mention my latest teaching assignment at the Paris School of International Affairs, Sciences Po. Several chapters in the book have been discussed in class there during the last few years.

I owe a special debt of gratitude to my collaborator in Paris, Selma Bendjaballah, for her extremely valuable contribution and her background work on the democracy chapter; my colleague in Athens, Nikos Koutsiaras, for his friendship, insights and wealth of knowledge; and Matina Meintani for helping me keep things under control.

I have benefitted from research assistance for individual chapters: Babis Avlakiotis on digital technology, Fabian Keske on climate policy and Christos Tsoukalis on inequalities. Emmanuela Doussis helped me understand better the intricacies of climate policy, Yves Mény helped to shed light on the crisis of democracy, and Jolyon Howorth shared some of his wisdom on matters of high politics. Jean Pisani-Ferry offered incisive comments and pertinent advice on an earlier draft of the book and so did three anonymous referees. I am deeply grateful to all of them.

In the last stages of writing this book, I was very fortunate to be offered a collection of essays published in my honour by Oxford University

Press. *Europe's Transformations* is an excellent book from which I have learned a great deal. It was an immense honour and I am deeply grateful to editors and contributors, all good friends and true Europeans.

I owe special thanks to John Thompson, who welcomed my manuscript to Polity Press, who masterminded the whole process leading to publication, and with whom I have had an extremely fruitful collaboration. Many thanks are also due to Fiona Sewell for her extremely meticulous copy-editing, and to Rachel Moore, Julia Davies and the whole Polity team for an excellent job done.

The book is dedicated to my sons Christos and Panos. They are both economists – they prefer the classical term 'political economists'. It seems to run in the family. They help keep me on my toes and abreast of some of the current literature. Together with other people of their generation, I hope they succeed in making our world better.

My wife, Maria Logotheti, has been a continuous source of support for me and much more. I have no words to thank her.

April 2022
Loukas Tsoukalis

Introduction: Declaration of Intent

This book draws on many years of study and periodic direct involvement, albeit modest, in the construction of a European economic and political entity that seeks to forge unity out of the wide diversity of the old continent. A strange entity indeed in a world of sovereign nation states, a revolutionary yet peaceful political experiment in a part of the world that had invented the nation state a few centuries back. I mean of course the European Union (EU).

Europe is certainly more than the EU, which sometimes tends to appropriate the name all for itself. Britain is an integral and very important part of Europe – no need to explain further – and so are not only Switzerland and Norway, but Russia too with a vast territory across Eurasia and a key role in European history and civilization. The EU does not represent the whole of Europe, but it is the only organized form of European integration (much more than cooperation) that makes a substantial difference in economic terms, and in political and potentially strategic terms as well. In other words, it is the only manifestation of European unity that has a significant impact on how individual European countries interact with each other and with the rest of the world.

For me, it has been a lifetime affair starting when I was a student and going on for several decades regardless of many let-downs. It has been an affair mostly of the mind and less of the heart. Difficult to fall in love with the EU, isn't it? Unless you succeed in purifying your love object from grey bureaucrats, interminable negotiations, often impenetrable jargon lost in translation, and long-winded compromises that make it difficult to inspire even those who approach it with the best of intentions. Yet I remain convinced, and increasingly so with time, that the construction of a European entity which is more than the sum of its parts represents the best hope for Europeans to preserve peace, freedom, democracy and prosperity at home. And it is the best hope for Europeans collectively to defend common interests and values in a world that is both dangerously unstable and highly asymmetrical in terms of the power and influence exerted by different actors, be they states or private companies.

But how much do Finns and Greeks, Italians and Irish really have in common, all of them proudly carrying their own very different baggage of history? Not much, would be the spontaneous answer, yet a rather superficial one. Because what brings all these different peoples together is precisely their shared experience of close cooperation and open borders over several decades, common institutions and laws, a common market with common standards, and a common currency for most of them. I would add basic common values as well for the large majority at least. All these things form part of shared citizenship in this postmodern European entity in the making, much more so than flags, hymns and myths, which had been essential ingredients of national sovereignty in the past – and they still are. But Europe is not a traditional nation state and will never be one. By necessity, Europe is therefore being built with different materials. And since there is no previous experience to rely on, it is largely a process of trial and error. It is also a hard slog because the forces of inertia are strong.

During more than seven decades, there have been many successes and failures, one of the biggest failures being Brexit. But the overall balance sheet is very positive. The best proof is that the EU has grown enormously over the years in terms of members and what it does. It has constantly accumulated new functions, including functions that lie at the very core of sovereignty, in a rapidly changing economic and political environment. European integration has reached a critical stage. The main argument of this book is that the old continent needs to become at last a political adult: Europe's coming of age.

Individual European countries today stand little chance of effectively defending their interests and values. This is also true of European Great Powers that are no longer global powers, such as France and Germany, as well as the UK, which has now decided to go on its own. Alas, war has not been banished for good from Europe and the post-Cold War order is no longer. Russia's invasion of Ukraine was a rude awakening. Meanwhile, the centre of gravity has been shifting to Asia and the Pacific, China has been challenging US hegemony, and Europe's protector of last resort is going through a deep internal crisis. In this world, the existential question for Europeans will be whether they are able to collectively define and defend common interests and values, defend their freedoms first and foremost. This inevitably raises the question of how to make the difficult transition from soft to hard power, which most Europeans have been trying to evade for far too long. Are they ready to take greater responsibility for their defence as part of the Atlantic alliance?

Europeans have lost their missionary zeal, which may not be necessarily a bad thing. Today, Europeans are mostly interested in preserving their way of life and prosperity at home and much less in trying to export them to the rest of the world. You may call it cynicism; others might prefer instead to think of it as hard realism based on experience. Without false modesty, we may recognize that Europe today is far ahead of most (if not all) other parts of the world in terms of individual freedoms, democracy, inclusive societies and sustainable development, even though lagging in terms of technological strength and military prowess.

The European model of intense cooperation among very different countries has been tried for many years and passed the test often against the odds. It can make a truly valuable contribution in a highly interdependent world in which both international cooperation and the defence of global commons are in woefully short supply. But no illusions: in a world with bullies, you also need to project hard power.

Meanwhile, the gap between policies and politics has grown ever wider. The old consensus is long gone. In times of large inequalities, growing uncertainty and rising social discontent, nationalism offers an easy but highly misleading and dangerous prospectus for escaping from today's reality of close interdependence. In some countries, it is already touch and go between the forces of nationalism and those who believe in a shared European future. Individual freedoms are at stake as well as institutional checks and balances. Democracy is not a given in any country. It constantly needs to be fought for. I believe that a stronger European centre can help in defending fundamental democratic rights in the constituent parts, sometimes protecting member countries from their own bad self. But can the centre hold when the extremes pull apart?

Running a common currency in a highly decentralized political system and relying heavily on non-elected technocrats to act as saviours of last resort is economically costly and politically risky – even more so while trying to steer a course between stagnation and inflation. These are not easy times. And they are also times of changing paradigms. Neoliberal ideas have been tried and found short on delivery. We are witnessing the return of the state for a variety of reasons including the unequal effects of market integration, rapidly growing politicization of international economic exchange, climate change, the pandemic and now much greater emphasis on defence. But what does the return of the state mean for this strange beast called the EU? Regression, further expansion or a new form of symbiosis with its members?

The first part of the book partly draws on personal experience, like extracts from a diary on the European journey. It is also a short and eclectic history of European integration of the last fifty years or so, concentrating on key turning points and drawing lessons from successes and failures. It ends with a provisional balance sheet in terms of the changing relationship between market and state, the limitations of common institutions, and Europe's manifest weakness in a world of power politics. When the facts change, can Europe adjust?

The second part is the most substantial part of the book and the more demanding for both writer and reader. It is also the most analytical, although written in plain English as much as possible, avoiding jargon and the introverted discussion among Europe experts. It deals with the main challenges and choices facing us today. They include the euro growing up to become a fully fledged currency; large inequalities between and within countries and the role the European centre can play in strengthening social contracts; Europe's lagging in high tech and its ambition to lead in the greening of economies; the fraught search for a common foreign and security policy that will require at some point the creation of a European defence pillar within NATO; and the equally fraught search for democracy beyond the nation state and still short of a federation.

The book looks at the bigger picture. I know it is risky because the bigger picture can easily turn fuzzy. The reader will be the ultimate judge. It is also a book with an argument, and it does not pretend to be value-free. But how can it ever be when trying to understand the economic not to mention the political process?

I am a Greek who loves his country and does not hate foreigners, a convinced European who is often critical of what the EU does and more often of what it does not do. I am a liberal democrat who believes strongly in the freedom of the individual and in policies that empower citizens. I recognize the strengths of the market mechanism, but I am not at all indifferent to the trade-off between efficiency and equity. I believe in inclusive societies and therefore in policies that correct and compensate for market weaknesses and failures. And I also believe that, in today's world, sharing sovereignty between a European political entity in the making and individual countries can deliver all the above much more effectively than European countries on their own.

I feel strongly about people who are indifferent to the plight of others outside their borders, yet I remain painfully aware of the threshold of tolerance of our societies to large and unregulated immigrant flows. I know that Europe's comparative advantage lies with soft power, but never forget it will not be enough in a world where Might often becomes Right. Notwithstanding, I feel extremely uncomfortable with Manichean views of a world divided between goodies and baddies – we being by an act of God always on the side of goodies.

If you think most of the above views are totally alien, you may not want to read further. If you have doubts about some of them, please give it a try. In any case, the reader has been warned.

In the concluding chapter, I come back to the broader questions. What does coming of age mean for Europe's fledgling political entity? Are enough Europeans ready for it? Who will lead in the next stage of integration? And crucially, what happens if they fail? In these times of transition – the end of an era? – Europe is facing choices that are indeed of an existential nature. My ambition in writing this book is to contribute to a better understanding of these choices and the high stakes associated with them. A better understanding is a precondition for an informed democratic debate leading to action – and we desperately need both. In times when fake news and conspiracy theories are in abundance, let us fight back with facts and rational arguments, and then act.

PART I

Extracts from a Diary on the European Journey

When Everything Seemed Possible

Discovering Europe

I discovered Europe as a political entity – or rather a political entity in the making – as a young student at the College of Europe in Bruges back in the early 1970s. The College was then more of a breeding ground for missionaries of the European idea, as we used to call it in those days, than the training centre for well-qualified, multilingual professionals that it was to become in subsequent years. Until then, I had a general, not very precise, notion of Europe as the centre of the world, that was perhaps no longer so, yet unwilling to admit it; a small continent very rich in history, science and culture, enormously diverse for its size, that had produced the best and the worst in terms of political, economic and social organization. The European history I had been taught previously was mostly about kings and queens, revolutions, wars and imperial conquests.

In Bruges, I discovered that some Europeans had begun in the decades following the Second World War to write a totally different chapter in European history: it was about peace and reconciliation between old foes, cooperation and the opening of borders. Those even more ambitious among them added an international dimension to it since no European country was any longer calling the shots. The two super-powers, the United States and the Soviet Union, had after all imposed the new order on the old continent, and former Great European Powers acted as auxiliaries at best. The aim was therefore for Europeans to regain through unity some of the power and influence they had lost on the global stage. But illusions of Great Power status die hard, while some people chose to concentrate their efforts in gaining influence by courting those with real power in Washington DC. In the UK, you usually found both types merged into one.

At the time, my native country, Greece, was under a military dicta-torship. On the periphery of the western side of the Cold War divide,

Greece had been previously rescued by the British and the Americans from communist rule during the civil war that followed a ruthless occupation under the Nazis. This in turn followed a long pattern of foreign interventions, for good and sometimes for bad, since the Greek war of independence in the 1820s, the first in the Balkans against the Ottoman empire. Greece was one more example of a country that had been for long the object rather than the subject of European diplomacy. For a young Greek such as myself, who had no intention of returning home to live and work under the colonels, this new phase of European history also offered the prospect of a democratic Greece as an equal (more or less) partner in the European construction. In my student days in Bruges, however, this looked more like a wild dream than a real prospect.

Back then, I was a young man who appreciated the virtues of democracy perhaps more than did my fellow students from luckier countries who enjoyed them in real life. Influenced by the May 1968 events in Paris and the general zeitgeist, my political reflexes were predominantly anti-establishment and left-wing, like those of so many young people at the time who felt ready to change the world. But I was also attracted by the ongoing integration project in Europe: revolutionary in some ways, I recognized, although essentially an elitist project run mostly by politicians who were at the opposite end of the political spectrum from me. A small number of *illuminati*, an enlightened minority consisting mostly of Christian democrats and liberals from different countries, were conspiring for the common good, or so they thought – and they were subsequently proved to be damn right, let us admit it – yet with little, if any, popular participation and support. Their hope was that if they succeeded in delivering the goods in the shape of peace and prosperity, people would follow. It was for me a crash course in both political realism and long-term vision. Yet even today, I often find it difficult to reconcile my support for the European project with some things done in its name.

I then returned to England, where I had done my undergraduate studies, to write my doctoral thesis in Oxford. I had extremely ambitious ideas: a young economist with a healthy dose of politicization who wanted to write a magnum opus in his early twenties on the new European political and economic system in the making. My Oxford professors tried to bring me down to earth, as should have been expected. They surely had much more experience than I had. But with few exceptions, they also treated the idea of a European system in the making as little more than daydreaming. The UK had just joined what for most Brits was a Common Market, with the appendix of that dreadful common agricultural policy, as they saw it. I insisted and ended up on a lonely path writing about the politics and economics of European monetary integration, a relatively small concession on my part. Believe it or not, the nine members of what was still then the European Communities, the UK included, had embarked on the most ambitious project yet, namely the creation of a full economic and monetary union (EMU) by 1980.

It failed abysmally and the UK was the first to abandon ship, while the rest were trying to keep it afloat in the huge storm unleashed when US President Nixon decided to unilaterally abandon dollar–gold convertibility and later fixed exchange rates. Those two decisions taken in the early 1970s marked the end of the Bretton Woods system that had been created by the Americans at the peak of multilateralist thinking (those good old days!) with the help of John Maynard Keynes as an economic adviser to their junior partner, the UK, back in 1944.

EMU in the 1970s proved to be a big non-event. In my doctoral thesis, I tried to explain the reasons it had been set up and later failed: a project of high politics with faulty economics, unrealistic political assumptions and disastrous timing. And yet, the main conclusion I dared put forward in 1975, when I submitted the thesis, was that monetary union was bound to resurface and become again a big issue on the European political agenda. I explained the reasons, political and economic, I thought it would be so at a time when monetary union looked deader than a dead duck. Luckily for me, a few people, including my examiners, thought there was something in this unorthodox thesis and decided to award me the degree. The thesis was further developed and published:[1] my first book at the age of twenty-seven. It was republished forty years later, and I was truly flattered to discover that people thought it still had some relevance.

Meanwhile, one pioneer Oxford don, Wilfrid Knapp, almost single-handedly raised the money and created a fellowship in European studies, the first ever in the University of Oxford. He thought that Oxford should develop knowledge and promote research in European integration now that the UK was a full member of the common enterprise, while most of his colleagues treated the subject (and the new post) with disbelief. An old university that respects its history and traditions cannot be expected, after all, to indulge in such trendy, if not vacuous, subjects.

I ended up being elected to this new fellowship, proud as anybody and fresh from my doctoral degree, yet from a country that had only very recently returned to democracy (miracles happened even then!) but was still a few years away from being admitted to the elite European club. Oxford may respect tradition but also prides itself on being unconventional. On this occasion, I was the beneficiary of Oxford unconventionality. And because the university had, and always has, connections in high places, I remember myself soon donning the (figurative) hat of a specialist adviser and helping the chair of the Select Committee on the European Communities of the House of Lords throw awkward questions at ministers and other lesser mortals, or being part of delegations to Brussels. Fellow German participants, among others, at those meetings often rolled their eyes in disbelief when they discovered that the long-haired and bearded young man with an unpronounceable name had only a Greek passport.

To my second country by adoption where I spent a quarter of a century, always an alien strictly speaking yet with the feeling of being warmly welcome, I owe a deep debt of gratitude for what I learned and the many opportunities I was offered. I never felt discriminated against as a foreigner – the idea, though, of being a fellow European meant little for many of my British colleagues. Tolerance and open-mindedness on the one hand, the provincialism of little England sprayed with a strong dose of nostalgia for the days of the empire on the other, have long coexisted. Alas, the balance risks tipping too much in one (the wrong) direction after Brexit.

From my youth, I have been a committed European, and am still hanging on, often against the odds and despite many disappointments on the way. The two countries I know best are the ones that have had the most turbulent relationship with European integration over the years. One has now left for good – perhaps too strong a term for a relationship so much shaped by geography and history – while the other has, remarkably, escaped a similar fate being thrust upon it during the euro crisis.

Many of my British friends still find it hard to believe that instead of Grexit we now have Brexit. True, the two countries are very different in so many ways. They are different also in the way they approach Europe. For the overwhelming majority among Greek politicians and the Greek public at large, Europe, unpleasant and punishing though it can be – and Greeks are always good at finding reasons to grumble and blame others for their misfortunes – is the only realistic option available. In Britain, on the other hand, many people believe they have many other options. They (and we all) will soon find out.

Ever bigger and more intrusive

One key feature of European integration over this already long journey that started more than seventy years ago has been its remarkable expansion in terms of both functions and members. Starting with two sectors of the economy, namely coal and steel, later destined for the dustbin of economic history (the former more than the latter), and ending up with just about everything being discussed in European councils, with virtually no national taboos left, and from six to now twenty-seven members (and probably more to come), it has been quite a journey.

Surely, there must be something in it, unless you imagine there is a never-ending epidemic of masochism on the European continent and/or an all-powerful conspiracy of elites against peoples. The rise of anti-systemic parties and movements, mostly on the right of the political spectrum in recent years, has given some political credence to the latter explanation. It has become fashionable to attack elites and the usual response of defenders of the 'system' has been to denounce populism. Yet, instead of simply indulging in a dialogue of the deaf, we need to try and understand why the anti-elitist message has gained considerable public support across Europe and beyond. Because the stakes are high, and because public discontent is real and not groundless. In simple words, we need to do something about it – and urgently.

But first things first. For several decades, the European idea turned into a project that kept acquiring ever more functions and members. In the process, it was itself transformed and not always by design. Events frequently have an independent logic of their own. From an economic liberalizer trying to eliminate all kinds of border controls, Europe turned more and more into a regulator writ large. The creation of the single market, a never-ending process which began in the mid-1980s, aimed at creating a large economic space with its own rules and the promotion of European champions able to withstand global competition. The single market contributed to growth and prosperity, but it also meant that Europe began to penetrate the nooks and crannies of our national systems and societies. And many people, including inveterate free marketeers who live under the illusion that markets do not need rules, were in for a shock.

Meanwhile, local dictators had fallen or just negotiated their exit in southern Europe. The young democracies rushed to join Europe, starting with my own country, Greece, which was finally admitted in 1981. It was surely a huge vote of confidence in the European project, but also a big challenge. New members brought with them relatively closed economies and societies, lower levels of development and fragile institutions. Democracy and modernization were hence added to the list of key objectives of European integration, while parts of the Brussels bureaucracy gradually turned into a development agency. It was a foretaste of the main and much bigger dish that was to follow with the accession of the former communist countries of central and eastern Europe.

There were surely many bumps and crises on the way, but over the long term the trend was blindingly clear, or so many people thought. European believers and the high priests in Brussels needed no further proof of the virtues and inbuilt automaticity of the whole process – with nuances if you cared to look closer. The European project enjoyed wide public support and looked even prettier from those countries outside queueing to join in. Europe's fathers (there were literally no mothers in the early stages of integration) were right after all: you lead the way with a visionary idea and people will eventually follow. But not to the point of enthusiasm and mobilization. True, the big majority of Europeans across countries (less so the Brits) over the years saw regional integration as a good thing, but never as a first, second or even third priority. This was still a matter for the *illuminati* and the growing numbers of Europe professionals. Hence, it remained an elitist project based, as the jargon goes, on the permissive consensus[2] of European citizens so long as it lasted.

In 1979, the first direct elections to the European Parliament took place. Combined with ever-growing powers granted to an institution that had begun life as a consultative assembly, direct elections were meant to inject more democracy into the European construction. But citizens were not wildly impressed: rates of participation in European elections were relatively low by national standards. European elections long remained essentially second-rate elections with mostly second-rate politicians who were much better paid than their counterparts in national parliaments, yet with usually less power than at home. It has been a slow climb for European democracy. Politics has remained essentially national and local; the rest is secondary. And Europe continues to this day to produce many more policies than politics.

As the project expanded, so did bureaucracy, together with all kinds of satellite agencies around it and, of course, numerous lobbyists. Academics specializing in European affairs were among those who were rapidly integrated (or lured) into the system. Research projects were offered in abundance, consultancy opportunities and lots of money to spend. European construction turned quickly into a big operation and a lucrative profession for many. For people armed with language skills and the right specializations, especially from poorer countries joining in successive rounds of enlargement, European institutions offered the chance of a lifetime: interesting jobs, multinational environment, lots of travel, and payslips that were a multiple of what they could get at home. As was to be expected, they voted with their feet and moved to Brussels.

With money and bureaucracy came waste and corruption. And to fight the latter, people invented more complicated rules and even more bureaucracy. But let us not make too much out of it. European bureaucracy is still small by the standards of any middle-sized country, while European waste and corruption is more often the product of malpractices at national and local level. Europe is surely not a family of saints, but whose family is? To be fair, some of our Scandinavian members, for example, with stronger traditions of good governance, have legitimate reasons to complain about the misbehaviour of several other members of their wider adopted family.

My own professional life almost coincided with the acceleration of European integration, taking place within the wider context of globalization and rapid technological progress that further facilitated mobility across borders. I was among the luckier of the post-war baby boomers in Europe – any comparison with the prospects of today's young generations is truly depressing for the latter. And in those earlier times, my career took off fast. I got a lifetime job in Oxford teaching international political economy and European integration, and returned to Bruges as a young, part-time director of the economics department. I also became the editor of a prestigious European journal, produced books and was always on the move. It was my fortune to work on what I really believed in, and I thoroughly enjoyed working with people from different cultures and backgrounds.

The number of Europeans who regularly crossed borders was still relatively small at the time; it grew exponentially in subsequent decades. Everything was possible, so it seemed, while I continued my balancing act between teaching and research on the one hand, policy on the other. During the 1980s, I worked for two Council presidencies of Greece, now a full member, with an ambassadorial rank. They were challenging experiences, to put it diplomatically, given Greece's idiosyncratic behaviour during its early years (and not only) of membership of the club.

I visited Brussels regularly as the capital of the European entity in the making, and also because I had so many friends there. My feelings, I must confess, were always rather mixed. I learned about current policies and future European plans straight from the source of power, which is often quite different from what you read in books – and I wanted that. But I also felt uncomfortable in the centre of Eurocracy: too much horse trading and double talk, short on meritocracy, while the mercenaries were fast taking over from the early missionaries. Perhaps all this is inevitable once an idea is translated into a political project. I continued my visits while choosing to keep a safe distance to preserve my own independence and the right to be critical. Speak truth to power: a good guiding principle for a young man with ambition and enough scruples to keep his ambition on a leash.

While things were going my way, I felt a strong itch for change and decided to leave Oxford for Athens. It was indeed a radical move and many of my Oxford colleagues and friends thought I was making a huge mistake. Oxford was offering me a highly stimulating environment and it was not stopping me from doing many other things. What did I want more? I always remember the conversation I had before I left with an older colleague who belonged to the traditional school of Oxford dons and who put a straight question to me: 'Why the hell do you want to leave? Isn't Oxford good enough for you?' In my answer, I mumbled all the obvious good things about Oxford and how much I had learned and enjoyed my life there. I meant every word. And I dared add: 'But Oxford doesn't have much to do with the real world.' To which, he immediately replied with a rhetorical question and genuine surprise: 'But do you like the real world?' That was the end of our conversation. We were clearly from different planets.

What I did not, however, confess to my interlocutor was that I was also flirting with the idea of becoming more actively engaged in public life, perhaps going into politics. And politics remained national, I never had any illusions about that. I later discovered through personal experience that if Greek politics was indeed the only available version of the real world, at least for me, my Oxford interlocutor may have had a point after all. But still, no regrets. Admittedly, if I were older and had made the move from Oxford to Athens say twenty or thirty years earlier, the change would have been much more radical. But in the age of increasingly borderless Europe and rapid technological change, mobility and regular exchange had become so much easier and actual location more relative – for some people at least, including myself.

Triumph and hubris

My return to Greece just about coincided with events in Europe that only happen once in a lifetime if that. I mean the collapse of communist regimes on the eastern side of the notorious Iron Curtain and the disintegration of the Soviet Union. We had so far learned from bitter experience (remember Budapest 1956, Prague 1968, Berlin and Gdansk in recurring fashion) that local totalitarian rule backed by Soviet tanks had created rock-solid regimes based on fear. Sovietologists explained how the system worked and most of them offered little hope of democratic change. And then suddenly, we were witnessing those regimes collapsing, because the top man in Moscow, named Mikhail Gorbachev, was no longer willing to support it. The Berlin Wall that had separated East from West for decades also came down peacefully.

Who would have guessed it? The honest answer was very few people indeed. Most of us were totally surprised and very pleasantly so. I for one knew precious little about those countries that were now celebrating their freedom and keen to join the liberal democracies and market economies of the West. In one of the few visits I had made to the 'other side', notably to Prague as a young student in the early 1970s, I remember discovering with real shock that the local variety of communism in the country 'liberated' once again by Soviet tanks in 1968 felt much worse than the military dictatorship we had back home. It was a political revelation for the young left-winger I was then, and I have never forgotten the experience. The colonels back home were ugly but true amateurs compared with communist apparatchiks in what was still Czechoslovakia. In 1989, communist regimes in Europe disappeared with a bang – or was it just a whimper?[3] It was, of course, a political triumph for the West, and indirectly also for the European integration that newly liberated countries wanted to be part of. The reunification of Europe at last.

We were soon to discover that Washington meant much more than Brussels for our partners-to-be, and for obvious reasons. They owed their liberation largely to the United States as leader of the Western alliance, and they have continued all along to rely on US and NATO guarantees for their security – at least for those who joined in time – against the big neighbour to the east and former oppressor, namely Russia as the inheritor of the Union of Soviet Socialist Republics (USSR). I was told the story of a senior Spanish politician on a visit to Poland after the fall of the Iron Curtain to whom his local interlocutor explained that Poland owed its liberation to the United States and the Pope. He replied, with tongue in cheek, that Spain owed something different to the United States and the Pope, namely forty years of dictatorship. In Greece, the Pope at least had nothing to do with our shorter-lived dictatorship. Try now to reconcile such divergent historical experiences and merge them into a common European foreign policy: it will take time and much effort at best.

In the context of European integration, 1989 was a huge turning point. The fall of the Berlin Wall raised the immediate prospect of German reunification, while the collapse of the old Soviet order produced a litany of countries keen to join common European institutions.[4] The response to this twin challenge, spread over several years, ended up changing radically the shape of the European project. It also changed the balance of power in Europe, a term that regional integration was meant to do away with.

François Mitterrand, Margaret Thatcher and Helmut Kohl, the political heavyweights of the time, knew they were taking decisions that would shape European geopolitics for many years to come. Neither Thatcher nor Mitterrand was keen on German reunification, to put it mildly, although the French president was quicker in realizing its inevitability. And once he did so, he decided to follow the example of Robert Schuman, the French foreign minister back in 1950 when faced with an earlier version of the German problem. Schuman had tried to bind Germany, back then a defeated and divided Germany, within a strong institutional framework of European integration. For Schuman, the instrument had been the coal and steel community; for Mitterrand, it was the currency.

A European monetary union once again as a means of achieving closer European integration: money is at the centre of economic policy and the currency one of the key symbols of sovereignty. What better way of getting closer to a true European union? Meanwhile, the Germans would have to give up their beloved Deutschemark, the strongest European currency, and the incarnation of the post-war German economic miracle. It was Cartesian logic and the French at their best as producers of big ideas and major political initiatives driving European integration. This was, however, only one side of the story. The other was that the Germans ended up drawing the red lines and shaping the economic content of monetary union: a familiar division of labour, as it was to develop later, between the two countries.

A currency union would require transfers of sovereignty that the French themselves were most reluctant to accept, and the Germans as well, although from a different perspective. However, in an imperfect monetary union with fixed exchange rates, the experience of the previous almost twenty years indicated that Germany would have a structural advantage. It was based on the country's capacity to produce lower wage increases and inflation than the rest and hence gain competitiveness at the expense of partners who could no longer resort to devaluations.

This structural advantage combined with size explained Germany's dominant position in previous European exchange rate arrangements. My old doctoral thesis on monetary union came in handy. But Mitterrand did not delve into trivial(!) economics, nor did Kohl; they only dealt with matters of high politics which they understood better. At the time, Jacques Delors was president of the Commission, the president with the biggest impact ever. Delors did understand economics well, but even he could not deliver the politics.

The result was Maastricht:[5] the most ambitious European treaty ever, which committed member countries to a monetary union by 1999, with formal opt-outs for the UK and Denmark. Cynical observers of the European scene hastened to remind people that a similar engagement had been undertaken back in 1970, and never fulfilled. 'Treaties are like roses and young girls [add boys and more to be politically correct today]. They last while they last', General de Gaulle had famously told us years back, to the shock and horror of disciples of international law. Yet this time was different.

Maastricht, linked in turn to German unification, was meant to shape things European for decades. It was a French initiative to deal with a German problem following in the tradition set by Robert Schuman, the initiator of European integration. It used economic means to achieve largely political ends, which was again consistent with the strategy of the earlier *illuminati*. And it was surely a project of elites who led the way hoping that people would follow once they began to see the material benefits resulting from the common European currency.

Germany provided the best illustration of the elites-know-best approach to politics. Opinion polls showed a majority among Germans did not want to replace their beloved Deutschemark with a common currency that would be jointly managed with other Europeans, many of whom they did not trust in sharing strongly held German views about monetary stability and rules-based budgetary housekeeping. But their representatives in the two houses of parliament voted overwhelmingly on a cross-party consensus in favour of the Maastricht treaty, because in Germany's representative democracy they were meant to know best, and they got away with it. It is difficult to imagine a similar thing happening today on such an important issue. Political elites are now kept on a short leash by their voters because the trust is no longer there. And they are thus given much less time to deliver. As for the French, who dared consult their citizens in a referendum in 1992, they only scraped through with a 51 per cent majority. Without that extra 1 per cent, none of us would have euros in our pockets today.

Maastricht created a very imperfect monetary union because that was all that was politically feasible, and reflected the economic ideas prevailing at the time. The signatories of the new treaty agreed to create a monetary union without being willing to endow it with the institutions and policy instruments necessary to make it viable in the long term. But was it not the way the European construction had been built all along? True in part, although this time Europeans were at risk of defying the laws of gravity. A common currency is a very different proposition from a single market. To add insult to injury, the plan for monetary union relied on very imperfect economics that assumed among other things efficient financial markets (really?), while just wishing for economic convergence, perhaps through the act of a friendly god. Wishful thinking instead of sound economics is often the weapon of last resort for politicians.

Finally, the euro did replace national currencies just before the turn of the century, according to plan and against the odds. More countries joined monetary union than anybody had imagined, Germans included, who had hoped for a small group of like-minded euro partners. It was one of those instances, decisive and hopefully not fatal in the long term, when Europeans collectively surprised doubters of the common project through their determination to fulfil joint objectives. Thus, unlike earlier attempts at monetary integration, this time high politics trumped economics.

There was surely an element of hubris with the decision to create the euro, and nemesis was bound to follow. Famous authors of ancient Greek tragedies had told us so thousands of years back. The creation of the euro did not only affect countries that decided to swap their national currencies for it. Monetary union also had a big long-term impact on the UK's reluctant membership of the European project. Maastricht was a big step too far for the British, who could not stop their partners from taking it. They surely did not share the political ambitions associated with the move to the common currency, although admittedly many of their economic objections were pretty much well founded. The British thus felt they had no option but to opt out, and this later proved to be only the first in a series of successive opt-outs, including notably the Schengen agreement that created Europe without borders.

The British felt increasingly uncomfortable with the accelerating pace of European integration. They could no longer reach the brake or get hold of the wheel, and they were not used to the status of a frustrated passenger in the back seat, unless of course the driver was an American. In the back seat with a French or, even worse, a German driver: it was too much for the British. After all, they had never been very happy with the journey, even less so with the pre-announced destination. With the benefit of hindsight, the creation of the euro was a key turning point for Britain's participation in the European project. The big financial crisis that followed a decade later, together with the immigration crisis and domestic British politics, finally combined to produce Brexit. But it had been a long process, an accident waiting to happen. It finally did when the passenger in the back seat opened the door and jumped out while the vehicle was in motion: usually not a wise thing to do.

2

Learning from Crises

Lopsided integration

In 1991, Oxford University Press published my new book on *The New European Economy*.[1] It was inspired by the new phase of integration and highlighted the emergence of a European economic system that was much more than simply the sum of highly interdependent national economies: a European economic system with its own rules and regulations.

I tried to understand the functioning of this new entity, the linkages between policies and politics, the single market and money, liberalization and regulation, efficiency and equity. I also tried to trace the ever-changing relations between the regional entity and its national parts, between Europe and the rest of the world. It was a highly ambitious exercise that went very much against the general trend of specialization. *Fachidioten* is an impolite term in German that describes experts with little or no understanding of the wider context of their specialization, literally translated as 'specialized idiots'. I have always struggled to escape in my work from narrow specialization and the artificial boundaries drawn by academic disciplines, albeit always at the risk of sacrificing depth for breadth. Many colleagues at university were never sure whether I was an economist or a political scientist, although they all knew I had this strange obsession with Europe.

Before writing these lines, I looked again at the three editions of *The New European Economy*, the last one published in 1997. I was concerned then about the growing gap between economic and political integration in Europe, the likely negative effects of the liberalization wave on market stability and social equity, the weakening capacity of the state to deliver its part of the domestic social contract in a world of high capital mobility and withering economic borders. I wrote among other things about the likely deflationary impact of monetary union, the unbalanced system created at Maastricht and the high risks associated with it. I was surely not the only one in doing so, yet a member of a dwindling minority back then.

In the concluding chapter of the third edition, I wrote about the losers from economic liberalization and technological change and reproduced a phrase from an article I had read in the *Financial Times* as early as 1994: 'In this bewildering new world the nation-state is no longer an engine of modernisation. Instead, it has become the "Jesus rail" – the handle that a white knuckled passenger clings onto shouting "Jesus", as the car he is travelling in hurtles round a blind corner.'[2] It was the new world of globalization in its neoliberal version combined with rapid technological change, the effects of which were to become blindingly obvious in the years to come.

I took up the issue of winners and losers and developed it further subsequently. I also had the opportunity to play a role in the creation of a European policy instrument that was meant precisely to address the problem of winners and losers within European countries. I did so while wearing the hat of adviser to the then president of the European Commission and – rather unexpectedly – succeeded in convincing the UK prime minister, Tony Blair, who held then the presidency of the European Council, to underwrite it. Blair was one of the few British prime ministers with a natural empathy for European integration, although he never invested enough political capital to help carry with him the rest of his party and British society at large. He also had Gordon Brown to contend with. The European globalization fund was finally set up in 2006. It was, I believe, a good idea although later reduced to a symbolic gesture, the kind that Europe often resorts to when consensus is superficial.

Winners and losers were strangely enough not much of an issue among followers of the Third Way[3] in Blair's New Labour. Together with sister parties of the centre left, they dominated the European political scene for several years before and after the turn of the new century. They believed in globalization and economic liberalization, including financial markets, which they wanted to complement with domestic reforms and effective welfare and empowerment policies. These were the years of triumph before the fall of the reformist centre left. For some years, I sat on the board of the European think tank of the British Labour Party and had the opportunity to take part in several 'Progressive Governance' gatherings that took place around the globe. Reformist social democrats did not, however, pay enough attention to the grossly unequal effects of globalization and technological change, or to the inherent instability of financial markets. They later paid a heavy political price for it.

Meanwhile, I had a spell of a few years in London when I took up a newly created university chair with Greek funds at the European Institute of the London School of Economics (LSE). London was growing fast as the most cosmopolitan city in Europe, a globalization hub, and a great place to be if you could afford it. Some of London's old inhabitants no longer could. They were gradually pushed out to long-distance commuter suburbs and satellite towns and replaced by wealthier foreigners with global skills and well-paid jobs, usually in the City, as well as by a motley collection of global oligarchs and rentiers.

London became a global city while remaining the capital of an increasingly unequal and divided country. The financial sector has a much bigger share of the economy in Britain than in most European countries, while the British political class took economic liberalism more seriously than most of their counterparts in the rest of western Europe. Economic liberalism and free trade had been, after all, one of the most successful exports of the erstwhile British empire. The result was a dynamic economy that acted as a magnet for foreign skills, yet with an increasingly unequal distribution of gains and hence more divided. Years later, the Brexit referendum of 2016 was like the opening of a Pandora's box that let out all kinds of internal divisions in British society.

Although standards remained, luckily, very high in both places, the academic environment in London around the turn of the century was quite different from the one I had been familiar with in Oxford. Better organized, run more like a company with regular assessment of measurable outputs and in constant search of funding as compared with the more decentralized and often anarchic system I had known in my earlier days in Oxford. The latter, however, showed more patience for brilliant minds who may (or may not) one day produce an idea that could change the way we think about the world. Oxford took a more relaxed approach with time, had more tolerance for eccentrics and perhaps also had a touch of decadence that mature societies (and universities) should be able to afford. It took me some time to realize that the difference was not just between LSE and Oxford. It had more to do with the big change in British universities and British society in general ushered in by the Thatcher revolution, for good and for bad.

The Thatcher revolution was a rather extreme version of the (neo) liberal revolution that spread throughout the Western world from the late 1970s and turned into an ideological monopoly (*la pensée unique*, as the French used to call it) after 1989, when the threat posed by Soviet communism simply disappeared. It was the end of History proclaimed by Francis Fukuyama,[4] although later proved to be rather premature. The acceleration of European integration, first with the creation of the single market followed by monetary union, was influenced by liberal economic ideas. In the process, the distribution of gains and losses became more unequal and European integration a more divisive issue within our societies. True, the direct effects of European integration are difficult to separate from the effects of globalization and technological change. But in popular perception this did not matter much. Large sections of our societies felt threatened by rapid change and Europe was increasingly perceived by those people as part of the problem and not part of the solution – not unjustifiably so.

The more the merrier?

If the challenge of exporting *Pax Europaea* to southern Europe after the fall of dictatorships had been a difficult one, yet executed with remarkable success, doing the same with many more former communist countries of central and eastern Europe was of an altogether different dimension. Like southern European countries after the fall of dictatorships, they started with closed economies and societies. But many of them also had much lower levels of income, and little, if any, experience of democratic institutions and markets. A few hardly had any experience of statehood either. Of course, numbers made a big difference too for the enlarged EU.

Adopting EU rules on the way to full membership was seen as part of the initiation process that central and eastern European countries had to go through to become like the developed democracies and market economies of the West. Europeanization was hence meant as a one-way process if a country wanted to become rich and democratic. Politicians and all kinds of experts in the West were on hand to provide valuable advice, usually sprayed with a strong touch of paternalism, while Brussels bureaucrats set conditions and timetables on the road to full membership – and paradise!

Back to earth, earlier experience with new members had taught applicants for EU membership to be on their best behaviour during the long rituals of initiation, knowing they would have more room to misbehave once they secured a seat around the European council table. Some of the new entrants were to do so with gusto years later, when their leaders began to denounce Brussels' interference in their domestic affairs and compare Europe's capital with Moscow. Of course, they never expressed any objection to receiving billions of euros in development aid from the EU budget. Václav Klaus of the Czech Republic was among the first to play the eastern version of the Eurosceptic game. He was such a contrast to his predecessor and namesake, Václav Havel, the philosopher-president who had overseen the transition of Czechoslovakia to democracy. Alas, the region gradually came up with more Klauses than Havels riding on a nationalist wave with a populist undercurrent.[5] The worst has been Viktor Orbán in Hungary.

With the benefit of hindsight, it is now clear that the transition to democracy and the market economy did not go as smoothly as many people had hoped for. Democracy takes time to spread roots, pluralism and tolerance of other people with different views even longer, especially after many years of totalitarian rule. Although standards of living are now much higher than they had been under communism, the transition to a market economy was painful and claimed many victims. People in central and eastern Europe have learned from experience that capitalism brings instability and uncertainty, while its gains are very unevenly distributed, especially when it comes in local versions of gangster capitalism.[6] Add declining populations and the exodus of some of their best and brightest to Brussels and western Europe in general, the takeover of much of the domestic economy by foreigners (meaning mostly other Europeans), as well as the feeling of being treated as second-class members inside the EU, and you end up with a heady mix.

It has been the right fodder for populism and nationalism. Even Poland, the country with the most successful economic transition, has not been spared. The consummation of the union between West and East Germany has not been an entirely happy affair either. What other conclusion to draw from the large share of votes that right-wing nationalists have been winning in the former communist land? Very large transfers from the rest of Germany, which reached as much as 50 per cent of the income of *Ossis*, the inhabitants of East Germany, were apparently not enough to ensure a smooth integration into the Federal Republic. You fill their pockets but lose their hearts – and the best and brightest vote with their feet.

I had direct personal experience of the early years of transition in several countries of the former Soviet empire. I paid several visits to Bulgaria, Moldova and Kazakhstan, among others, on European missions and on behalf of a consultancy firm I had then set up to work on programmes of technical assistance for transition countries. Such programmes were financed by Brussels: well-paid Western consultants and considerable waste on one side, local chaos, big-deal corruption and a lot of human suffering on the other. The European bureaucracy had enormous difficulty in handling large sums of money and so many programmes, while most people on the receiving end of European generosity found it very hard indeed to adjust to the new political and economic reality. As always when the old order collapses and a new one takes its place, the transition period was painful for the many while offering great opportunities for the few. Former communist apparatchiks were usually much more capable of seizing those new opportunities by establishing profitable contacts with foreign businessmen and the more unsavoury representatives of Wild West capitalism who rushed there to make a quick buck.

After the fall of the Berlin Wall and the disintegration of the Soviet empire, EU enlargement to the east had to happen. Anything else would have constituted an outright denial of what the European project has always stood for. Of course, perspectives and interests differed considerably among the old members. Some reminisced with a camouflaged German accent of historical alliances and spheres of influence that no longer dared speak their name. Others with a French touch were not so keen on countries they knew little about, even worse countries that could turn into economic competitors starting from a low-wage base. And there were those who saw further enlargement not just as the means to extend the European order to the east but also as making sure that a wider and much more diverse Europe would never be united. They spoke in impeccable Oxford English. Many Republicans in the

US enthusiastically sided with the British view: they did not take kindly to the prospect of a more united Europe that might one day challenge American hegemony within the Atlantic alliance and beyond.

Thirteen new members have already joined the EU since 2004. Successive enlargements of the EU have indeed contributed to peace, democracy and prosperity on the continent. Sure, it has not been an unqualified success, but when in doubt think of the alternative. The EU provided the political framework and the destination, large transfers of funds, a wide range of rules and norms as well as a process of socialization. EU membership has been indeed Europe's answer to high politics, although surely not a magic potion to cure all national ills. And it has also come at a price. Increasing numbers and growing diversity have taken their toll in a Union where the centre is weak, the unanimity rule still largely prevails, and the legitimacy of common institutions remains fragile.

The attempt to combine the euro and big bang enlargement with a stronger European centre failed abysmally. The constitutional treaty, itself an awkward attempt to reconcile treaty and constitution, which are two very different things, hit the rocks in 2005 when it was rejected in referendums held in France and the Netherlands. Strange coalitions were formed and became the precursors of things to come. People concerned about further loss of sovereignty allied themselves with those opposed to new enlargement and immigration. They were also joined by others who were unhappy with the weak social dimension of the European project. It was an ad hoc alliance of voters of right-wing parties with frustrated socialists, old-style nationalists with the new losers in times of rapid economic transformation and neoliberal policies. They all came together to vote against the constitutional treaty, perceived as one more project of political elites.[7]

The consensus on European integration lasted longer within political elites than within the public at large. In the early 1990s, that consensus helped to get the Maastricht treaty through, although only just. More than ten years later, the same could not be repeated with the constitutional treaty. Growing divergence among national political elites and the disconnect between elites and the public were added to the unanimity rule and frequent recourse to referendums. It looked like the perfect combination for political gridlock in the new century.

When financial hell broke loose

In 2009, as Europeans were celebrating the tenth anniversary of their common currency, the biggest financial tsunami since 1929 reached their shores. For the Western financial system and Western capitalism in general, the big crisis that began in the US in 2007 and continued longer in Europe constituted a huge failure of markets, institutions and democratic politics. It was also a crashing failure of the economics profession which had provided, with notable exceptions, the intellectual and ideological justification for the deregulation and liberalization of financial markets, those markets that were now collapsing with the risk of causing an economic Armageddon.

The international financial crisis exposed in a big way the flaws of the euro construction. It also exposed deep internal divisions. Europeans were surely unlucky when the international crisis hit their young currency. They were careless too and totally unprepared.[8] They lacked the institutions and policy instruments. The Union had no fiscal capacity of its own and no political authority to take quick decisions in an emergency. The only institution that could act quickly and decisively was the European Central Bank (ECB), which was, however, forced to fight difficult battles to be allowed to operate like a half-normal central bank. And with no political counterpart at the European level, the ECB repeatedly ventured into unchartered waters. In times of big crisis, the European monetary union was faced with fundamental questions about authority and legitimacy, solidarity, responsibility and trust. The architects of the euro had shied away from such questions, which were now back with a vengeance to torment their successors. Rigid rules could be no substitute for discretionary policies when reality deviated from the preordained path.

In the beginning, Europeans were simply in denial. Gradually and reluctantly, they began to react, always a dollar short and a day late, in the words attributed to former President Obama.[9] As the crisis deepened, political leaders at the European Council took centre stage, pushing both the European Commission and the Parliament to the side. In conditions of emergency, the famous Community method of decision making thus morphed into a more traditional intergovernmental conference where the will of the strongest usually prevailed. And the strongest was

Germany, no doubt about it: the biggest creditor with the strongest economy and with political leaders who dominated the European stage.

Germany was a reluctant and unhappy leader with strong views about how to run the economy. Old fears about having to share a currency with countries that did not share their views about sound finances were now coming to haunt the Germans. They were not at all keen on saving irresponsible partners by lending them their money. They already had enough of calls for solidarity given their long and costly experience of paying solidarity taxes for eastern Germany after reunification. They insisted instead on austerity policies. It was all the fault of fiscal laxity, we were told by German disciplinarians. They, however, conveniently forgot the active participation of German banks in the big bubble. They also forgot the persistent and ever larger German trade surpluses with other European countries and the rest of the world, sustained through their membership of the euro. After all, what are surpluses if not a sign of economic success and virility? A model for others to follow, they thought. Not everybody agreed with the Germans, but they usually did not dare to express different views too loud: it was a sign of the times.

Germany defined the terms and drew the red lines for national bailouts that had never been supposed to happen. It did the same with European measures to bolster the collective defences of the euro. Poor French, they had been the prime movers behind the creation of the euro in the first place as a means of containing reunified Germany within a stronger European framework, and they were now facing a German-run monetary union in deep crisis. As for the British, they kept more distant from a badly governed Eurozone, yet were deeply worried that a euro crisis running out of control would unavoidably spill over across the Channel.

Between 2007 and 2013, real growth in the Eurozone was below zero: it was the Great Recession. Furthermore, the burden of adjustment was very unequally distributed. In the worst-affected countries, the younger generations were disproportionately hit and the number of people below the poverty line rose fast. For them, the 'Jesus rail' of the nation state came unstuck and Europe became a threat. The negative effects of the euro crisis were thus added to the long-term trend of higher inequalities and slower growth. And while the adverse long-term trend could be attributed, at least in part, to forces beyond the control of European policy makers, a bit like the weather, the euro crisis was mostly made in Europe. Between 2011 and 2013, trust in the EU reached a historical low according to Eurobarometer figures.

Living in Athens and commuting regularly to the main centres of power, I found the years of the big crisis a personal ordeal even though I knew I still belonged to the privileged few. My own country was imploding – or was it just about to explode, I was not sure. The domestic economy lost more than a quarter of its output in less than six years, unemployment skyrocketed, many young people lost hope of ever finding a decent job and left in increasing numbers for other countries. The centre of Athens was constantly under siege by thousands of demonstrators, soup kitchens for the poor spread in the big cities, and politicians were sacrificed on the altar of economic adjustment. Greece had not experienced a crisis of such dimensions since the end of the civil war in the 1940s. Surely, much of the blame lay with the Greeks themselves, principally those who had mismanaged the economy for years. In 2009, Greece was insolvent not illiquid. But hardly anybody in Europe was prepared to face up to the truth. They were all terrified of the prospect of Greece – Ireland as well because of its banks – becoming a European version of Lehman Brothers that could cause a financial meltdown while markets were in a state of panic.

I received many invitations to speak and consult during the crisis because I was Greek and spoke European, although I was surely not the only one. I had access to the corridors of power and select international gatherings with representatives of political and economic elites meeting behind closed doors. Some of those elite gatherings were like Davos without journalists and in much smaller numbers, hence the subject of popular conspiracy theories. I had the opportunity to meet and interact with people with enormous power in their hands, wise people and dedicated Europeans among them, also quite a few I choose to forget. I learned a great deal, although for sure it was not always uplifting. Such is the world of power. It was, however, painful to witness so much self-righteousness, arrogance and intolerance verging on racism within what I had always considered to be my European family. But after all, such things can happen in the best of families when misfortune strikes.

Can elections change economic policy in a Eurozone country, and who decides? It was an interesting debate of sorts between Wolfgang

Schäuble, Germany's finance minister throughout the long crisis, and Yanis Varoufakis, Greece's short-lived rock star finance minister in a coalition government of the radical left with right-wing nationalists: another product of the crisis. Schäuble used dry language and a loaded gun against the flowery rhetoric of his opponent, who really had no weapons.[10] Guess who won! The Greek threat, which ultimately depended on Greece's readiness to exit the euro and thus (possibly) destabilize the common currency, proved empty. And economic policy did not change. Grexit was only just avoided through the intervention of the French president, François Hollande, and the president of the European Commission, Jean-Claude Juncker.

The international implications of the euro crisis were no less severe. A high-ranking European official once told me the story of a conversation he had with a top politician from China a few years back. His interlocutor said that from the Chinese perspective Europe was a kind of greater Germany until the euro crisis came and they discovered that Europe was more like Greece writ large. The crisis cut Europe down to size.

The US Federal Reserve provided ample liquidity to the dollar-based international monetary system through swap agreements with foreign central banks, including notably the ECB and the Bank of England. It was the kind of action, although not widely known, that helped to prevent an international financial meltdown. It could also have served as a warning to Europeans and others of their dependence on the United States in a dollar-based international financial system. This was to become painfully obvious when, a few years later, the Trump administration began to use it as an instrument to force banks and other companies based in foreign countries to conform to unilateral US sanctions.

The International Monetary Fund (IMF) became directly involved in the management of the euro crisis despite early statements by European political leaders that the Washington-based international organization would have nothing to do with an internal European problem. After all, the United States does not invite the IMF to deal with an economic problem in Louisiana or Nebraska. The same should therefore be true of any issue arising within Europe's monetary union, so we had been told at the beginning of the crisis. But when markets began to speculate on euro divorce, we all realized that Greece was not Louisiana.

Creditor countries, especially Germany, insisted on the participation of the IMF, because the latter had the experience, which is true, and because they did not trust their Commission – and they said so in public. It was not a glorious chapter in the history of European institutions, to put it mildly. And the IMF did not come out of the whole affair with flying colours either. The representatives of China, Brazil and other countries on the executive board did not mince their words when criticizing the involvement of the Fund in rescue programmes for Eurozone members much richer than themselves. At least, IMF officials had the courage to be critical of their own policy on the matter, which is more than their European counterparts were able to do for a long time.

Transatlantic divisions and European frustrations

The Cold War had frozen regional conflicts and put a lid on irredentism in several parts of Europe. Once it was over, nationalist forces were unleashed, first in Yugoslavia where a bloody civil war broke out in 1991. Instead of the end of History, we were unfortunately witnessing the return of History on the old continent. European countries were divided and totally incapable of dealing with a war in their own backyard:[11] surely not the 'hour of Europe' as was prematurely proclaimed by the foreign minister of Luxembourg. Instead, it was a US-led NATO operation that finally put an end to the war and set the terms for peace. Yugoslavia was divided into no fewer than seven independent republics, and Europe was then brought back into the picture. Incapable of dealing with matters of war, the EU was meant to help consolidate a rather fragile peace in what used to be Yugoslavia. The instrument to achieve this objective would be the prospect of EU membership for the successor republics: the magic potion we talked about earlier. Slovenia and Croatia are already members of the EU, and all the other five republics aspire to join at some stage, although the wait has already proved to be terribly long.

Divisions within the EU on key issues of high politics became more pronounced with the arrival of new members from central and eastern Europe carrying their own historical experiences and political sensitivities. Such divisions were exposed with a big bang when President George W. Bush, with the support of the Blair government in London, launched the Iraq war in 2003. It was a war against a terrible dictator,

Saddam Hussein, but based on false premises and with no realistic plan for the day after. The US administration at the time made no distinction between allies and obedient followers, exerting strong pressure on all and sundry to toe the line.

Transatlantic unity forged in the aftermath of the 9/11 attacks on the US had not lasted for long. France and Germany took a strong stance against the war on Iraq, together with a small number of countries in western Europe.[12] But there were not many who could afford the luxury of disobeying the leader. With characteristic arrogance, US Secretary of Defense Donald Rumsfeld spoke of new and old Europe and made his contempt more than clear for the latter. For Rumsfeld, new Europe showed the way forward. He meant the new democracies of central and eastern Europe, ready to follow the US lead with enthusiasm and no questions asked – plus the UK, which thought of itself as co-leader in this ill-fated enterprise.

Those Europeans who later appeared to be genuinely shocked by President Trump's unilateralism and his aggressive stance towards allies with views of their own chose to have short memories. Prominent politicians of the Republican Party in the US had long laid the ground. The Iraq war exposed deep fault lines in how different European countries perceived external threat and in turn defined their relations with the protector of last resort and leader of the Atlantic alliance. Visiting Washington in those days, I had the feeling I was visiting the capital of the new Roman empire – and I was not the only one. It was unchallenged power in a now unipolar world and in the hands of politicians with little time or patience for Europeans coming from Venus, unlike them, who apparently came from Mars.[13] What has come out of America's Martian approach to Iraq and other places is, however, a moot point at best.

Europeans from Venus, usually divided among themselves, were perhaps bound to have a troubled relationship with Russia, with which they now shared borders and neighbours. A postmodern EU makes indeed an awkward pair with post-imperial Russia. When the Soviet empire collapsed, it left behind a power vacuum extending to the whole of central and eastern Europe and the former Soviet republics further to the east, which then gained their independence. It also left a big mess behind, as disintegrating empires often do.

The United States and western Europe rushed to fill this vacuum, directly by acquiring a political and economic foothold in those countries and indirectly through NATO and EU enlargements, which happened in stages. In the process, the relationship between Russia and the West turned increasingly sour, while Russia became more assertive under Putin's leadership and began to challenge the rules of the game set by the West. As the latter came closer to the Russian border, it found countries with large Russian or Russophile minorities, countries often internally divided and over which an increasingly assertive Russia claimed a *droit de regard*. The Baltic countries, with large Russian minorities of their own, had been quick enough to join both NATO and the EU. But when others tried to follow their example a few years later, they found the road was filled with landmines.

The EU offered association agreements to former Soviet republics on the European side. They were meant to open the way – sometime in the distant future – for full membership of the EU. In fact, the Union was short on actual concessions and long on vague promises. Ukraine was destined to become the key testing ground. A country whose history has been closely intermeshed with that of Russia, strategically important and economically dependent until then on its much bigger eastern neighbour, Ukraine was also a divided country in terms of ethnicity, language and religion, with the eastern part looking more towards Russia and the other looking to the West. That is how it was back then. Henry Kissinger,[14] with deep knowledge of History and a cynical master of realpolitik, strongly cautioned against treating Ukraine as part of the East–West confrontation, but in vain.

In 2014, the Maidan revolution finally forced the then pro-Russian president to flee – one more corrupt government to go – while Putin treated the whole affair as a direct provocation and an opportunity. He seized Crimea and fomented revolt in the eastern regions of Ukraine. He found local support with large Russian-speaking populations. It is worth recalling that Crimea had been transferred from the Russian to the Ukrainian Soviet Republic by Khrushchev in 1954. A generous gift back then, it did not have important political and strategic implications so long as the USSR existed. Now, with an independent Ukraine that might end up as a member of NATO and the EU and with Russia's Black Sea fleet still headquartered in Sebastopol in Crimea, it did.

The annexation of Crimea and war in the eastern regions of Ukraine inevitably turned the large majority among Ukrainians against Putin's Russia, as had happened with Georgians when the Russian army had come close to their capital Tbilisi in 2008. President Putin did, however, draw a line on the map then that would prove difficult for Europeans and Americans to cross. It was later to become painfully clear with Russia's invasion of Ukraine in 2022. Back then, Brussels wanted to believe it was all about association agreements, and they were proven wrong. High politics was not a game they knew how to play, especially when others around the table carry guns and are ready to use them. Once again, Europeans dithered; they were also divided. Having lost the game, Berlin and Paris then took over responsibility in what was clearly a damage limitation exercise.

Immigrants, nationalists and populists

It was not the end of Europe's troubles with the neighbourhood. The big immigration crisis in 2015, when around one million people arrived in dinghy boats in Lesbos and other Greek islands adjacent to the Turkish coast, exposed once again deep divisions, the fragility of common policies, notably free internal movement and open borders, as well as Europe's very limited capacity to influence developments in its neighbourhood. Mostly refugees from the war in Syria, those arriving on European shores were in search of a haven and Germany was their preferred destination. They were joined by many others from the troubled region of the Middle East and further afield trying to escape from war, persecution and abject poverty, usually a combination of all three.

The neighbourhood was exporting instability and insecurity to Europe in the form of large numbers of refugees and immigrants, as well as terrorists, which surely made things much worse. A long series of terrorist outrages in European cities reached a peak in 2015. The jihadi threat, home-grown or imported yet all in the name of radical Islam, was growing. The resulting sense of insecurity in European societies provided fertile ground for far-right parties to sow the seeds of fear and hatred in the face of an alleged invasion of people of alien religions and cultures.

European countries had already experienced the rise in popularity of nationalist right-wing parties addressing concerns among ever-growing sections of their societies about loss of control over their lives and their immediate environment. It was the fear of accelerating change and the fear of modernity that parties on the far right tried for years to address and cultivate. Europe was generally perceived as a vehicle of change and such parties proposed national solutions instead, offering protection in a rapidly changing world. Immigration figured most prominently on their agenda: numbers of immigrants had been rising and many European societies appeared to be dangerously close to their threshold of tolerance for the Other. In 2015, immigration became the number one issue of concern for people across Europe, according to Eurobarometer polls. It has occupied one of the highest ranks in notoriety ever since.

For Brussels, a clear distinction is always made between immigration from outside, subject to international law and conventions, and the free movement of European citizens inside the Union. The latter is treated as a fundamental right, indeed sacrosanct, as David Cameron, former UK prime minister, was to discover when he tried to restrict the entry of other Europeans into the UK and failed. In the earlier period of European integration, only a small number of mobile Europeans had exercised that right. But when poorer countries joined the Union, numbers increased significantly. The economic crisis added further to European internal migration.

It is a long and inconclusive debate whether cultural or economic factors[15] have been more important for the rise of nationalist right-wing parties in European countries and beyond. In practice, it is difficult to separate two sets of factors that are more likely to be mutually reinforcing than mutually exclusive. What we do know is that supporters of such parties are mostly male, older, with low education and income. The same was true of many supporters of Brexit and former President Trump. The financial crisis and the immigration crisis came at the tail end of a long period of low growth, widening inequalities and increased uncertainty for large sections of European populations. And they provoked a big blast in the political systems of many European countries, as well as across the Atlantic. The result has been fragmentation, radicalization and polarization, which were bound to spill over into European integration.

Anti-systemic parties and political movements gained votes at the expense of the old parties of the centre right and centre left that had been alternating or sharing power in most European countries for the biggest part of the post-war period. Social democrats were the ones who suffered the most across Europe.[16] With the blurring of ideological lines, social democrats had become part of the neoliberal consensus, but many of their traditional voters were not at all happy with the results. The same happened when social democrats adopted a liberal stance on immigration. As a result, large numbers of blue-collar workers ended up voting for nationalist parties of the far right.

In northern and western Europe, the immigration crisis combined with the rising threat of terrorism was a golden opportunity for parties on the far right – and they used it unscrupulously. Earlier, they had already made political capital out of their strong condemnation of rescue programmes for southern countries. Solidarity with foreigners, including fellow Europeans, was surely not one of their strong points. Meanwhile, the political scene in the weaker countries of the south had become more varied. It included parties on the radical left with an anti-capitalist discourse making political gains out of the deep recession and high unemployment in their countries, especially among the young who feared they had no future at home. There were also parties on the far right raising the nationalist flag and targeting immigrants as scape-goats. Cross-migration of voters between these two extremes was by no means a rare phenomenon: a sign of the times. It was even worse in the countries of central and eastern Europe, even though many of them had suffered less during the financial crisis and had so far not seen that many immigrants coming their way.

Anti-systemic parties, especially those on the right of the political spectrum, are branded as populists. They don the garment of the only true representatives of the will of the people against corrupt elites. Such parties propose simple solutions to complex issues and are usually led by demagogues. Athenian democracy in ancient times had a rich collection of such people, hence the Greek origin of the two words 'democracy' and 'demagogues'. However, populists do not come out of nowhere. They generally arise in response to real problems and failures of democratic systems, of which there have been plenty in recent years. With crises succeeding one another, more and more people in our societies came to believe that the rules of the system were stacked against them. Alas, they were not completely wrong. To brand as populists all those who try to take political advantage of public discontent, often well founded, hardly solves the problem, and nor does complacency among the old systemic parties.

At the peak of the refugee/immigration crisis, Chancellor Merkel took the lead and tried to provide a European solution. One part of her strategy was to stem the flow by steering an agreement between the EU and Erdoğan's Turkey: European money and visas in exchange for Turkey keeping most refugees and immigrants at home. Critics denounced the agreement as being against European values. Do we sign deals with authoritarian rulers at the expense of desperate people fleeing war and persecution? But if not, how can we cope with growing resistance at home to rising immigration flows and the threat of right-wing extremists? For those who have read the classical work of the German sociologist Max Weber, it was the best illustration of the dilemma between the ethic of conviction and the ethic of responsibility.[17]

In other words, how do we reconcile humanitarian values with hard political and economic realities? I remember telling the person in charge of the migration centre at the think tank I was presiding over in Athens that her liberal views, which I instinctively shared, risked providing fodder for all kinds of racists and fascists at home – their numbers increasing fast during successive crises. The path to hell is often paved with good intentions and large doses of political innocence.

The other part of Chancellor Merkel's strategy was to achieve a more equitable distribution of the burden through an intra-European agreement to reallocate people among member countries of the EU. Such an agreement was indeed reached by majority vote in the Council but never implemented, because of viral opposition from countries in central and eastern Europe. 'Over our dead bodies' was the answer given by some political leaders who saw the arrival of large numbers of immigrants from faraway lands as an existential threat to the national and Christian identity in their countries. European decisions were thus pitted against national political realities under extreme conditions, and the fight was unequal.

As a measure of last resort, Merkel opened the German border and took more than one million refugees in one year. It was a bold decision for sure, an act of generosity to people in distress, and an act of solidarity with other European countries. Merkel thus played the role of the *deus ex machina*, the Latin term for 'the god from the machine', the outside intervention used in ancient Greek theatre to resolve conflict and thus conclude the drama. It was precisely the role she had repeatedly refused to play during the euro crisis. Alas, many people at home did not appreciate Merkel's decision at all. The far right received a big boost in popularity and we all then understood better why Merkel had been previously so reluctant to do for Europe the right thing at the right time. The reason was blatantly simple: many Germans had not considered it to be the right thing and the right time, and they were after all the ones who voted her in to power.

The immigration/refugee crisis of 2015 had many similarities with the euro crisis earlier on. Both were imported into Europe and quickly transformed into big internal crises, because of weaknesses in the European construction and deep divisions between and within countries. To be sure, a complete breakdown was avoided at the last minute, which was no small achievement. Cassandras who had repeatedly prophesied the breakup of the EU were proved wrong. But the EU paid a high price in terms of political cohesion, economic performance, social welfare, international credibility, you name it.

The Ability to Surprise

Washington is not London

If Britain had chosen early enough to engage actively, it could have played a leading role from the very beginning and could have shaped the European model much closer to its own image. Luckily, it chose not to, ardent supporters of European unity now hasten to add, liberated after Brexit from the constraints of political correctness. Britain joined late in 1973 in what always looked from its side like a business affair based mostly on a narrow calculation of economic benefits and costs.[1] There was little love at best and a mismatch often resulting from poor understanding of the motives and intentions of Britain's European partners. For a former imperial power, proud of its navigating skills in the rough seas of international diplomacy, Britain's turbulent relationship with European integration does not score high marks.

All countries of the EU are different, but the UK was always more different than the rest. Confident they could make a difference and really convinced they had alternatives to being part of the European project, British politicians and the public at large never took much interest in European integration. The exceptions proved the rule. For most Brits, it was always about 'us' and 'them'. Several decades back, Winston Churchill had summed it all up very aptly: 'We are with Europe but not of it. We are linked but not comprised. We are interested and associated, but not absorbed.'[2] In his famous speech delivered in Zurich in 1946, he spoke in favour of the United States of Europe, but Britain was not meant to be part of it.

I remember Margaret Thatcher's famous Bruges speech delivered at the College of Europe in 1988. At the end of the official ceremony in the impressive Gothic Hall in Bruges, we all listened to the 'Ode of Joy' from Beethoven's ninth symphony, which serves as the European anthem, and we all stood up, Thatcher included – she had no other option. Her people had earlier tried in vain to ban both European flag and anthem from the ceremony. After all, non-political entities such as Europe are not entitled to a flag or anthem, they firmly believed. But College authorities and most people present at the ceremony, including many of Europe's *illuminati*, thought otherwise. The symbolism was stark and so were the two contrasting views of Europe.

Britain has a more global outlook than almost any other country in Europe. But as a member of the EU, it consistently tried to put its foot on the brakes and restrain the pro-integration zeal of its partners on different fronts, resorting to exceptions and opt-outs when everything else failed. And this happened more and more as European integration shifted into a higher gear from Maastricht onwards. Exceptions and opt-outs in turn led to more isolation, which is often a self-fulfilling state of mind. During Europe's multiple crises in the 2010s, I had the privilege of taking part in high-level informal meetings in Brussels in which small numbers of participants discussed the general direction of European policy. It was brainstorming in an emergency and off the record. I was then struck by the absence of Brits in most meetings. It would have been unthinkable twenty or even ten years earlier. I began to feel then that the UK was already on the way out.

In 2013, I was invited to give the Alcuin Lecture, set up by the late Lord (Leon) Brittan at Cambridge University.[3] The UK prime minister had already promised a referendum, and I thought at the time that such a referendum could indeed be desirable more than just unavoidable. It would force a proper debate with facts and arguments, which would be good for democracy and good for the cause of Britain in Europe, so I thought. Although aware of the risk of demagogues trying to hijack the referendum, I believed it was a risk worth taking. Obviously, I had grossly underestimated the problem back then. But with the benefit of hindsight, Brexit looks like an accident waiting to happen in a country that had never been reconciled to its participation in a European project leading to ever closer union.

The campaign leading to the referendum of 2016 revealed big cracks in the British political system and British society in general. Something had gone badly wrong in previous years. However, the domestic campaign also had things in common with the debate taking place in other countries in those times of crisis: polarization, mistrust of political elites, and fake news. For somebody like me with deep affection for the country, it was shocking to watch British politics sink so low.

A former colleague from LSE, Iain Begg, very succinctly described the majority that won the referendum as an unholy alliance between members of golf clubs in the English countryside and the *sans culottes* in the decaying heartlands of British manufacturing industry. In other words, it was an alliance of old-age nationalists and well-off conservatives joining forces with people who had long felt left behind and now seized the opportunity to vent their anger against the system. Such alliances can indeed win elections – referendums even more easily – in times of political flux, but they usually fail to deliver the goods once they have won. Within the winning alliance, some talked of global Britain and free trade, while others yearned for protection.

The result of the referendum came as a shock. Such things were not supposed to happen. People in Brussels tried to explain the unthinkable with reference to British exceptionalism and Cameron's gross mishandling of the whole affair. But they knew all too well this was only part of the explanation. They were deeply worried about political undercurrents that threatened the European political order. And some drew comparisons with what had happened back in the 1930s.

We learned that the transition team of President Trump, elected a few months after the Brexit referendum, called the Brussels officialdom asking which countries would follow the UK on the way out. They were apparently convinced that Brexit was only the beginning of an unstoppable process of disintegration.[4] So much for understanding Europe. True, the narrow victory of Brexiteers was greeted with enthusiasm by leaders of nationalist/populist parties in other European countries, notably in France and in Italy. But such enthusiasm did not last long. Witnessing the ever-growing difficulties in negotiating divorce after the referendum, and, even more, the obvious asymmetry of power between a united EU-27 and a deeply disunited UK, early enthusiasm among those who might have contemplated following the UK towards the exit quickly withered away.

The rest of Europe closed ranks and they ended up setting the terms of the negotiation. Britain's old policy of divide and rule did not work this time for two simple reasons. One is that the single market and the rest of the *acquis*[5] are powerful common instruments that help to bring EU members together. The other is that the UK is no longer in the top power league, difficult though it may be for some people in the British Isles to accept. Thus, instead of more disintegration, Brexit rather unexpectedly helped to unify the rest of the Union and increase public support for the European project. Europeans who had long been critical of the way Brussels and member countries (mis)handled successive crises now had the opportunity to see live what divorce meant – and they did not like it at all.

In a lecture tour in Australia and New Zealand in the autumn of 2017 and in Vancouver, Canada, a few months later, I often spoke about Brexit and its likely consequences. Many people in the audience had family roots in the UK and I thought my critical remarks would not go down well with them. Instead, I was surprised that my audience often went much further than me in their criticism. Even from a long distance, people recognized madness when they saw it.

It was also the revenge of History in a way. The main stumbling block to reaching an agreement on the transition period following Brexit was the so-called Irish backstop provision, introduced by the EU and meant to ensure there would be no hard border between Northern Ireland and the Republic of Ireland after Brexit. Many Irish on both sides felt strongly about it: preserving peace on the divided island was at stake. With the support of its European partners, the former colony was thus imposing conditions on the old master. Boris Johnson finally decided to cut the Gordian knot, only to change his mind later by trying to rescind the agreement he had signed. Admittedly, it was a rather impossible agreement to apply that created a frontier between Northern Ireland and the rest of the UK.

Some people in Brussels initially toyed with the idea that the Trump presidency, like Brexit, could act as a further catalyst for European unity. The former US president called for the breakup of the EU, adopted unilateralism as the key principle of his foreign policy and made little distinction between allies and foes. Granted, US criticism of Europeans free-riding on defence within the Atlantic alliance had a long history and valid reasons. However, the Trump administration stretched criticism beyond the limit. Diplomacy turned into outright bullying. Meanwhile, his emissaries openly flirted with the far right in several European countries.

But Washington is not London. Donald Trump was an extreme populist yet with enormous power in his hands, hence the great difficulty for Europeans in turning adversity into unity as they did with Brexit. The old European political establishment cajoled and bided its time, while Trump was the source of inspiration and a model to follow for European populists with an authoritarian streak. Virtually all leaders in central and eastern Europe, irrespective of political persuasion, felt they had no choice. For them, the Russian threat continued to loom large, and the US remained their protector of last resort.

In 2016, I taught a course on policy issues and choices for the EU at the Kennedy School of Harvard University. It was the only course on Europe offered at this famous school of government during the semester. I had many Europeans in class, which was to be expected, also Chinese, other Asians and Latin Americans, and only one US citizen. It was telling. Americans were at best interested in their own backyard and most of all in China, which was increasingly perceived as a strategic threat. Trump was extreme in many ways, but he also represented a certain way of looking at the world which is popular in the United States.

Faced with the steady weakening of the post-war multilateral order, with the global balance of power shifting to the east and US leadership under Trump turning into unilateralism, Europeans were able to preserve their unity in trade matters – and unity was in turn translated into negotiating power. They were much less successful, though, in matters of high politics, where disunity often went hand in hand with powerlessness and marginalization. The Middle East was another good example. This turbulent region of the world continued to be of strategic interest for Europe. It also remained an endless source of frustration and a testimony to Europe's inability to exercise influence in its close neighbourhood. The long and bloody civil war in Syria provided a painful illustration.

Reversing the populist tide

With Brexit and the election of Donald Trump, nationalists and populists were in the ascendant. The year 2016 was truly an *annus horribilis* for those defending the old order of things and they had plenty of reasons to fear it would only get worse. The next big battle was to be fought in France, a leader in European integration although for years feeling it was losing ownership of the common project. A neoliberal economic model, too many new members who looked to Washington rather than Brussels (or Paris), a German-run common currency, growing numbers of immigrants and leaky external borders: this was not what the French had bargained for in Europe.

In the last few years, I have been teaching at Sciences Po, one of the elite schools in Paris; about Europe, what else? Spending time in the most beautiful city in the world is indeed a great privilege. Interacting with colleagues who share a strong interest in Europe is also very rewarding. And teaching a class of very bright and well-educated young graduates from all over the world, with English as the common language of communication in a top university in Paris, is an experience typical of the world in which some of us have been living in recent years.

In one of my classes, we were discussing the distinction introduced by David Goodhart[6] between *Somewheres* and *Anywheres*, which was meant to capture the new important line of division shaping identities and ideologies in our globalizing world. A student from an Asian country made the rather obvious remark that all of us in the class were typical representatives of the *Anywheres*. Another added jokingly that we should unionize! My own response was that instead of the privileged acting collectively to defend their interests, it would be much wiser if they tried to better understand the other side and begin to bridge the gap with practical measures, not just words. Otherwise, they risk losing much more than their privileges and economic rents. The reversal of globalization in its liberal version could indeed take a nasty turn.

The second round of the French presidential election in May 2017 was a straight fight between the nationalist right and a reformist, pro-European candidate who had blazed his way through old established parties. Such things could only happen with a presidential system and when politics is in a state of flux. It was a battle for France and a battle for Europe. The spectacle of the newly elected president of the French Republic walking up to the podium in front of the Louvre to deliver his victory speech to the sound of the European anthem was something nobody could have imagined only a few years earlier. The battle was to be repeated between the same two combatants, Macron and Le Pen, in the second round of the 2022 presidential election. Luckily, for democracy and Europe, Macron won again in a deeply divided country where the main parties of centre right and centre left have been pulverized.

Macron has been by far the most European-minded president of the Fifth French Republic. A powerhouse in terms of ideas and proposals, he has tried to change the shape of European integration from common institutions and democracy to security and defence, the Eurozone, migration and common borders, although arguably not sensitive enough to the concerns of *la France profonde*. Macron spoke of sovereign Europe, a revolutionary idea in many ways although hard to translate into concrete policies.[7] For him, Chancellor Merkel was the obvious interlocutor, and he tried hard to convince her. But it proved a hard slog. His repeated overtures to Berlin for a Franco-German alliance to lead Europe with bold initiatives and reforms met for a long time with little response. Merkel was apparently not interested in meeting him even half-way while other Europeans, especially those in central and eastern Europe, were much less diplomatic in their rejection of Macron's radical ideas. He had few allies.

At least, the populist tide was in retreat. Pro-Europeans were winning in national elections across Europe. Brexit surely helped, so did economic recovery and the creation of new jobs across Europe. But while nationalist/populist parties were toning down their anti-European discourse, their views on immigration became part of the mainstream political agenda. 'Fortress Europe' was now the answer to unregulated immigration flows. And the attempts made by autocrats in neighbouring countries, starting with Erdoğan in Turkey and continuing with Lukashenko in Belarus, to use immigrants as the way to extract concessions from the EU made the reality of 'Fortress Europe' even stronger.

The European Parliament election of May 2019 was another important turning point. Europe-wide issues were debated across borders more than ever before and voters elected a clear pro-European majority. Nationalists and populists received around 25 per cent of the votes cast. They were divided among themselves since nationalists do not easily get on with each other across borders. Participation rates also rose for the first time, although numbers were still depressingly low in the new democracies to the east. But a pro-European majority to do exactly what? The political landscape was more fragmented than ever. The old parties of the centre right and the centre left, which together had provided since the very beginning a solid base for consensual politics in the European Parliament, suffered a big decline. Greens and new parties were on the rise, filling the gap.[8]

The great accelerator

European economies enjoyed a modest but sustained recovery after 2013. But private debt continued to rise and the ECB, like other central banks in the developed world, was printing money on a large scale and buying mostly government bonds in secondary markets. Believers in austerity policies, mostly in Germany and countries of the north, were deeply concerned about rising levels of debt and the effects of zero or negative rates of interest for savers. They also wanted to make sure that fiscal policies remained under tight control. On the opposite side, there were those who worried about insufficient demand and called for fiscal expansion. They were the usual suspects in France, Belgium and the European south.[9] This debate was, however, rendered irrelevant when Covid-19 hit Europe together with the rest of the world.

The coronavirus pandemic is the kind of crisis most of us had thought belonged to the distant past. With a heavy toll in terms of human lives, stretching health systems to their limits and beyond, with societies and economies going through long periods of lockdown and experiencing an even worse recession than the one caused a few years earlier by the financial crisis, the pandemic further exposed and indeed magnified large injustices in our societies. This new crisis was also the great accelerator of trends already happening,[10] including the return of the state, more divided societies in terms of economic inequality and vulnerability to external shocks, more debt both private and public, much greater reliance on digital technologies, as well as globalization going into lower, if not reverse, gear.

The social and political aftershocks of big crises usually stretch out in time – more than one butterfly flapping its wings in China and causing a hurricane in Europe, north America and the rest of the world. To the great surprise of seasoned observers, the pandemic has also acted as a great accelerator for European integration. Based on experience from recurring crises, believers in the common project together with all kinds of infidels had reached the conclusion that muddling through was the

49

best that Europe could do in such difficult times.[11] They were proved wrong.

The sequence of events followed a familiar pattern, albeit with some new variations. It all started with one more Franco-German initiative originating in Paris and ending up with Berlin taking over the helm. It was followed by the Commission helping to translate rough ideas into concrete policy proposals and further raising the stakes. Then came the usual hustle and tussle of intra-European negotiations, with shifting alliances in a complex decision-making system always hostage to veto threats. But for a change, decisions were taken remarkably fast by European standards, and they were a real game changer. Imagine what would have happened – or rather not happened – in such a difficult negotiation over very large amounts of money and high stakes, if the UK were still in. Brexit made a crucial difference for the outcome because the biggest veto player of them all was no longer there.

The compromise was made possible through Germany's sudden conversion to Keynesian economics. It was a spectacular shift in terms of attitudes and policy, pointing to a pragmatic streak in the German soul that many people had not suspected before. It happened under the pressure of an unprecedented shock that hit Germany as well. It was no longer something terrible that only happened to others. The German U-turn had been preceded by strong pressures for the issue of a European corona bond to help deal with the economic effects of the pandemic. And it was in response to growing fears this could very well prove to be one big crisis too many for European integration.

Chancellor Merkel finally yielded to President Macron's wooing. Or was it more in response to the rising threat of populists taking over in Italy and elsewhere, hence provoking the mother of political crises that so many European leaders had been fearing all along? When it came to the crunch, it was not entirely clear who was the most persuasive in Berlin, the French President Macron or Salvini the Italian populist, each one of course for very different reasons. The fear of Matteo Salvini taking over the reins of power in Rome had long kept many Italians and other Europeans worried. They knew that the EU and the euro had survived the Greek crisis with difficulty and at a great cost. And they were not at all sure they could survive a similar crisis of much bigger dimensions in Italy.

The main package of European measures was agreed during the second half of 2020 under Germany's rotating presidency of the European Council, which was a truly happy coincidence that placed the most powerful country officially at the helm of the EU. European gods conspired and Chancellor Merkel apparently wanted this to be her strong European legacy before leaving the stage. The most important decision was the adoption of a large European financial package of €750 billion branded as Next Generation EU. It was directed mainly at the weaker and worse-hit members, more in the form of grants than loans. Of course, redistribution continues to be a taboo word in the European official vocabulary, but actions count more than words. It was also decided that European recovery funds would be directed mostly towards public and private investments, with a strong emphasis on the green and digital transformation of European economies. The new Commission under Ursula von der Leyen had already announced in December 2019 the European Green Deal as its key priority for the next five years.

The Commission borrowing hundreds of billions of euros on behalf of the Union? It is the stuff of Eurodreams now come true. Sure, EU borrowing will not be called Eurobonds, which is another taboo word for many, but does it matter much? The recovery programme as a response to the pandemic, together with the new EU budget extending over a seven-year period, amount to close to two trillion euros. Add to them the pandemic emergency purchase programme, which gives the ECB the power to buy close to two trillion euros' worth of private and mostly public sector securities. Combined with the temporary lifting of EU rules on national fiscal policy, ECB action allowed member governments to borrow and spend at very low cost – close to zero – to prevent their economies from imploding. For disciples of fiscal and monetary prudence, the world had turned upside down. The Commission was also given a coordinating role in the provision of vaccines and their distribution across the EU, to avoid an undignified and highly divisive scramble among national governments. Health had remained essentially a national prerogative until the pandemic struck, and now the Commission was trying to make the best of a weak mandate and with precious little experience in this field.

When European gods conspire, miracles can happen even in the most unlikely of places. Instead of Matteo Salvini, Italy ended up in 2021 with a broad coalition government led by Mario Draghi, the erstwhile saviour of the euro. Another high-profile Italian technocrat, like Mario Monti at the peak of the debt crisis a decade earlier, Draghi was imported from Europe to save the country in difficult times. Italy is the biggest beneficiary of the European recovery programme: one more chance for Italy, as for other European countries where EU funds can make a big difference. Those in trouble need Europe the most. The future of the European project will at least partly depend on the use made of EU funds under the recovery programme and the domestic reforms it helps to bring about, especially among the weaker members.

Or will it depend much more instead on the big question of war and peace in Europe? Russia's brutal invasion of Ukraine in early 2022 came as a huge shock: the first large-scale war on the European continent since the end of the Second World War. A few European leaders had made strenuous diplomatic efforts to prevent it, and failed. Europe did not count for much in Moscow and President Putin wanted guarantees from Washington. Thus, EU countries were reminded once again of the limitations (illusions?) of their soft power as war came closer to their borders. We shall come back to the war in Ukraine and its broader consequences in subsequent chapters.

Much of the writing of this book was done in conditions of intermittent lockdowns and restricted travel during the pandemic. By necessity, a large part of this fragmentary diary on the European journey was mostly written at home. I surely had more time and the opportunity to reflect on the accumulated experience of almost half a century. Of course, I also missed out on the stimulus and feedback that close interaction with colleagues and fellow Europeans across borders normally provides, including access to corridors of power. Online exchange surely helped to keep us all in contact during these difficult times, but virtual contact is not a good enough substitute for the real thing, at least not for my generation.

For me, the European journey has been extremely rewarding. I feel more European today or rather more aware of my multiple identities, European being a very important one among them. Sure, I have not succeeded in changing Europe, but I think I know much better now what the making of Europe as an economic and political entity is all about and what the stakes are. In the long process of learning about it,

I may have also helped others to understand better this extraordinary political experiment and become more committed Europeans as a result.

One huge consolation for me during the pandemic was the publication by Oxford University Press[12] of a collection of essays in my honour. They were written by leading experts and policy makers from different countries. The book in hand is also an attempt to pay back my debt and engage in a constructive debate with the large community of people who have invested their hopes in the European project. I hope they will not be disappointed.

When the Facts Change

Going with the liberal tide

European integration started as a project for peace and reconciliation after the end of the Second World War. And because it had to rely on economic instruments to achieve those political objectives, leaders who took the initiative bet on rising prosperity for the many as the way to convince citizens it was a good thing. A benign conspiracy of political elites, it was meant to gain public support by delivering the goods; it did both, for a long time.

The project was premised on liberal economic ideas and was thus consistent with the international economic order set up after the end of the war under US leadership. This new order included freer trade, fixed exchange rates, limited capital movements across borders, and multi-lateral institutions; in other words, liberalism in moderation, carefully administered doses and common rules. The treaty of Rome, signed in 1957, took this international economic order as a given and built on it for the six founding members while taking special characteristics of Europe into account. Typically, lawyers and Europe professionals always refer to the four fundamental freedoms of the founding treaty as the main pillars on which the European construction rests, namely the free movement of goods, services, people and capital.

It could not get more liberal than this, although – to be fair – it was never meant to happen at one stroke or in an undiluted fashion. Liberalization took place in stages and was extended over many years. There were also exceptions, agriculture being the most prominent among them. And so were coal and steel, with which European integration had started in the first place. For all those sectors, the gradual elimination of national protection was meant to be accompanied by the creation of common policy instruments. The architects of the European project were economically liberal, but they were not politically naïve. They knew the long history of heavy government intervention in all those sectors as they also knew full well the reality of mixed economies in Europe.

The treaty of Rome was therefore intended to gradually liberalize economic exchange between highly protected national economies destroyed by war and in which the state had historically played a major role. Hence the implicit division of labour that developed over time between European and national institutions. The former concentrated on liberalization while the latter continued, in ever-increasing doses, to provide redistribution as well as economic stabilization through fiscal and monetary policy.[1]

National governments thus remained the ultimate guarantors of the social contract, which in turn ensured a modicum of social peace. The power of governments over markets steadily increased during the first thirty years or so of the post-war period; it was the triumph of social democracy writ large. In some European countries, more than half of GDP went through the hands of governments. A liberal Europe with social democratic states: it was a paradox that all kinds of purists could not understand. But so long as levels of prosperity rose fast and the gains were perceived to be fairly distributed between and within member countries, this unorthodox division of labour between European and national institutions worked reasonably well. In fact, it did so for several decades.

The next stage of integration was about transforming a very incomplete customs union into a single market. It was an ambitious exercise, still ongoing, which was again fully compatible with the latest phase of economic liberalization that the world experienced for the next almost forty years. In fact, during this period starting in the 1980s, European integration and globalization were two sides of the same coin and free capital movements under flexible exchange rates were the main driver for both.

Of course, some things were done differently in Europe. The EU became not only a liberalizer but also a regulator on a big scale. Zealots for free markets were shocked as a result, as zealots habitually are when confronted with reality that does not conform to their own ideological purity. True, zealots of a different kind were also to be found among some Brussels bureaucrats who looked for ways to stretch their administrative power. And local demagogues had a field day; for them the whole exercise of European standard and rule setting, a typical feature of advanced economies, was just a conspiracy by foreigners and technocrats (God only knows who is worse!) to regulate our lives. British tabloids excelled in this sport.

Orthodox economic theory told us that trade and market liberaliz-ation would bring material benefits, although it was less clear how those benefits would be distributed between and within countries. In fact, views about the unequal effects of free trade combined with economies of scale and very imperfect competition have become mainstream in the economics literature for some time now.[2] In the crucial early stages of the transition to the single market, the president of the European Commission was Jacques Delors, a French socialist and a moderate who had never been elected to political office. He believed that markets should be guided by the hidden (or otherwise) hand of governments, which have the responsibility to stabilize their economies and better distribute the benefits from free economic exchange. He also believed in Europe as a political project. He thus seized the opportunity provided by the single market programme to add new items to the European political agenda.

New members had already been added and the single market programme was meant to apply to a very diverse community of countries and economies. Delors argued that the way to convince less developed countries and regions to accept more competition and the breaking down of national economic barriers was through the provision of development aid through the EU budget. Some people were tempted to call it a bribe. Delors preferred the name Structural Funds. The latter contributed much to the opening and modernization of countries such as Ireland, Spain and Portugal, while also playing a big role in making poorer members love Europe.

Admittedly, large transfers of development aid came with considerable waste, because of administrative failures at all levels, not to mention corruption. European institutions do not have a strong record in tackling corruption, nor do they have the resources, political and administrative, to deal effectively with malpractices at national and local level. It may be part of the price to pay for a highly decentralized structure and diverse traditions within Europe's fledgling political entity. On the other hand, Structural Funds added an element of redistribution in the European contract, although in low-key fashion because many Europeans were still not ready to officially recognize that redistribution may be part of the overall European contract. Delors also tried to strengthen the social dimension of European integration by linking it to the single market, although he was much less successful on this front.

The implementation of the European single market programme coincided with a big liberalization drive on a global scale. Keynesian economic ideas began to retreat. The rise in inflation reinforced by the oil shocks of the 1970s was the catalyst. Reagan and Thatcher borrowed from Hayek and Friedman[3] to provide the ideological justification for a new, stronger version of economic liberalism, while Deng Xiaoping brought capitalism to China and opened the country to the world economy. It is impossible to think of this more recent era of globalization without Reagan and Thatcher, equally impossible to do so without China, which practised capitalism under the control of the Communist Party: a novel experiment indeed.

During this period, the relationship between state and market shifted in favour of the latter. The pendulum swung. It was a conscious decision: economic liberalism dominated the political agenda. Freer markets and technological change brought with time more integration and trade, global supply chains and the prevalence of the financial sector. They brought considerable material benefits as well. But benefits were unevenly distributed. Hundreds of millions of Chinese were taken out of abject poverty as Chinese GDP multiplied more than seventy times in forty years. This had never happened before in world history. Meanwhile, earnings of blue-collar workers in the US remained stagnant for decades, much of the middle class was hollowed out and the top 1 per cent captured a much larger share of income and wealth across the world.

Economic insecurity was also very unevenly distributed in this new liberal world, with segments of the labour market operating again in conditions similar to those prevailing in the early capitalist era, all in the name of flexibility. 'Gig economy' is the term to describe the growing segment of developed economies relying on workers with temporary, part-time jobs and little social security. Zero-hour contracts, mostly used in the UK, are the epitome, forcing workers to be constantly on call without any guarantee of minimum hours of work. Such flexibility is good so long as it applies to others. The Italian term, *precariato*, provides a more accurate description of the conditions under which many people live and work today. These people have coexisted for years with the growing numbers of *Anywheres* in our cosmopolitan metropolises and beyond: an uneasy coexistence.

In most of Europe, inequalities within countries increased, although less than in the United States or the UK. National welfare systems and state intervention continued to play an important role as an economic and social Leveller,[4] although under growing pressure from both within and without. Solidarity was less in fashion in increasingly individualized societies and trade unions were in decline, while global competition and capital mobility put pressure on wages and government tax receipts. Governments need borders to exercise their authority, and borders became increasingly permeable in this era of global capital mobility.

Thus, political and market forces combined to weaken what used to be generally referred to as the European model, an attempt in other words to reconcile efficiency with equity. Of course, there have always been different national versions of this generally defined European model, ranging from its most advanced form in Scandinavia and much of north-western Europe to lighter versions in southern Europe and the more recent extra-lite versions in former communist lands to the east.

Things were not made any easier by slower output growth and productivity experienced during the same period, a declining trend that became much more pronounced during the financial crisis. Slower output and productivity growth in the developed world in recent decades have been the subject of much analysis and debate within the economics profession, leading to different explanations. In one of the most celebrated works, Robert Gordon[5] analyses the reasons behind lower long-term trends of productivity growth in the US economy with an emphasis on the role of new technologies. His explanation is also relevant for the rest of the developed world. Theories of secular stagnation,[6] on the other hand, concentrate on the long-term decline in demand related in turn to demographic trends and rising inequalities. Theories of declining productivity growth and theories of secular stagnation make for a depressing combination. Solutions to the problem have been sadly more difficult to design and are most unlikely to be created by markets operating on their own.

Meanwhile, Europe was losing out in the race for new technologies, which only made matters worse in this part of the world. The existence of a large European market without internal borders was apparently not enough on its own to create the conditions for European firms to win in the global race, although research in Europe was usually in the top league. There was a problem in matching research with entrepreneurship in the old continent, and it was not new.

Widening inequalities and slow growth are not a good recipe for happy societies, nor are they a good base from which to build a more united Europe. The gradual worsening of the economic environment, after a long honeymoon period that had lasted until the early 1970s, was therefore bound to take its toll. Defenders of the European project tried to argue that Europe was a victim of collateral damage, but how many out there were willing to listen? For those on the losing side of economic change, Europe could not provide a substitute for the waning protection of the nation state.

In this changing environment, the early division of labour between Europe and member states became more tenuous. Except for Structural Funds specially designed for less developed regions, Europe had effectively no instruments to help the growing number of people who found themselves on the losing side of economic liberalism and the technological revolution. Instead, Europe was perceived by losers as a vehicle of change, hence part of the problem and not part of the solution.

Economic games political adults play

Meanwhile, the euro had come into the picture. This was an altogether different ball game from the one European institutions had learned to play so far. EMU involved the core economic functions of the modern state, a game for political adults in other words. The architects of Maastricht tried to tackle the problem by drawing a clear line of division between monetary and fiscal policy. The former was to be centralized and reserved for technocrats operating within a narrowly confined mandate – less politely called a straitjacket – while the latter would remain the responsibility of national governments under joint supervision and subject to rules.

Monetary policy in the hands of experts and away from the reach of (irresponsible) politicians would ensure price stability. Constraining rules on national fiscal policy would prevent large deficits and, God forbid, there would be no transfers across borders. Free markets, notably unregulated financial markets, would take care of the rest. It was economic liberalism with a special kind of rules: Germans call it *Ordnungspolitik*. The combination of market competition and rules is the key principle of ordo-liberalism, on which Germany's post-war economic miracle has been based. Germans have tried to export ordo-liberalism to the rest of the Eurozone, although forgetting welfare policies and the crucial role played by social partners in Germany's coordinated capitalism[7] – Germany Incorporated in simpler terms. Marcel Fratzscher, a leading German economist and strong critic of the official orthodoxy, writes that *Ordnungspolitik* 'tends to treat economics as a moral science which judges policies primarily through their compliance with rules rather than by outcomes'.[8] Listening to top German officials at the peak of the euro crisis, it was difficult to disagree with him.

Were Europeans ready to assume the responsibilities that come with sharing a common currency? Judging from the Maastricht treaty and early responses to the euro crisis, the honest answer would be 'No', although Europeans have been trying hard ever since. They know that any attempt to go back to national currencies would have made the management of Brexit look like a trivial operation by comparison. This is a key point that helps to explain why the overwhelming majority among European political leaders – citizens as well, judging from opinion polls – have never been willing to contemplate a possible breakup of the euro. It is exactly what has kept the common currency alive in times of crisis, forcing decisions and policy measures that would have been simply unthinkable before. They include national bailouts that had never been supposed to happen, the creation of a European monetary fund (alias European Stability Mechanism – ESM), more stringent rules and procedures for the coordination of national fiscal policies, a banking union albeit still incomplete, and, last but by no means least, never-ending large-scale interventions by the ECB.

Only a few years after they had managed (and how?) to bring the euro crisis under control, the pandemic forced governments to act again as saviours of last resort. They needed to spend huge sums of money to deal with an unprecedented downturn in economic activity, in turn forced by lockdowns to save human lives. But the capacity to borrow differed widely among member governments. Therefore, if member governments were left on their own, the euro and the single market could be in grave danger. The strong EU fiscal stimulus programme adopted in 2020, backed by a decision to mutualize part of the new debt, was therefore meant to complement national efforts, and it was extended to all EU members. It went hand in hand with an expansionary and unconventional monetary policy. Thus, successive crises were forcing the ECB to behave more and more like a normal central bank.

The pandemic came at the tail end of a succession of big shocks that radically transformed the context within which European integration was taking place. Shocks came together with the debunking of economic dogmas and myths. Growing inequalities and large-scale financial instability had already exposed the faults and weaknesses of unregulated global markets. European integration was no longer working like a convergence machine and the weakness of the euro construction had become all too obvious. Meanwhile, climate change was forcing (almost) everybody to revisit economic models that left a heavy carbon footprint. And unfair trade with China's state capitalism was acting as catalyst for the politicization of international economic exchange. The reversal of the previous liberal trend had already begun before the pandemic arrived; it was much reinforced when it did.

The new crisis threw a large spanner into the wheels of market globalization. Global markets and supply chains took a big hit, while countries and individual producers began to think and act more in national or regional terms. Thus, the European decision to strengthen the regional project came precisely at a time when globalization was faltering. This parting of the ways between European integration and globalization is bound to have major implications for a whole range of EU policies.

In the 1970s and 1980s, most of my British colleagues in Oxford referred to European integration as the Common Market. For them, it was all about a Common Market – and they often meant it rather disparagingly. The management of the European single market is now almost all-encompassing, from regulation and standard setting, competition, industrial and environmental policy, to taxation and redistribution. Most countries have already replaced their currencies with the euro. In the name of the Union, political leaders now take decisions amounting to trillions of euros and the ECB holds about a third of all government bonds in circulation. Talk of a Common Market: it is a very different world today.

The Union has been steadily encroaching on the core of economic sovereignty while having an ever-increasing effect on domestic social contracts. This trend has accelerated in recent years. Some EU members have been kicking and screaming, but they have not been able to stop it. Is it all part of the old plot of the *illuminati*? A more realistic explanation would instead focus on the need to respond to new challenges and recurring crises in a rapidly changing economic and political environment, as well as to protect a very imperfect monetary union set up initially for geopolitical rather than economic reasons. As a result, the division of labour between the EU and its member states has been shifting inexorably, albeit with fits and starts.

Where is the team spirit?

It is a strange team, this United Europe. There are players of very different classes: some are fast and extremely skilful, others with little training, dragging their feet – we may sometimes wonder how they got in. Some are highly respectful of rules and others often cheat and complain loudly once caught. And with a lot of quarrelling among players: the team spirit leaves much to be desired. Seen from outside, what is truly surprising is that the United Europe team, although very uneven in its performance, sometimes plays well. It scores and wins a few championship matches – not at all obvious.

True, the United Europe team benefits from technical support and coaching provided by common institutions, many and varied, resorting to conventional and less conventional methods. Conventional methods include traditional intergovernmental negotiations, the less conventional ones the so-called Community method. The United Europe team also has an organized fan club through the European Parliament as Europe's direct source of democratic legitimacy, which provides the link with hundreds of millions of (lukewarm) supporters. Fan clubs of national teams that lend their top players to play with the United Europe team are to this day far more devoted.

In principle, all players are equal, although some are much more equal than others – everybody knows this. The team has two undisputed leaders: they are from France and Germany, for whom the club was created a long time ago with the aim of getting them to play together instead of constantly fighting each other. When the two leaders coordinate, they usually lead the team to victory. In the jargon, Franco-German cooperation is a necessary but not sufficient condition. What is also important is that the two leading players have very different backgrounds and skills, which allows other players room to express their own talent.

Another very talented player was from the UK. He left, though, less of a mark than expected for the simple reason that he never felt terribly comfortable with the rest of the team. The UK player has now decided to play only for the national team, and it has not been a smooth exit. And there is one more player to keep a close watch on, namely the goalkeeper, who comes from Italy. He is talented but unstable. Everybody on the stands keeps a close watch on the goalkeeper, knowing that his unstable performance may cost the club some crucial matches, if not the entire championship.

But enough with the football metaphor. Let us get back to politics. France and Germany have been from the very beginning at the centre of European integration, because of history, geography and size. Their bilateral relationship has evolved enormously during the last seventy years or so and has been directly linked to the multilateral European framework. The former foes now interact and cooperate very closely at all levels, bilaterally and as partners in the European project. Not always successfully, it should be said, because on many issues they start from different ends of the spectrum, be they economic policy, foreign policy or the overall direction of European integration. Trying to find a compromise somewhere in the middle, they usually allow room for other countries to express their views and promote their interests. When sober, the other members recognize that this peculiar European arrangement of consensus politics in which some are clearly more equal than others is still much better than the old concert of European powers, which had left little room for smaller countries to manoeuvre.

The central role of France and Germany is widely acknowledged. In the 'EU Coalition Explorer' survey conducted by the European Council on

Foreign Relations (ECFR),[9] based on expert opinions of more than 800 respondents from all twenty-seven members, the two countries clearly stand out from the rest as potential coalition partners in the EU. In other words, they are the countries that count the most and the countries to be contacted first on a wide range of policy areas. Of the two, Germany holds a more pivotal position while France has rather weak links with countries of central and eastern Europe. Perhaps surprisingly given its size, the Netherlands ranks third in terms of relative importance in the eyes of EU partners, albeit at some distance from the two leaders.

French and German views on Europe have evolved over the years while the balance of power between them shifted. The French increasingly felt they were losing ownership of the European project, which they believed was rightfully theirs. Being overtaken by Germany, France also became more supportive of the old Community method and common institutions. At the same time, Germany moved in the opposite direction: a reluctant leader during Europe's recent multiple crises, drawing on its economic strength and creditor power and more Gaullist in its attitude towards European institutions. Strange games history sometimes plays. Working through the Council as the European intergovernmental institution par excellence was seen by the Germans as the best way to defend their interests and protect their purse from the greedy(!) hands of their European partners.

The Franco-German relationship[10] has had its ups and downs and personalities have played a major role in shaping it. The peaks have been usually associated with the Giscard–Schmidt and Kohl–Mitterrand eras from the 1970s to the mid-1990s, which also suggests that ideological and party preferences are not necessarily that important in shaping a close relationship across the Rhine. It became increasingly uneven during the long Merkel era until Macron came to power. France then took the initiative in a variety of fields and Germany's role was reduced to choosing between modest concessions and outright '*Nein.*' France was taking bold initiatives from a position of relative weakness, while Germany was in a stronger position – a successful country on many fronts – yet behaving more like a merchant than a leader. Admittedly, the word 'leader' in German (*Führer*) carries very strong negative connotations both at home and abroad. And finally, Merkel took the big decision to join Macron in a bold joint initiative to strengthen Europe during the pandemic. Merkel then donned the mantle of the stateswoman, as she had already done before during the immigration crisis.

With the UK now out of the picture, Italy is the only other country with the potential to belong to the big league of European powers, yet a potential that has rarely been translated into reality. During the previous two decades, economic stagnation and populism created a vicious circle from which it proved extremely difficult for Italy to escape.[11] Unhappy with the straitjacket of the euro and the lack of European solidarity on the immigration front, the erstwhile fervent supporter of European integration turned more and more Eurosceptic. And then came the pandemic, which hit Italy hard while also exposing the fragility of its health system and its finances. The size of Italy's public debt makes it a prime example of a country that could be too big to fail and too big to save. Yet so long as the ECB continues buying bonds on a large scale and keeps interest rates low, the problem will be shifted to the future.

The north–south divide has become wider in recent years. It is largely of an economic nature and related to the difficulties experienced by southern countries in adjusting to globalization, the strictures of euro membership, and EU enlargement to the east, all combined and in succession. In turn, the difficulties experienced have much to do with production structures and the position of their economies near the lower end of the international division of labour, which means they produce price-sensitive goods in direct competition with those produced in emerging economies. Are those economic factors more important than gridlocked political systems and a strong aversion to reform, which are also real? This remains a highly contested argument, albeit with crucial policy implications.

The east–west divide is more political and cultural. The latest big bang enlargement has been the most difficult ever for the EU to digest. Countries in central and eastern Europe benefitted from large-scale foreign investments and were quickly integrated into global supply chains, mostly German-owned. They also benefitted from large inflows of EU funds. They became much richer and more unequal. They also lost many of their best-educated and most mobile people, who emigrated to the more developed countries of the EU. At the peak of the euro crisis, some of the former communist lands were more royalist than Queen Merkel and Prince Schäuble in support of economic austerity. The zeal of new converts to neoliberal ideology combined with weak trade unions and weak civil societies.

But they also ended up with more than their fair share of populists who showed little respect for democratic pluralism, combined with strong nationalism also directed against Brussels and visceral reactions against immigration from non-European countries. They wanted EU funds but no EU interference in domestic affairs. The so-called Visegrád[12] countries, comprising the Czech Republic, Hungary, Poland and Slovakia, formed a group of their own. Hungary and Poland usually led this pack and were treated as Europe's ugly ducks. During the euro crisis, Greece had played a similar role as the black sheep of monetary union – we use different animal metaphors in the United Europe team! How to deal with misfits and laggards has always remained a sensitive issue, since all players are supposed to have a contract for life.

There are subgroups and constantly shifting alliances within the EU. Numbers and diversity offer plenty of opportunities for participants to jostle around during the long negotiations that are the trademark of European decision making. The old Benelux group consisting of the three smaller founding members is no longer as operational as it used to be. Mainstream political elites in Belgium and small Luxembourg are very European, while the Dutch have remained Dutch and more Eurosceptic. In the past, southern countries had rarely succeeded in forming solid alliances, but they have done so increasingly in recent years, especially within the Eurozone in support of Eurobonds and more risk sharing. France has often acted as the informal leader of the southern group, while simultaneously looking towards Berlin.

Germany has been the natural leader of countries with strong economies and a strong aversion to risk sharing and spending more money on common policies. The Netherlands acts as the deputy leader and takes the helm whenever Germany shows too much of an inclination to compromise with France. The Dutch have acted as informal leaders of the so-called Hanseatic league comprising fiscally conservative countries that are also staunch believers in market integration – more recently also of the smaller group of 'frugals' including all Scandinavians. As cool northerners, the latter do not naturally belong to the category of Eurodreamers, although the Finns at least have decided to throw in their lot with the most advanced group of integrationists through their participation in the Eurozone. A common border with Russia surely has something to do with this decision.

Europe's political geography is extremely colourful and varied, as might be expected given so much diversity bequeathed by History in a relatively small continent. Running the United Europe team is surely no easy affair, to put it mildly. The real power rests with the heads of government – and of state in the case of France, which has a presidential system. They are the ones with whom the buck stops, in the famous words of a former US president, Harry Truman. With time, the European political system has turned more intergovernmental, especially when important decisions are at stake.

It is of course a good thing that the top people in each country have become directly involved. But ruling through conferences held under the name of the European Council, deciding mostly by unanimity, with a president who is more of a facilitator and mediator, and through exhaustion in long sessions that often last for several days until the early hours of the morning, is not exactly the most efficient way to run Europe.[13] The European decision-making system hardly matches the importance of decisions it is meant to produce. As a political entity in the making, Europe has become more ungovernable with the accrual of new functions and the addition of new members in an ever more challenging environment. Watching the United Europe team play is indeed a nerve-racking experience that often leaves the fans hoping for a miracle to save the match. Remarkably, though, miracles sometimes happen.

The team and the fans

An elite-driven process based on wide cross-party consensus, dealing with issues of limited political salience, and enjoying passive public support: it would be a good summary of what happened with European integration for several decades. In the words of a former French foreign minister, it was enlightened despotism.[14] But it could not (and should not) last forever.

Talk of a democratic deficit in European integration goes a long way back. 'Decisions taken by foreigners and technocrats behind closed doors' was always an easy and, indeed, misleading way to portray the

European method of decision making. The fact that national, democrati-cally elected representatives took part in those decisions, usually taken by unanimity, was conveniently forgotten. But convinced Europeans wanted to go further anyway. Thus, direct elections to the European Parliament (EP) were introduced as early as 1979. For diehards of national sovereignty, it was a direct affront, if not a useless operation, since for them there can be no democracy beyond the borders of the nation state. If anything, attracting public attention to the workings of the EP has proved a steep upward climb.

The EP acquired ever more powers with time and hence played an increasingly important role in the drafting of European legislation. But all big decisions continued to be taken elsewhere. This was not, however, unique to the EU. Parliaments were fast losing power to the executive branch in all parliamentary democracies. There was, nevertheless, a crucial difference. Unlike its national counterparts, the EP had no say over who runs the executive in Europe's fledgling political entity. Most European citizens do not understand the nuances of the extremely complicated governance structure of the EU, and they do not care either. But they have a pretty good sense of where real power lies. And they know it does not lie with the EP.

The European Council is the closest we have to a European government, and its members are elected by and accountable to national parliaments, not to the EP. An attempt was made in recent years to link the election of the president of the Commission to the directly elected EP, which was meant to provide the Commission with a source of direct legitimacy and make it more political. It was, however, short-lived: national political leaders reinstated their control in 2019 by choosing Ursula von der Leyen to run the Brussels machine.

Europe's democratic deficit grew bigger as the scope of integration widened and thus entered more sensitive areas of national sovereignty. It reached dangerous peaks during recent crises, when the asymmetry of power within the Council also became much more pronounced. In the name of whose democracy exactly were decisions taken that dictated economic policy in certain member countries or decisions about the number of immigrants to be allowed in? It was difficult to explain to people in Madrid or Athens, Budapest as well, who felt strongly that the European Council – often personified by Chancellor Merkel as the obvious *prima inter pares* – had no legitimacy to take such decisions on their behalf.

The problem with democratic legitimacy has both a national and a European dimension. As executives and national bureaucracies constantly gained space at the expense of parliaments, as power shifted from states to markets and national borders became more permeable, and as ideological convergence between mainstream political parties grew further, political choices in national democracies shrank as a result. European integration was one factor, but nevertheless an important one, contributing to this effect.

One of the leading European political scientists, the late Peter Mair,[15] wrote some years back about states that ended up ruling the void as key decisions were steadily taken away from them. Margaret Thatcher put it differently in her inimitable and rather extreme fashion. She often defended her policies in the name of TINA, which stood for 'There Is No Alternative.' In this world of the single truth and no real choices, or at best a choice between Coca-Cola and Pepsi Cola as proudly proclaimed by Thomas Friedman,[16] a leading advocate of market globalization in the early years of optimism, voters on the losing side of economic change felt disenfranchised. And their numbers grew with time, especially with the advent of the financial crisis. TINA and the liberal consensus were not delivering the goods for many people: the numbers of disenfran-chised losers were growing fast. Sooner or later, this was bound to find a political expression. History habitually punishes hubris.

The result was the rise of anti-systemic and populist parties to give voice to popular discontent. Often, there was not much to distinguish between the two categories. National politics thus became more fragmented and polarized, while the old mainstream parties that had ruled for many years in coalitions or in succession rapidly lost votes – in some countries, they also lost power. The credibility of political elites naturally suffered as well. Hence, national democracies became more difficult to govern and all the key political ingredients of the early success of European integration, notably an elite-driven process, wide cross-party consensus and passive public support, were no longer there.

Of course, fragmentation and polarization in individual member countries, coupled with political instability and leaders who burn all too quickly in populist bonfires, also made for an increasingly ungovernable

Europe. The national problem was multiplied at the European level. It had been difficult enough when centre-right and centre-left parties converged in their policies and tried to run the show for years, while allowing themselves, if only occasionally, the luxury to think long-term. Now, they needed to fight new contestants at home under the unforgiving rule of the ephemeral, and often with little distinction made between real and fake news in social media as now the main source of information for most people. No surprise, European policies became much more difficult to decide and implement. It was hardly a consolation that the problem was not unique to Europe.

The EU is an essentially confederal political system[17] with some original elements of supranationality and federal touches here and there: a unique legal system with the European Court of Justice (ECJ) at the top (now being challenged by some of its national counterparts), a politicized bureaucracy and special powers for the Commission, plus a multitude of agencies, a federal central bank and a directly elected EP, alongside prime ministers and presidents, finance ministers and others who represent the member states. Although the general direction of policy and the most important decisions remain under the control of member states, it is also true that Europe has more than its fair share of governance by rules and technocrats. It is part of the DNA.

The goal of effectiveness and legitimacy presents a tall order for the European system, especially since there is no historical precedent or anything similar in other parts of the world to learn from. Take the example of the Eurozone as the most advanced form of European integration, which is also an extreme example of governing by rules and ruling by numbers.[18] Too many rules are there because there is not enough trust among participating members. But this is hardly an effective or efficient way to run the Eurozone, as became obvious in times of crisis. Rules are needed for sure, but so are institutions and people vested with the authority to exercise discretion and take difficult decisions. Such decisions inevitably have distributional effects. Alas, no politically sterilized way has been found anywhere yet to run an EMU.

The economic (and not only) functions that Europe has gradually undertaken, sometimes in an absent-minded fashion or more often forced by events, are not matched by the legal and institutional structure within which the EU operates, nor are they backed by the necessary political legitimacy. Policies without politics, in other words. The EU is like a team playing in a world championship with clothes that are too tight, inadequate training, and many frustrated fans in the stadium shouting in different tongues and disagreeing among themselves about how the team should play. The treaties are certainly too tight for what the EU is tasked to do today, but hardly anybody wants to have another go at revising the treaties. They still remember what happened with the European constitution less than twenty years ago. A new treaty or a constitution to be agreed by unanimity, ratified by twenty-seven parliaments and approved in successive referendums is a nightmare for many of Europe's political leaders today.

Unaccustomed to rough play

European integration was born in times of benign US leadership of the West and with active US support. It was perceived as an integral part of efforts to strengthen the Western alliance during the Cold War. Sure, Washington was not always in agreement with specific European policies, and with time was getting increasingly apprehensive of European negotiating power based on unity. Yet strategic interests usually prevailed, as expressed by the Department of State, while the US continued to provide the ultimate guarantee for the security of its western European allies. The latter were in turn forced to recognize that geopolitics was now mostly in the hands of the leader of the alliance. This was made painfully clear to both British and French in the Suez debacle in 1956.

Steadily expanding its functions and taking in new members, the EU learned to make more out of its joint negotiating power, which was indeed substantial and drew mostly on the size of the single market. The EU has always been a trade power, first and foremost. With time, it also became an economic power more broadly as a global rule-setter and provider of large amounts of economic aid. In contrast, the introduction of the euro has not been translated yet into similar influence in monetary and financial affairs.

Europeans often like to think of themselves as being different from the rest in international relations. European integration was meant from the very beginning as a rejection of traditional power politics. Soft power, civilian power or normative power are terms often used to describe the role of the EU as international actor. A strong advocate of global multilateralism and common rules in trade, the European bloc, however, always had some difficulty in reconciling this principled stance with the reality of many preferential agreements signed with neighbours and former colonies. It was not the only contradiction that Brussels had to deal with. EU institutions focused on trade and economic instruments of foreign policy and were strong advocates of democracy and human rights, while member states kept for themselves the more traditional instruments of foreign policy that went with a more pragmatic (cynical?) approach to power politics. It was another example of an implicit division of labour between European institutions and member states, albeit with an element of hypocrisy hidden in it. The dirty work was left to national chancelleries, which in turn operated within the cocoon provided with the compliments of NATO and the United States in the time of the Cold War.

Only France seemed to dream of an independent (and French-led) Europe as an international actor, although this dream carried for a long time too little conviction with most of the other European partners. Hence, foreign policy cooperation among member states registered very slow progress despite lofty declarations issued by European foreign ministers. Internal European divisions, coupled with the need for unanimity in foreign policy cooperation and a general unwillingness to commit resources, especially soldiers, to operations beyond national borders, meant that the influence Europe could exert in its neighbourhood and beyond was limited at best. The so-called High Representative of the European Union for Foreign Affairs and Security Policy (a long name with limited substance) is usually a frustrated person trying to articulate a common European stance where unity usually does not exist.

Geopolitics has essentially remained out of bounds for Brussels with one important exception, namely enlargement. By opening the doors to new members, the Union played European high politics. The year 1989 was indeed a big turning point. The Cold War was over, at least temporarily, and the Soviet Union was dismantled together with the Soviet empire that had extended all the way to Berlin. In the famous words of its first secretary general,[19] NATO had been meant to keep the Soviets out, the Americans in and the Germans down. After 1989, the only element of the old equation left was the American military presence in Europe. The breakdown of the post-war political order on the old continent thus presented the European regional entity, limited until then by necessity to the western side of the Iron Curtain, with new and difficult challenges. And Europe did best what it was always good at, namely in extending *Pax Europaea* to other parts of the continent.

The solution to the new German problem, so to speak, was found in the context of the EU: it meant more and stronger Europe. Thus, the former German Democratic Republic became part of the Federal Republic and hence part of an EU determined to proceed to the next stage of integration, including notably monetary union. In other words, German unification became part and parcel of a much bigger European contract, in the same way as the integration of Germany into common European institutions has been all along a key part of peace and reconciliation in Europe after the Second World War. Similarly, the extension of EU membership to the former communist countries of central and eastern Europe was an integral part of the post-1989 European order and the transition of those countries to democracy and market economy. This is undoubtedly one of the great achievements of the European project, despite the many difficulties experienced with the new enlargement.

The EU has been much less successful in handling traditional power politics. Its soft power reached its limits as it came nearer Russia's hard power. To make matters worse, EU members were divided on how to deal with the big neighbour to the east. Germany, France and Italy tended to see Russia as a strategic partner in terms of energy and trade, as well as a difficult neighbour with whom one needs to find a peaceful modus vivendi. In contrast, Poland and the Baltic countries, often led by the UK while still a member and strongly supported by anti-Russia hawks in Washington DC, perceived such attitudes as unacceptable appeasement of the aggressive Russian bear always ready to attack.

Different perceptions about Russia in turn strongly influenced the relationship of individual European countries with the leader of the Atlantic alliance. During the war in Iraq, the administration of George W. Bush Jr had successfully played the divide-and-rule game in Europe. More than ten years later, President Trump was much blunter in reminding Europeans of their limited degree of independence. President Macron gave his own answer: he called NATO brain-dead[20] and insisted on European defence cooperation, European sovereignty and strategic autonomy. Most central and eastern Europeans were apoplectic. They did not want to undermine the Atlantic alliance in any way while being always ready to follow the US lead to anywhere, even under President Trump. For them, it was an existential issue, rightly or wrongly.

After Russia's seizure of Crimea and the eruption of war in the eastern regions of Ukraine in 2014, the US rallied the troops in Europe and sanctions were imposed on Russia. But the US later also threatened sanctions to halt the construction of a new gas pipeline intended to bring additional Russian gas directly to Germany under the Baltic Sea, thus bypassing Ukraine. US sanctions in relation to a joint project between Russia and Germany while the latter remained a major ally of the US were not at all obvious.[21] EU members in central and eastern Europe were only too pleased. But things changed radically once again when Russia invaded Ukraine in 2022. It was a huge shock and members of the Atlantic alliance quickly closed ranks. Will Putin inadvertently also become Europe's ultimate unifier by forcing Europeans to take more collective responsibility for their defence?

Europe has repeatedly offered itself as an easy playground for outside powers – foes, rivals, also allies – to play divide-and-rule games. The Chinese as well were quick in learning to play such games. Individual European countries tried to outcompete each other in attracting Chinese favour and investment, especially during difficult times. And the Chinese were only too pleased to accommodate them.

One of the few examples of Europe playing an international role with effect was the Iran nuclear deal, in which France, Germany and the UK were actively engaged, together with the EU Commission. It was the deal that President Trump later denounced when he came to power, leading to US withdrawal. In contrast, the civil wars in Syria and Libya were examples of European frustration and/or internal divisions. In both cases, Russia and Turkey ended up as power brokers.

In a world where the geopolitical tectonic plates are shifting fast and security concerns take over from economic efficiency, in a world where Russian revisionism takes a nasty turn and US unilateralism sometimes turns ugly, the EU has had enormous difficulties in grappling with the reality of power politics. It is precisely power politics that the EU had long tried to negate if not hide away from. But power politics is now back with a vengeance and Europe's soft power cocoon is no longer. The facts have changed.[22] Can Europeans begin to think and act collectively as an international power? It would be the surest sign of Europe's coming of age.

PART II

Main Challenges and Choices

5

How Many Presidents and Crises for the Euro?

The optimist of the will

'How many presidents and crises will it take before Europe acquires a fully fledged currency in a properly functioning economic and monetary union?' This is the question any seasoned observer of the European scene would be tempted to ask, looking back at the long and chequered history of the euro and its antecedents.

The pessimist, and equally the non-believer, would give a short and straight answer: 'Not in your lifetime – or the next one.' The pessimist would surely remind the curious observer that a currency needs a state and that no European political union can be seen on the horizon. The up-to-date pessimist might perhaps concede that state and currency may no longer remain inextricably linked in the digital age, although nobody can be sure except for visionaries and libertarians mostly inhabiting the Silicon Valley – and such people have no interest anyway in the European project.

Your mainstream pessimist would therefore conclude that Europe is doomed to live with an incomplete EMU and a dysfunctional currency for as long as we can see, without excluding the possibility of disintegration in the next crisis, or the one after next, to be followed by a chaotic return to national currencies. This is what happens when you try to defy the economic laws of gravity, the hard-nosed economist might add. Pretty dismal stuff, as should be expected, from disciples of the dismal science.

Optimists, on the other hand, usually rely on either ignorance, dogma or sheer perseverance. I would opt for the last or rather for what Antonio Gramsci, the Italian political thinker and activist of the interwar period, described as the pessimism of the intellect and the optimism of the will.[1] Gramsci was writing in a prison cell in Italy under fascism. Since European integration has been shaped by a relatively small number of people determined to change the course of history and try things that the large majority considered as unrealistic or downright mad, with remarkable successes so far and many failures, let us hear what Gramsci's politically committed optimist might say about the euro and EMU.

He or she would probably start by reminding us of key turning points in European monetary integration[2] going all the way back to the late 1960s and the Werner report of 1970, which was the first official report outlining a plan for a complete European EMU. It was named after the then prime minister of Luxembourg, who chaired a committee of high-level experts. EMU died a quick death back then, a victim of international monetary instability, internal economic divergence in Europe and muddled thinking. But it was never buried.

Instead, European political leaders kept trying with more modest versions of a regional currency bloc. And they did so with new plans being constantly tested by successive crises until the end of the Cold War and German reunification, which finally provided the decisive political catalyst for another go at a proper EMU. It was a happy coincidence that a committee chaired by Jacques Delors, then president of the European Commission, had laid the ground only a few months before the post-war European political order collapsed. The Delors report was followed a few years later by the Maastricht treaty. And by 1999, eleven EU countries had replaced their national currencies with the euro. The number has grown to nineteen, which means that today approximately 350 million people in the EU (and more outside) have euros in their pockets and their bank accounts. No small feat.

The Maastricht treaty of 1992, which gave birth to the euro after years of pregnancy, was the product of political feasibility and economic orthodoxy. Unfortunately for Europeans, what had been politically feasible back in the early 1990s proved to be totally inadequate when the big international financial crisis struck in 2007, while economic orthodoxy also suffered a big blow to its credibility. The result was a real mess. But the euro survived against the odds and contrary to all kinds of doomsday predictions from non-believers. Reforms were introduced under duress during the crisis. The Four Presidents' report in 2012 and the Five Presidents' report one year later went much further. They were signed by the heads of all major EU institutions and called for much bolder reforms to complete the EMU construction, alas with limited effect. They received praise from representatives of member states, although a blocking minority among them made sure that collective presidential ambition was kept on a short leash.

However, big crises sometimes make the politically unthinkable happen. And this proved to be true once again when the Covid-19 pandemic struck in 2020. The result was the large fiscal package financed through European borrowing in capital markets, with an explicit redistributive dimension in favour of the weaker and/or hardest-hit economies, and a strong emphasis on investment to help bring forward Europe's green and digital transition. It was not exactly Europe's 'Hamiltonian moment' as the United Europe faithful, including Germany's new chancellor Olaf Scholz, would have liked to believe. A few centuries back, Alexander Hamilton, one of the founding fathers of the United States of America, had played a key role in transforming the debt of individual states into federal debt. And in so doing, he had laid the foundations of a fiscal union and paved the way for the transition of the US from a confederation to a federal union. Surely, the EU is nowhere near, yet the decisions taken in 2020 constituted a major turning point. Thus, a deadly virus succeeded where several presidents combined had previously failed.

Based on historical experience, the long-winded answer of Gramsci's optimist of the will might conclude as follows: 'A fully fledged European currency in a properly functioning EMU is bound to be a difficult and long-drawn-out process, with many crises and failures. Although the price of an incomplete EMU in times of crisis was high, the long-term objective is of strategic importance. We are already more than half-way there and trying hard to get closer everyday.' With a cynical touch, he or she might also add that all you need is a visionary French president and a determined German chancellor, with an Italian populist looming on the horizon, to turn a big crisis into another opportunity to forge closer European unity.

After all, Jean Monnet,[3] the key figure among Europe's *illuminati* of the earlier period, had predicted that much. A French entrepreneur and diplomat, Monnet had been highly influential in the creation of the European Coal and Steel Community (ECSC) and the first president of the High Authority of the ECSC. He was also the founder of the Action Committee for the United States of Europe in 1955 and never elected to office: the *illuminati* often prefer to work behind the scenes.

The elusive goal of symmetry

One of the key drivers all along for monetary union has been the search for stability in intra-European exchange rates, seen as a necessary element for the proper functioning of the common and later the single market. The issue first arose in the late 1960s with the growing instability of the post-war Bretton Woods system and hence the perceived need to insulate Europe from the vagaries of the US dollar. Unlike academic economists, most European policy makers have never been much convinced about the virtues of floating rates for internal European trade. This strong preference for at least some degree of exchange rate stability has in turn much to do with the European reality of relatively small and very open economies tied together in a common economic and political project.

In the early days, European political leaders were broadly in agreement about the objective, although they could hardly agree about ways to achieve it. They disagreed about specific steps to be taken and the link between the fiscal and monetary aspects of EMU-to-be. But virtually all seemed to believe that the irrevocable fixity of intra-European exchange rates as the end goal depended on economic convergence. And for them, this could only be brought about through the progressive harmonization of national economic policies, hence ultimately a function of political will.

Economies shaped by policies, markets under the control of governments: it was an illusory view of the world soon to explode with a big bang. And the ammunition for the explosion was provided by increasingly mobile international capital and the inherently unstable financial markets. The post-war international economic order was undergoing a radical transformation at the time. Market forces were being unleashed and government policies hence became much more constrained. Few policy makers realized at the time the full consequences of this transformation. In other words, the first attempt at EMU was premised on a crucial assumption about the relationship between state and market that no longer held true.

Governments were no longer masters of the economic universe and monetary union was therefore not something that could simply be decreed. It took Europeans many years and successive crises before and after Maastricht to reconcile themselves to this hard fact. For the French, with a long tradition of *dirigisme*, this was even more difficult to accept. Nevertheless, despite many difficulties, most Europeans stuck to the objective of stable, if not irrevocably fixed, intra-European exchange rates all the way. And they ended up years later with a common currency, having thrown national currencies into the dustbin of history. That surely was a revolutionary act – non-believers would call it an act of irresponsibility. European political leaders have been struggling to defend that decision ever since.

The second key driver has been the search for further integration. EMU has always been not just an end but also the means to achieve closer economic and political integration. This is a crucial thing to understand, yet also a highly controversial issue between friends and enemies of a united Europe. From the very beginning, it was abundantly clear that the creation of a common European currency would be much more than simply another step towards economic integration. It would directly affect the exercise of macroeconomic policy in general, thus entailing a major transfer of economic sovereignty from the national to the European level. And much more: money is about symbols, also part and parcel of high politics.

The link between EMU and political union was established from the very beginning, although a big gap always existed between lofty declarations about long-term objectives and concrete commitments in terms of policies and institutions. The big change came with the fall of the Berlin Wall and German reunification. The link with EMU was established by President Mitterrand of France and Chancellor Kohl of Germany. And this in turn created a strong political momentum that led to Maastricht and ultimately to the creation of the euro in 1999. During the negotiations for the Maastricht treaty, the UK prime minister, John Major, said that support for EMU had 'the quaintness of a rain dance and about the same potency'.[4] He obviously got it wrong. It was neither the first nor the last time during the post-war period that British political leaders failed completely to understand what was happening across the Channel.

During the euro crisis of the early 2010s and more recently with the pandemic, many 'unthinkables' happened to protect the common currency and the European construction in general. It was this crucial link between the euro and the whole European project that many non-Europeans failed to grasp when making their predictions about the imminent demise of the euro at the peak of the crisis.[5] But it helps to explain a whole range of difficult decisions taken in Berlin, Paris and other capitals over the years and why Grexit was avoided against all odds. It also helps to explain the urge felt by Baltic countries to join the Eurozone in times when the euro faced an existential crisis. Currency and defence make an interesting link: for the Baltic countries, participation in the core group of European integration was tied to the perceived threat from Russia.

The euro remains to this day the most important act of European integration, more important than the single market or anything else that Europeans have achieved together in this novel exercise in sharing sovereignty through peaceful means. It is undoubtedly a powerful instrument that binds Europeans together. But the combination of an incomplete EMU and wrong policies came at a big price. At the peak of the euro crisis, EMU became a major factor of European disunity, creating a north–south cleavage and adding fuel to centrifugal forces within European countries. It also seriously undermined Europe's international credibility as an entity capable of managing its own affairs. If in doubt, ask the Chinese.

The third key driver for European monetary integration has been the search for symmetry, both internal and external. It all started with the perceived need to provide a collective European response to international monetary instability in the late 1960s that morphed into US unilateralism. Back in 1971, the US Secretary of the Treasury, John Connally, had referred to the US dollar 'as our currency, but your problem', addressing himself to European finance ministers. It was apparently his Texan version of diplomatic finesse.

Europeans were not ready then to face up to this challenge. They all wanted a more stable and more symmetrical international monetary system, but, France excepted, they felt they could not go too far in antagonizing their US protector of last resort. Each time the US pushed things to the limit, the Europeans backed down, usually divided among themselves. After all, the 'exorbitant privilege'[6] of the dollar has always been premised on US leadership in the Western world and beyond. Did anybody ever seriously believe that money can be divorced from geopolitics?

It has hardly changed to this day. The creation of the euro has not led to any fundamental change in the distribution of power within the international monetary and financial system. This is very different from what has happened with international trade, where the European single market, backed up by a common external trade policy, has enabled the EU to become a major actor on a par basis with the US and now China. In the monetary and financial area, the euro has essentially replaced the Deutschemark as the second most important international currency, albeit still a long distance behind the US dollar. And the distance grew bigger during the euro crisis.

Then came President Trump, who ruthlessly made use of the international dollar standard and targeted economic sanctions to impose his foreign policy choices on other countries, including Europeans. He did so with respect to Iran, he tried to do the same with the Nord Stream 2 gas pipeline, and increasingly as regards relations with China. Europeans (and others) thus painfully realized that, unless they conformed to US foreign policy choices and unilateral sanctions, they risked being completely cut off from the US market and the dollar-based international financial system in general. No global company can afford to do so today. As a result of these developments, the euro came to be seen increasingly as an important instrument that Europeans might employ to achieve strategic autonomy in a world where multilateral rules were being replaced by aggressive unilateralism.

Symmetry vis-à-vis the Americans, but what about symmetry within the European currency bloc? This is an issue that also goes back to the first discussions on EMU. Symmetry, or lack thereof, within a fixed exchange rate system is determined by markets and rules. The latter at least are in the hands of policy makers. During the Bretton Woods negotiations in 1944, Keynes had raised a fundamental question about how the burden of adjustment would be distributed between surplus and deficit countries in any system of fixed exchange rates. Keynes understood only too well that lack of rules would shift the burden of adjustment to deficit countries, and this would in turn have a deflationary impact for all concerned. But since the Americans wrongly believed at the time that US external trade surpluses would last for ever, they fought against such rules and made sure nothing happened.

The same issue arose in relation to European EMU both before and after Maastricht. It has never been properly resolved until now. Asymmetry is a key element of EMU,[7] and it has been so throughout its history, starting with the first attempts back in the early 1970s. Asymmetry manifests itself in terms of both the distribution of decision-making power inside the regional bloc and the distribution of the burden of adjustment between surplus and deficit countries. They are closely interrelated, although by no means the same.

EMU has been the epitome of Franco-German leadership in European integration, or the Franco-German axis for those tempted to see the negative side of it. In the big negotiations that marked the history of EMU, the two countries usually started with very different views on a wide range of issues. But once they reached a compromise, they began to set the agenda and build coalitions of the willing. And they ended up with a powerful political momentum that left little room for dissent on the basics, although enough space for haggling on side issues. It happened with the early attempts to set up a regional currency bloc in the 1970s, again with the Maastricht treaty, and more recently with the large recovery fund to deal with the pandemic.

However, if we look more closely at what happened in between those big turning points, a different picture emerges. It is the picture of a frustrated France, together with Belgium and Luxembourg, trying with little success to achieve symmetry within the European currency bloc. The so-called snake in the tunnel in the 1970s was the first attempt to create a European exchange rate arrangement. It became, albeit unintentionally, the first manifestation of German de facto leadership. The Deutschemark soon established itself as the pivotal currency and Germany ended up as the country that set policy priorities for the rest. In turn, German leadership was a function of economic size, export-led growth, and a strong currency backed by domestic policies and consensus among social partners aimed at price stability.[8]

It has not been much different within the Eurozone. Writing about the euro project during the crisis, Jean Pisani-Ferry[9] referred to the

Franco-German couple as sharing one bed and different dreams. It was a very apt description. If anything, there have been many more partners and many more dreams which have proved difficult to accommodate in the same bed. They include different expectations about the link between EMU and political union, as well as the division of powers between the Union and member states. They also include different ideas about the conduct of common monetary policy and the use of fiscal instruments. In real life, some people's dreams have proved to be more realistic than those of others.

When the euro crisis struck, several countries lost (or came very close to losing) access to markets and borrowing. It was not exactly what they had dreamt of when they struggled to fulfil the requirements for euro membership back in the 1990s. Particularly for southern countries, membership of the euro meant being part of the European core. They had hoped to borrow credibility and stability by sharing a common currency with countries that had more of both, as well as through the external discipline imposed by their membership of the euro. Alas, reality turned out to be very different from their dreams, but it was largely their fault. They borrowed cheaply and irresponsibly through the banks or the state, thus taking advantage of the credibility of the common currency, while running ever-growing external deficits and feeding domestic bubbles. The latter were of course part of the much bigger international bubble that burst in 2007. Ireland became then an honorary member of the southern group with one of the biggest domestic bubbles, financed by Irish and international banks.

All those countries were then put in the dock, pronounced guilty and punished with strict austerity policies as a condition for being bailed out by creditor countries in the Eurozone and the IMF. Their accusers, however, conveniently forgot that in a debt crisis there are both irresponsible borrowers and irresponsible lenders. Hence, most banks in creditor countries escaped scot-free. While recognizing that countries with large deficits surely had to adjust, a near-consensus view now among economists is that the scale of austerity imposed during the crisis was a very costly mistake. As early as 2013, Olivier Blanchard,[10] then chief economist of the IMF, recognized that his organization had grossly underestimated the negative effects of restrictive policies on economic activity.

During the euro crisis, surplus/creditor countries lent their money and set the conditions. Germany was the biggest creditor of them all. German political leaders drew the red lines for all to keep to and released credit on punishing terms. And they often did so with an ideological obstinacy that left little room for the democratic sensitivities of those on the receiving end of their generosity. True, they had to answer to German taxpayers who were livid because they were being asked to bail out irresponsible partners. They forgot, however, to tell them that German (and other) banks were up to their neck in loans to countries bailed out by taxpayers: they had not made the best use of German savings, to put it mildly. Even more important, Germany remained all along the biggest beneficiary of the euro. With the strongest economy and a heavy reliance on export-led growth, Germany benefitted more than others from unrestricted access to a large European market with no exchange risk internally and a favourable exchange rate vis-à-vis the rest of the world. Just think of what the exchange rate of the Deutschemark would have been like in a world without EMU.

During the crisis, the main burden of adjustment fell on deficit/debtor countries, which were forced to adjust in a short period of time through painful internal devaluation that brought about deep economic recessions. Meanwhile, German and Dutch current account surpluses kept rising. The Dutch current account surplus hit 10 per cent of GDP in 2019. New rules were introduced during the crisis to deal with macroeconomic imbalances within the Eurozone, of which current account imbalances were considered a key indicator. But the rules were never applied in a symmetric fashion. The distribution of the burden of adjustment between deficit and surplus countries was clearly a function of the political balance of power. Economists beware!

Things changed radically during the pandemic when EU rules on deficit financing were temporarily lifted, thus allowing member governments to borrow and run large deficits to save their economies from implosion. Part of the new debt was mutualized through a joint fiscal stimulus package of an unprecedented size. Meanwhile, the ECB continued with its quantitative easing programme, throwing large sums of money at financial markets on the brink of a nervous breakdown and keeping interest rates close to zero or below zero. It is difficult to imagine how the weaker countries could have coped with the pandemic without European solidarity expressed through fiscal and monetary measures. Therefore, much of our analysis about economic asymmetries in the Eurozone no longer holds. The key question is how long the new situation will last.

Responsibility and solidarity

Europe's monetary union consists of very diverse national political economies. They are different in size, structure, level of development and quality of institutions, hence also different in their capacity to adjust to shocks. It is not an optimum currency area,[11] in the jargon of economists, meaning that automatic market mechanisms are unlikely to compensate even partly for the loss of two important policy instruments at national level, namely the interest rate and the exchange rate. But it could eventually become a functional currency area – like the US? – if several political and institutional conditions were to be fulfilled. The final objective of 'Elysian harmony',[12] which is how a German finance minister had described a complete EMU several decades back, is still a long way away. Even short of 'Elysian harmony', membership of the euro looks with time more like a Catholic marriage – never mind it is a polygamous affair – with no possibility of divorce. Although we can never say never in a world of rapid change and much uncertainty, the experience from a succession of big crises suggests that exit from the euro for any member has a very low probability indeed.

The question is how to make this marriage, if not always pleasant, at least as tolerable as possible for the parties concerned. In times of crisis, the debate among euro partners often sounded like those dialogues of couples in distress shouting at each other, only occasionally listening, and rarely trying to reach a compromise. One side invariably insisted on individual country failures. In simple words, they tended to blame the other side for being weak and irresponsible. They were the ones who generally had the upper hand in this untypical marriage and felt strong enough to weather storms on their own. They almost instinctively stressed the need for individual responsibility before anything else. In contrast, the other side put the emphasis in every misfortune on structural economic differences, systemic failures or wrong European policies, usually a combination of all three. In the conjugal jargon, they complained of unreciprocated love, even of an inherent mismatch they belatedly discovered. They were the ones who constantly appealed to European solidarity and burden sharing.

The two sides in this debate correlate closely with the north–south division inside the Eurozone, the north calling for responsibility and the south for solidarity. Members of the Eurozone from central and eastern Europe usually found themselves in alliance with the north, with their fortunes closely tied to those of German industry. But as with other issues, nationality often trumped political ideology, albeit not entirely. Thus, German social democrats were more sensitive to appeals to European solidarity than their compatriots on the right, while market liberals in the south were more willing to recognize the need for reforms at home.

Those who speak of responsibility are allergic to what economists call moral hazard. Too much insurance breeds irresponsible behaviour, they claim, and they are surely not at all keen on extending their economic and social safety nets to other Europeans. A transfer union is indeed a dirty word. They remind all concerned that European integration has not reached the stage when it can be complemented with generous welfare provisions and transfers across borders. The feeling of a shared community (*Gemeinschaft* in German) is still not there, and the legitimacy of European institutions is limited as well. No doubt, these are valid arguments.

Yet good Europeans with a strong upbringing in the values of a social market economy in its different national variations should not be entirely comfortable in arguing that a single market and a common currency can survive in the long run without automatic adjustment mechanisms and without solidarity and transfers. They know this well from their own national experience and from the experience of other monetary unions, such as in the US. They therefore want to make sure that the long run lasts long enough. In the meantime, they will try to minimize costs for their own countries and adopt rules that constrain irresponsible behaviour among their partners. The truth is that they do not trust some of their partners, and often for good reasons. Clientele politics, inefficiency and corruption are endemic features in several parts of Europe, although surely not a monopoly of the south or the east.

The EU is a highly decentralized political system with very diverse economies and insufficient trust among partners, in which economic integration has run far ahead of political integration. This applies even more to the Eurozone. Bridging the gap between the two is likely to be a long slog marked by tension that periodically blows up in crises. In such a political entity in the making, solidarity among partners is bound to come in limited doses and be tied to conditions for those on the receiving end. It is therefore crucial that conditionality (another popular term in the EU jargon) enjoys as wide support as is politically possible.

No doubt, fiscal responsibility is highly desirable, so long as it is not hijacked by zealots. Equally, structural reforms are both urgent and necessary in times of rapid change, but again so long as they are not just being treated as a synonym for market deregulation, especially of labour markets. The European Commission will need to improve its credibility as a fair and efficient monitor of European conditionality. The Commission is indispensable because this is not a task that can be left to governments to administer in relation to each other; it would be politically explosive.

During the euro crisis, Eurozone finance ministers set up a fund to lend to member governments in emergencies, with a maximum lending capacity of €700 billion. In the future, banks in trouble will also be potential beneficiaries. The European Stability Mechanism (ESM), which is the official name, is already one of the biggest financial institutions in the world. The architects of the Maastricht treaty had failed to make any provision for such a fund because some of them believed that insurance policies breed irresponsibility – the moral hazard argument. Alas, they did not avoid irresponsible behaviour by governments and banks alike. And when the Eurozone caught fire, there were no fire extinguishers to put it out. The ESM started as an intergovernmental arrangement to deal with the fire emergency by lending money, together with the IMF, to Eurozone countries that had lost market access and hence the capacity to borrow during the euro crisis. However, it did so under conditionality rules that gave it a bad name in debtor lands. The ESM thus became identified with strict austerity policies, and it is being treated almost as a no-go area by several Eurozone governments.

In the European debate on banking union, solidarity and responsibility have code names: risk sharing and risk reduction respectively.

The Maastricht treaty had left the overseeing of banks to national authorities. After all, the big threat to EMU was supposed to come from uncoordinated government policies, not from private banks meant to operate like good, rational actors according to neoclassical economic theory. But the outbreak of the big financial crisis[13] shattered such illusions, while also creating the so-called 'doom loop' between banks and sovereigns in the Eurozone. Many banks had invested in large quantities of government bonds of the country each knew best, to use the politically correct language of Brussels officials when referring to their mother country.

It was nothing new. The close relationship between banks and the state goes a few centuries back to the Renaissance period, when banks were in a close embrace with Italian city states. Now, fast forward to what happened only some years ago. With the possibility of a breakup of EMU at the peak of the euro crisis, doubts about bank solvency were extended to state solvency, and vice versa. Such doubts risked turning into self-fulfilling prophecies through market speculation. One side effect of this vicious circle was the fragmentation of financial markets along national lines, which was exactly the opposite of what proponents of EMU had in mind in the first place.

When markets begin to think the unthinkable, governments need to do the same. Hence the decision in 2013 to proceed with a European banking union, which meant the adoption of a common rulebook for all financial actors in the EU. It also meant the transfer of responsibility for the supervision and resolution of big banks from the national to the European level, hence the creation of new European agencies under the aegis of the ECB. The European banking union marked a new, big step in integration. It was a difficult decision taken under intense market pressure.

However, European banking union remains to this day an incomplete construction. The main thing missing is a European deposit insurance scheme that would provide the same kind of insurance for people who deposit their money with banks in different parts of the Eurozone. Not surprisingly, countries with more vulnerable banks stress the need for risk sharing. They are in favour of a European deposit insurance scheme and in favour of common funds for the resolution of banks. On the opposite side stand those who insist that risk reduction through the cleaning of balance sheets of banks in trouble should precede further risk sharing across national borders.

To put it bluntly, when and under what conditions would Germany or the Netherlands be ready to underwrite Italian and Greek banks, among others? Potential underwriters have already had some traumatic experiences with their own banks and naturally they are not at all keen to take on other people's burden as well. Until that happens, in this life or the next the hard realist might interject, governments of highly indebted countries will be equally reluctant to cut the umbilical cord with their banks.

Several economists have tried to break the deadlock by offering ways of treating risk sharing and risk reduction as complementary activities. For example, some leading French and German economists[14] jointly proposed measures for a more complete EMU, including a full banking union. Franco-German cooperation takes, indeed, many different forms. If there is political will there is the way, these economists tried to tell us. We are still not there yet, although perhaps not that far off either. A watered-down version of a deposit insurance scheme with a European and a national component looks like a possible compromise, together with a more determined effort to clean the balance sheets of banks in trouble. In European politics, the sequence of such actions of course matters a great deal, as well as the perception of who gives in to whom.

What role for central bankers?

Monetary policy in the euro area is in the hands of independent techno-crats appointed by European governments on long, non-renewable contracts to run the ECB with a narrow mandate that focuses exclusively on price stability. This is the product of a mindset prevailing at the time of Maastricht: that monetary policy should have only one objective and thus refrain from trying to influence output and employment. But things have turned out differently from what was expected. The financial and euro crisis forced the ECB to interpret its mandate as broadly as possible in trying to save the common currency and European economies from implosion. In doing so, it took highly controversial decisions.

The ECB is the most important institution and the only federal one in EMU. Big crises have forced the European Central Bank to act more and more like a normal central bank, a lender of last resort for commercial banks, if not strictly speaking a lender of last resort for sovereigns. Like other central banks in the developed world in times of low demand and low inflation, it purchased ever-increasing quantities of financial assets, mostly government bonds in secondary markets since it is not allowed to finance member governments directly. It already holds more than one-third of the total stock of government obligations of Eurozone member countries. But contrary to the fears of austerians, inflation in the Eurozone remained for years significantly below the official target of close to 2 per cent per year.

In the process, the ECB stretched the limits of its legal powers and its legitimacy. Most importantly, it took decisions that brought it into direct confrontation with national governments. Thus in 2011, the president of the ECB, Mario Draghi, asked for economic reforms in Italy as a precondition for continuing to purchase Italian government bonds and played a key role in forcing the resignation of the government led by Silvio Berlusconi, a media mogul and populist leader. In 2015, Draghi again forced the hand of Alexis Tsipras, a left-wing populist who then led the government in Athens, in accepting a painful compromise with Greece's creditors by withholding liquidity from Greek banks. Draghi's predecessor, Jean-Claude Trichet, had earlier threatened to do pretty much the same in a letter addressed to the Irish finance minister in 2010, if Ireland decided to restructure bank debt.

They were all highly political and indeed controversial decisions. In times of big financial crisis and with Europe's fiscal hand being tied for years, central bankers occupied centre stage. And they took decisions with important distributional effects, be they decisions on quantitative easing programmes or choices they made between bailing out and bailing in of shareholders and bondholders of banks in trouble, with important implications for taxpayers and the economy in general. The ECB was for years a favoured target for the German right's collective hatred, because of money easing programmes and persistently low or even negative interest rates that hit the proverbial German saver. In other countries, European central bankers had a better reputation, though. In 2011, the former vice-president of the ECB, Lucas Papademos, became prime minister of Greece in crisis. And ten years later, Mario Draghi was called upon to lead a government of national unity in Italy. Central

94

bankers taking on the political mantle is, however, not a good omen for democracy.

For obvious reasons, problems with Germany and creditor countries in general proved more difficult to handle. The fast-expanding programmes of bond purchasing by the ECB caused much controversy within its governing board and beyond. German members of the board disagreed and resigned, while ECB programmes were challenged in court, both the German constitutional court and the ECJ. It is, however, open to speculation whether the German government found it convenient during the euro crisis to hide behind ECB actions to save the euro, instead of relying more on fiscal instruments that would have required approval by the Bundestag. Unaccountable technocrats occasionally provide a useful fig leaf for politicians.

Having fired early warning shots, the German constitutional court finally decided to launch a frontal attack. In a decision issued in May 2020,[15] the court in Karlsruhe challenged the legality of actions undertaken by the ECB through its quantitative easing programme and rejected in strong terms an earlier favourable decision on the subject issued by the European Court of Justice (ECJ). In doing so, the German court challenged the supremacy of European law and the European Court, hence one of the fundamentals of European integration. Imagine what would happen if other national courts were to follow the example of the federal court in Germany in ruling that ECJ decisions are 'arbitrary from an objective perspective' and beyond its competences.

But here again, the law of unintended consequences may have worked in favour of more integration. It is not at all implausible that the decision of the German constitutional court may have encouraged Chancellor Merkel to go ahead shortly afterwards with the ambitious European recovery programme, coupled with large-scale borrowing in the name of the EU. She had to reaffirm Germany's commitment to the European project and help salvage it from yet another big crisis. At long last, the EU then began to walk on two legs, the monetary and the fiscal leg.

Back in 1969, Milton Friedman had coined the term 'helicopter money'[16] to deal with the problem of deflation. He meant that central banks could make direct payments to citizens, like dropping money from helicopters. In the years of low growth and low inflation, 'helicopter money' became more popular among economists as an alternative to central bank policies of quantitative easing. The main advantage would be that money would be distributed to everybody instead of simply buying financial assets, which is an operation that feeds asset bubbles and subsidizes the wealthier few who hold most of these assets. Writing cheques for everybody would also be a non-reversible act, unlike the purchase of assets, which is meant to be of a temporary nature.

Can such decisions be left entirely to the collective wisdom of unelected and largely unaccountable experts? What should be the boundaries between elected representatives and independent agencies, notably central banks that have steadily expanded their remit and power in times of crisis? And how should central bankers become more accountable? Such questions are not confined within Europe's boundaries. They are major issues facing all mature democracies in today's world. They are even more sensitive within the EU because of the fragile legitimacy of common institutions. By necessity more than by choice, the president of the ECB and colleagues have been walking a legal and political tightrope for years. Relying too much on central bankers to run Europe's monetary union is bad for democracy and dangerous for European integration.

The ECB is now ready to undertake a direct role in Europe's green transition through its asset purchasing programmes. This is indeed a welcome move. But more responsibilities need to go hand in hand with more effective democratic accountability and more attention to the distributional effects of ECB policies. Unaccountable experts are no longer acceptable in our increasingly unequal and fragmented societies.

Waiting for the next crisis?

The pandemic did not hit thriving economies or a well-functioning currency union. And conventional truths about economics had already turned upside down. It was a world in which advanced economies, including European ones, were already caught in a double trap. One part is called secular stagnation, a term that traces its origins back to the 1930s. It denotes a state of semi-permanent low demand attributed mainly to large inequalities, the rich having high savings, and new technologies requiring relatively low capital investment, a state into which advanced economies have arguably been locked for some time now. The other part is the old Keynesian liquidity trap created when interest rates are already close to zero and people expect deflation and hence hoard cash. The Eurozone and the ECB more particularly had been fighting to escape the liquidity trap for years. And then came the pandemic with prolonged lockdowns and an unprecedented downturn of economic activity.

Borrowing our way out of economic depression looked indeed like the only realistic strategy available at the time, at least for those countries in the developed world that could sell debt in their own currency, including of course members of the Eurozone. Debt levels no longer acted as a constraint on governments able to borrow on interest rates close to zero or even below zero. With the money borrowed, they could support ailing firms and citizens who lost their jobs. They could also help to turn idle savings into investment.

This is what Sebastian Mallaby[17] called the age of magic money, and he did not mean it to be a dangerous fantasy. In his 2019 presidential address to the American Economic Association, Olivier Blanchard, the former chief economist of the IMF, went further: 'put bluntly, public debt may have no fiscal cost' so long as interest rates for government safe assets remain below the rate of growth.[18] And the so-called modern monetary theory went even further in seeing ample opportunities for money creation by central banks until the economy hits full employment, hence triggering inflation.[19] Even the managing director of the IMF, Kristalina Georgieva, was preaching large-scale borrowing by governments to cope with the economic effects of the pandemic. For an international organization such as the IMF that had always been a paragon of fiscal responsibility – and market deregulation, let us not forget – this was a remarkable policy shift. The world had indeed changed. Because of a virus, or was it more because the virus forced us all to focus better by magnifying already existing problems?

The EU together with national governments temporarily freed from fiscal constraints were all pouring large amounts of money into economies that would have been otherwise half dead. Repayment of new debt will be stretched out over a long period. At the time of writing, Europeans have not yet decided how EU debt will be repaid and which new taxes will be levied. It all made sense at the time so long as the ECB succeeded in keeping interest rates very low and inflation remained under control.

But how long is long, the worried economist asked. At what point will inflation strike back?

Inflation in fact reappeared in 2021 as a by-product of economic recovery that came together with disruptions in global supply chains and the explosion in the price of energy and raw materials. Things became even worse with the war in Ukraine. What should then be the policy priority: fighting inflation or preventing another recession? Of course, the answer to be given will have major implications. Or will it be a new financial crisis that strikes first when the non-performing loans of firms in trouble hit the roof and the liquidity of still highly leveraged banks begins to melt away? Many people have been worrying about a new asset bubble in the making. Is Europe well armed to fight a new financial crisis? A list of key questions with no obvious answers.

Crises are succeeding one another and the Eurozone, together with much of the rest of the world, will continue to navigate in dangerous seas. European institutions and national governments will be judged on their navigational skills and their capacity to reach (soon?) a haven. How well or badly Europe comes out of the latest crisis – or crises – and what follows will largely determine the future course of European integration.

European rules on fiscal policy will need to become more flexible, symmetrical and transparent, concentrating on debt levels, setting limits on the growth of expenditure while making more room for public investment. Hopefully, Europe will not rush in restoring strict fiscal discipline too soon. Both the IMF and the Organisation for Economic Co-operation and Development (OECD) have been telling us so. We should also have learned something from the previous crisis. In the meantime, debt levels in some countries have reached those of Japan, a long-time leader in the public debt race. A combination of growth, responsible national policies and ECB support could render even such debt levels sustainable; but will this materialize? Alternatively, debt restructuring may become the instrument of last resort in the future. Historically, countries have dealt with high indebtedness through a combination of growth, inflation and debt restructuring.[20] We have been here before.

The quality of projects financed with European funds and the speed of implementation will be crucial in the next few years. For some countries, it will be their last chance to change domestic economic structures and catch up with new technologies. State institutions will be stretched to the limit, some much more than others, and so will European institutions that are meant to monitor the use of EU funds. Those less enthusiastic about risk sharing and redistribution at the European level will be constantly on the alert, scanning the horizon for new cases of inefficiency, waste or corruption.

EMU was the child of German reunification. It went through a difficult adolescence with the financial crisis and is forced to become an adult because of the pandemic and the war. Surely, it is a hard way to grow up and learn the ropes in the world of adults. Big events or crises have repeatedly forced France and Germany to converge and lead the rest: this is how it usually goes. In the case of EMU, it has, however, developed into an unequal partnership between the two. A successful country with the biggest economy, Germany usually keeps the last word for itself. It has the ultimate veto right. The large EU stimulus package to deal with the effects of the pandemic was a big and unexpected German concession. But more concessions on a similar scale may not be forthcoming – unless necessity dictates? It would, however, help if German politicians became more honest with their citizens about the real stakes with EMU and the responsibilities (not only gains) of a benign hegemon. It would surely also help to have partners Germany can trust and rely upon, in Paris most importantly, where presidents as elected monarchs have the luxury to think long term, in Rome, where the quality of economists is not usually matched by the wisdom of politicians, and in other places as well.

We have learned from experience that common institutions and common instruments matter a great deal. The ECB made the crucial difference for the survival of the euro in the worst moments of the financial crisis. The creation of a proper European monetary fund and the completion of banking union are still pending. At some stage, the president of the Eurogroup will need to be promoted to the status of European finance minister in charge of a still relatively small-sized budget targeted towards stabilization. It could include a common unemployment insurance scheme and more European taxes. The fiscal package agreed in 2020 should not be a one-off operation. And the Eurozone will surely need more effective democratic accountability.

Deciding behind closed doors in the Eurogroup, which is still an informal institution, is no good.

EMU is the most important manifestation of a two-tier Europe. It also became one of the catalysts for Brexit, although it had never been meant to. Short of a major disaster, euro membership can be expected to increase further, and it will be up to individual countries to weigh the costs and benefits of joining. The decision to join will be as much a political decision as an economic one. It has always been so and treaty obligations in this respect will continue to make little difference. In other words, it is in nobody's interest to force countries to join if they do not want to. Denmark, for example, will probably continue shadowing the euro from outside for domestic political reasons, unlike Sweden, which has opted for more autonomy. On the other hand, Bulgaria and Croatia may join soon. So long as some EU countries remain outside the Eurozone, the boundaries between members and non-members will need to remain flexible. After all, Europe has managed to cope with more demanding cases of legal ambiguity. And there are plenty of highly qualified lawyers within the Brussels bubble.

The euro will be faced with at least two more major challenges in the years to come: adjusting to the digital world and developing further its role as an international currency. Cryptocurrencies are already there and digital platforms such as Facebook have declared their intention to launch private currencies. Will sovereign currencies go into retreat in our digital era? It would be an irony of history if this were to happen precisely when the state is making a comeback in times of crisis to provide economic stability, social protection and public goods in general.

The ECB is thinking about the introduction of a digital euro while defending the role of sovereign currencies more generally in their capacity to provide safety, stability and protection from illicit activities. A digital euro would enable citizens to have direct access to the central bank without the need for intermediation, traditionally offered by commercial banks. This would constitute a major break with a long tradition. Will commercial banks be among the main victims of this new technological revolution? As if the financial crisis followed by close-to-zero interest rates were not bad enough.

Many years back, some Europeans began to talk about the exorbitant privilege of the US dollar that allowed Americans to borrow at will in their own currency and indirectly impose uncomfortable choices on their partners. These Europeans were treated then as exotic creatures by the large majority among politicians and economists who doubted the substance of the argument and/or felt it was an improper criticism to make within the Alliance. Things have changed since then. Stripped of emotional language, there is little doubt that the use of a national currency as the international standard creates a large asymmetry.

This now mostly boils down to the capacity of the United States to impose its foreign policy choices on others through the dollar-based international financial system. The repeated use of targeted sanctions has become a favourite instrument of US foreign policy in recent years. It reached an unprecedented level with the sanctions imposed on the Russian state, companies and individuals in the joint response of Western allies, led by the United States, following Russia's invasion of Ukraine in 2022. And the threat of secondary sanctions loomed large on the horizon against any other country that might find itself on the wrong side of the divide, China of course included.

In the Ukrainian case, sanctions served a good purpose as a financial weapon short of direct military intervention that could have provoked a third world war. However, the long-term effect is likely to be a more fragmented financial system in which China, Russia and other countries try to protect their interests by reducing their dependence on the dollar: the weaponization of economic interdependence is a double-edged sword. In such an increasingly fragmented world, Europeans as well will need to strengthen their strategic autonomy through an extended international use of the euro. But of course, this is easier said than done.

An international trading currency that also serves as an international reserve asset for central banks and private companies alike requires access to a large financial market with a very wide choice of instruments to invest in and a deep pool of government safe assets denominated in that currency. Furthermore, it requires the existence of a strong financial centre open to the rest of the world. Judging from the experience of the British empire and later the US, such a currency also needs a major political power to back it up.

For all the above reasons, the EU surely has some way to travel before the euro can compete as an international currency on (more or less) equal terms with the US dollar.[21] But given the growing need globally for risk diversification and reduced dependence on a single country and a single currency in what is very likely to be an increasingly multipolar and multi-currency world, there is potential demand for a stronger international role for the euro. On the other hand, China will have difficult decisions to make with respect to the liberalization of capital movements as a necessary prerequisite for the internationalization of the renminbi. Today, China ticks fewer boxes than the EU in this respect.

Issuing more triple-A-rated debt in euros would surely help in gradually creating a bigger pool of safe assets for non-Europeans to invest in. A first big step was taken with the decision to finance the stimulus package in 2020 through EU borrowing. They are not called Eurobonds, God forbid, but what's in a name anyway? Further progress towards the creation of a true European capital market as part and parcel of the single market would add to the attraction. The City of London could have played the role of the international financial centre for the euro. But it is most unlikely to do so as an offshore centre after Brexit. Would Paris or Frankfurt be able to provide credible alternatives any time soon?

An international currency needs both markets and politics to back it up. Other countries would be interested in diversifying their portfolios and holding more euro assets. Discussing such issues with politically less obvious interlocutors would be indeed a difficult threshold to cross. It would therefore be easier to start by engaging in such dialogue with neighbours, including large parts of Africa, countries which are of strategic importance for Europe. The crucial question is whether Europe is ready to think and act strategically.

The privileges of an international currency come with responsibilities. Europeans would have less control over their monetary policy. They should also be ready to cooperate through swap agreements with other central banks when needed. And they might have to accept at times a higher exchange rate for the euro: mercantilists would not be happy. In other words, Europeans will need to be gradually socialized in the role of a big international actor. This role would come with privileges as well as responsibilities, much more so than the trade power which the EU has exercised until now.

Europeans might want to start with easier tasks to send a clear signal to the rest of the world that they now mean business. For example, what about France and Germany announcing their joint representation at the

IMF and the World Bank? Once they did, could many EU countries afford not to join as well? They would just follow the precedent set by the common trade policy, with spectacular effects in terms of collective negotiating power. Is it not high time they started doing the same with international money and finance? The euro is there to provide the instrument.

European countries, together with the United States, are grossly over-represented in international economic institutions such as the IMF and the World Bank. Their shares in management and votes are now totally disproportionate to their respective shares in population and GDP. The era of Western-dominated multilateral institutions has run its course. It would therefore be a matter of consistency for Europeans who proclaim their strong attachment to multilateral institutions to correct this anomaly. And the transition would be made easier if they joined their votes together, hence also increasing their collective weight.

'That's Your Bloody GDP, Not Ours'

The shape of the elephant

The title of this chapter is from a quote in an article published in the journal *Foreign Affairs*. The author, Anand Menon, one of the most knowledgeable British academics on European integration and a former student from Oxford days, was speaking at a public meeting in Newcastle in the north-east of England ahead of the 2016 referendum on Brexit. He was trying to explain that leaving the EU would entail a drop in GDP, based on the views expressed by a large majority of economists. And somebody shouted back at him from the audience: 'That's your bloody GDP, not ours.'[1]

This angry response summarized very aptly the problem that much of the developed world has been faced with in recent years, especially the Anglo-American world. Large numbers of people who felt left behind by economic and technological developments, afraid and resentful of immigrants coming in increasing numbers, people who felt ignored by mainstream politicians and for whom much-quoted averages, such as GDP figures, meant nothing at all. They were people with little interest in, even less respect for, experts who were telling them what was good for the country and the economy. Many of them vented their anger and frustration by voting 'Leave' in the UK referendum in 2016. They were similar people who voted for Donald Trump in the US presidential election in the same year. Until then, they had been relatively inconspicuous politically and under the radar of most pollsters. Hence, the failure of opinion polls to correctly predict those results.

The developed world experienced big and rapid changes after the 1980s: a liberal revolution that swung the pendulum from society to the individual and from state to market; a new era of globalization with the emergence of new economic powers and growing migration; and the ongoing technological revolution of automation and digitization that have radically transformed conditions of work and the way we live.

The overall economic dividends have been less than anticipated or hoped for. Average economic growth since 1980 has been much below what the West had experienced during the first thirty years after the end of the Second World War. For Europe, the comparison between those two periods is even more depressing: from an average of 5 per cent rate of growth per year in the early period down to less than 3 per cent during the 1980s and 1990s and declining much further since then, with the accompanying rise in unemployment for much of the period.[2] All the way down, in other words, ending up with the biggest financial crisis since 1929 and its long aftershocks – and later the pandemic. Even worse, slower growth was combined with a more unequal distribution of the economic dividend from growth, exacerbated by one crisis internally created, namely the financial crisis, and the more recent one which looks like the act of a vengeful god through the spread of a killer virus. Not the kind of story that can cheer up the domestic audience, poor politicians!

The best way to summarize the distributional effects during this period is the so-called elephant curve that first appeared in an article by Lakner and Milanovic,[3] in a World Bank publication covering the period between the fall of the Berlin Wall and the Great Recession that began in 2008. Lakner and Milanovic divided the world population into income groups from the lowest percentile to the highest. The graph that emerged from numerous surveys and the trove of World Bank data showed how the growth dividend had been shared between different income groups. And it looked like the shape of an elephant, starting with the big hump and ending with a long, raised trunk.

Updated versions of the curve covering longer periods have been published periodically in the *World Inequality Report*,[4] produced by a team of economists in Paris including Thomas Piketty, whose books bear titles intended to remind readers of the classical work of Karl Marx and sell like hot cakes. Piketty, Milanovic and others have played a big role in turning economic inequalities into a major political issue. International organizations as well have devoted much of their attention to economic inequalities in recent years, with the OECD leading in this respect. The titles of successive publications of this organization based in Paris that now serves thirty-seven developed market economies are highly indicative.[5]

The story that different versions of the elephant curve tell us is both simple and powerful. I have borrowed figure 1 from the latest *World Inequality Report*. The shape of the elephant in this graph is less easily recognizable than in its original version, although the message is still both clear and strong. Two different groups emerge as the big winners. The hump of the elephant represents around half of the world's poorest people, including the hundreds of millions of Chinese and others in emerging economies who have been lifted from abject poverty in record time. But since they started from a very low base, they ended up capturing only 9 per cent of total growth between 1980 and 2020. The trunk represents the world's few: the richest 1 per cent of the world population, to be found mostly in Western countries but also in China, Russia and elsewhere, who have captured 23 per cent of total growth during the same period: a truly astounding figure. Squeezed between the two groups of winners, we find the lower and middle classes of rich countries.

If you are not an economist, forget precise numbers and technical discussions about models and data employed. The message delivered across a wide spectrum of the economics profession and international organizations, corroborated by an abundance of data, is strikingly clear:

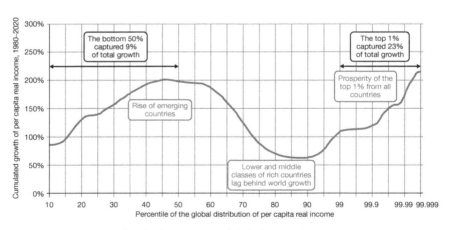

Figure 1 The elephant curve of global inequality, 1980–2020
Source: *World Inequality Report 2022*, 61

the latest era of economic liberalism, globalization and technological revolution has produced a very unequal distribution of gains and losses. While world inequality has been significantly reduced because emerging economies, most notably China, grew very fast and thus narrowed the big gap that had separated them from the West, inequalities within developed countries grew considerably. Those poorly paid and economically more vulnerable were later called upon to take more risks with their lives in keeping the economy and hospitals going during the pandemic. The latest crisis has exacerbated deep injustices within developed countries; the political aftershocks may follow later. In an IMF report, the authors found a strong historical correlation between pandemics and social unrest, the latter following with a time lag.[6]

Economists have come up with a host of factors that help to explain the highly unequal distribution of the growth dividend in this latest phase of global capitalism – and global capitalism it surely is. Even communists in China have adopted the market model, albeit with the strong guiding hand of the state and the party, which allows little space for democracy and individual freedoms but has had remarkable success in turning their vast country into an economic powerhouse in a little more than three decades. This is presumably what makes the authoritarian regime in China enjoy wide popularity at home, if not just benign tolerance.

Is the rapid shift in the distribution of global economic power in favour of emerging economies linked to the more unequal distribution within countries in the developed world? In other words, should the new poor and the squeezed middle classes in much of the Western world blame globalization and China for their ills, foreigners in general, including notably immigrants? No doubt, these are politically loaded questions with huge policy implications.[7] The answer that former President Trump gave to both questions was an unqualified yes, and he managed to convince millions of his compatriots who elected him to power in 2016 with the promise he would do something about both foreign trade and immigration. And he did, in his own unilateral and arbitrary fashion under the motto of 'America First', while trashing global cooperation and multilateral rules in the process. He also succeeded in making the richest Americans even richer through more favourable taxes and deregulation. Was it meant to be part of the deal?

In the era of globalization, the opening of economic frontiers and the rapid growth of global supply chains surely benefitted capital owners more than labour, for the simple reason that capital is much more mobile than labour across borders. Ample supply of cheap labour in the emerging economies led to job losses and put a downward pressure on wages in the advanced economies, especially among the lower skilled. Immigration further added to this effect. The bargaining power of trade unions was hence reduced. The ratio between profits and wages changed significantly in favour of the former during this period, and so did the ratio between the earnings of top managers and lower-skilled workers.

At the same time, the rapid growth of the financial sector further widened the income gap and regional disparities within countries, while capturing an ever-growing share of the economic pie and offering more opportunities for high returns on capital to the well-off. And when the financial crisis struck, it was with taxpayers' money that governments bailed out shareholders and bondholders of financial institutions, while austerity policies hit hard the poorer members of society. It was adding insult to injury and many people on the wrong side of the divide saw it as such. In subsequent years, trying to fight deflation through quantitative easing programmes, central banks in the developed world have contributed significantly to asset bubbles. No need to remind the reader that people with lower incomes do not have large amounts of savings to invest in shares and therefore cannot benefit much from the rise in asset prices.

Globalization led to tax competition among governments in their efforts to attract mobile capital, and hence to lower taxes on personal income and capital. It was fully consistent with the prevailing liberal ideology. In fact, those lower taxes were often not paid, since tax avoidance and tax evasion turned into a cottage industry for the benefit of large multinationals and rich people, who have many more opportunities than lesser mortals to hide their wealth in offshore locations.[8] On the other hand, a large concentration of economic power at the global level, especially in digital technology, was translated into abnormally high profits.[9] Market conditions under which Google, Apple, Facebook (Meta since 2021) and Amazon operate today are millions of miles away from the perfect competition model we used to be taught at university. Technological innovation, hugely important and beneficial as it surely is, should not necessarily allow for rigged markets and winner-takes-all behaviour.

In the early years of euphoria about the benign effects of globalization, Thomas Friedman,[10] a leading US journalist and commentator, welcomed with glee the 'Golden Straitjacket' that global markets imposed on economic and political choices for governments. Autonomy would be willingly sacrificed at the altar of prosperity, thus Friedman concluded. More realistically, Dani Rodrik,[11] a Harvard professor of Turkish origin, saw a trilemma between free global markets, sovereignty and democracy. Rodrik argued that governments could only choose a combination of two out of three, which meant that globalization was forcing individual governments to choose between sharing sovereignty (a global version of the EU?) and forgetting about democracy at home, and thus willingly donning Friedman's 'Golden Straitjacket'. These were no doubt difficult choices that turned into explosive political issues as more and more people began to realize with time that the straitjacket on offer was comfortable for some and too tight for others – more than a few people simply could not breathe in it.

Based on empirical evidence, many economists attach more importance to technology as the key driving force behind the rise in inequalities within the developed world. Automation and digitization have placed an economic premium on high skills, while killing off millions of jobs on the middle and lower end of the technology ladder. Numerous studies[12] thus conclude that the effect of technology has been much stronger than the direct effect of trade or immigration on the lower end of the labour market. The effect of technology has been indeed fast and pervasive. And it will continue, most probably even faster, with the new revolution in artificial intelligence and robotics. However, many economic studies tend to underestimate the broader effects that the opening of economic frontiers have had on the relative bargaining power of different interest groups, more specifically business and labour.

For whose benefit?

Should we submit ourselves to the inexorable logic of progress, be it technological progress and/or globalization? Are growing inequalities within our societies the inevitable price to pay for progress? The more extreme advocates of the Brave New World in the neoliberal era have often pointed the finger at Luddites for erecting obstacles to such progress. But then come Piketty and others who argue that 'Inequality is neither economic or technological; it is ideological and political.'[13] Could they be right?

In today's developed economies, governments continue to play a large role in economic affairs through taxing and spending, as well as through a wide range of policies from labour market regulation to health and education, housing and much more. In an average European country, government spending represents today approximately 45 per cent of GDP – you wouldn't call them typical laissez-faire economies. It is significantly less in the United States, where a long tradition of individualism and distrust of the state has gone hand in hand with market fundamentalism even among those on the losing side: ideology is not always backed up by facts.

Progressive taxes on income and wealth make a difference. So do welfare policies that offer a safety net to those who risk falling, as well as empowerment policies that attempt to ensure equal opportunities. Competition rules are meant to create a level playing field among economic actors. Minimum wages in general and the regulation of the gig economy more particularly try to improve conditions for the weaker and more vulnerable members of the labour force, and so on. These are policies meant to deal with market failures and/or to alleviate the unequal effects of the market. They recognize among other things the existence of a trade-off between efficiency and equity[14] and try to deal with it as best as they can. Such policies formed the basis for the post-war social contract in western Europe.

Global economic competition and technological progress have increasingly constrained government choices, but only up to a point. Institutions still make a big difference and so do political choices translated into specific policies. Of course, the bigger the country and the less dependent its economy on the world outside, the wider the range of choices available. Americans have known this all along and take it for granted, while Europeans have been gradually discovering the same through their experience of shared sovereignty and the joint management of a large internal market.

In most studies, the US today is near the top or at the very top in terms of income and wealth inequalities among developed countries. Income and wealth shares of the bottom 50 per cent were for long steadily declining in the US, while corresponding shares of the top 10 per cent were rising fast, and much more so for the top 1 per cent. For the period 1980–2015, average income growth before tax for the bottom 50 per cent of the population was 37 per cent in Europe and only 3 per cent in the US.[15] The data therefore suggest that markets had different distributional effects on the two sides of the Atlantic, which may in turn be explained with reference to different power relations between business and labour as well as the role played by state intervention.

A similar picture emerges as regards wealth distribution. According to the latest *World Inequality Report*, the top 1 per cent in the US were the proud owners of more than 35 per cent of total wealth in the country. Only Russian oligarchs were doing better! Piketty makes the point that the unequal distribution of wealth becomes self-perpetuating so long as the average rate of return on capital exceeds the rate of growth, thus further widening the gap between rich and poor.[16] Furthermore, social mobility between generations in the US has fallen far and is now lower than in most European countries. This has much to do with the high cost of education and the privileged access of sons and daughters of rich people to elite universities: so-called legacy turns into inherited meritocracy. What happened to the American Dream? What indeed!

Money buys power, especially in the US political system, and power usually brings more money. This is the definition of plutocracy. In the words of Warren Buffett, the sage of Omaha, a business guru and philanthropist: 'There is class warfare, all right, but it's my class, the rich class, that's making the war, and we're winning.'[17] I don't think he meant it approvingly when he said that back in 2006. In the United States, plutocracy has gone hand in hand with the rise of populism in recent decades. Apparently, much of the Republican Party concluded years back that allying themselves with religious fundamentalists, conspiracy theorists and all kinds of populists often verging on fascism was the best way to defend the interests of plutocrats. Major US business groups connived with them and reaped the benefits. Now, the Biden administration is struggling to reverse the trends of the last thirty to forty years, which proves to be an extremely difficult task. Woke zealots within his party are not making his task of winning the hearts and minds of many middle-of-the-road Americans any easier. In conditions of deep polarization, democracy in America is under threat.

Europe has more equal societies than the United States, although the European average hides large differences between the north and the south, the west and the east. In Europe as well inequalities have increased across the board, including in Germany. Europe's economic leader has become more unequal: stagnant or falling real wages for the bottom half of German workers during the last fifteen years were coupled with a large increase in the numbers of people with precarious jobs and close to or already in poverty, including many immigrants.[18] Admittedly, reunification also played a role.

Are growing inequalities a relevant factor for European integration?[19] And if so, is there much that European institutions can do about them? In the early years of high growth and limited liberalization, European integration was generally perceived as a positive-sum game. But the successful recipe mixing liberalization with some redistribution reached its limits as growth slowed down and the pendulum shifted to more market. It got much worse with the financial crisis that brought lower incomes, more divergence between north and south, and more inequalities within countries. The European convergence machine thus ceased to function.

Meanwhile, the old recipe was being applied to eastern enlargement although the context had changed. The accession of central and eastern European countries, plus the two Mediterranean islands of Cyprus and Malta, happened when resistance to liberalization measures was already mounting in the old members. More competition from trade and the outsourcing of production to countries with lower wages and lower labour standards created more losers in the old members, while the extension of the internal market programme to services led to more resistance. Intra-EU migration added further to the problem.

The spectre of the proverbial Polish plumber taking the job of locals became an effective political slogan in France against both enlargement and immigration. And the fear of 'posted' Latvian workers doing construction work in Sweden with their lower wages and labour standards made local trade unions extremely unhappy and forced difficult decisions upon the European Court. Domestic social contracts were coming under strong pressure and more layers of the old permissive European consensus were successively being peeled off. Growing numbers of Europeans became disenchanted with the common project and the way the world was changing around them: the two being in fact inseparable in their minds. More competition, more immigrants, and growing insecurity for those on the lower end of the economic and social ladder created a pool of discontent that the EU had no instruments to deal with. Sure, it had the Structural Funds. But was there much in them for the French or Belgian industrial workers who were losing their jobs to lower-paid workers in Poland, in Slovakia or further away in China? The European globalization adjustment fund created in 2006 was precisely meant to address this problem, but with little money and even less effect.

Countries of central and eastern Europe benefitted from large-scale foreign investments and generous EU transfers as they gradually integrated into the European and global economic system, while becoming part of international supply chains. They benefitted from the catching-up process as late arrivals and their fortunes became closely tied to those of German industry. Sure, the early years of transition had been difficult. And later came the big shock of the financial crisis. Tough adjustment programmes in several countries led to big losses in incomes and employment, while domestic welfare systems were too weak to alleviate the pain. Latvia was an extreme example. As a result, the exodus of people who took advantage of free movement inside the EU accelerated further. Between 1989 and 2017, Latvia lost 27 per cent of its population, Lithuania 23 per cent and Bulgaria 21 per cent. After EU accession in 2007, almost four million Romanians left their country looking for a better future elsewhere.[20] The last one to leave please turn off the lights!

Many of the better-qualified and more mobile citizens in the new members chose to seek their fortunes in countries with better job opportunities. In the words of Ivan Krastev,[21] it is much easier in Europe today to change your country of residence than to change your government. It was the first time in the history of European integration that the right of free movement of people across borders was exercised on a relatively large scale. It had not happened with southern enlargement or before. And it did cause friction on both sides.

In countries on the receiving end, resistance to immigration grew, especially among the poorer and the lower-skilled. It was further multiplied in regions that felt left behind. It was not an unblemished picture either for the countries of those leaving. Emigration provided a safety valve for unemployment at home. It also provided remittances that migrants sent back home: a welcome economic boost for their close relatives and the domestic economy in general. But large-scale emigration was as well a severe haemorrhage for the home country. For example, a large exodus of Romanian medical doctors left local hospitals without adequate staff. Those doctors had been trained with the money of Romanian taxpayers. The loss of many of their best and brightest, accompanied with rapid demographic implosion, was indeed a big price to pay.

Regional disparities within countries grew fast as foreign investment and technology concentrated around large urban centres and a few growth poles, while much of the hinterland was being deserted. The per capita GDP in Warsaw, Bratislava and Budapest quickly overtook the EU average. At the same time, the gap at home between city and countryside grew ever wider. European agricultural subsidies and structural aid were not enough to compensate.

The economic gap was perhaps unavoidably translated into political terms. The countryside ended up voting for nationalists and populists: this is where Orbán in Hungary, Kaczyński in Poland and others drew most of their electoral support from. Conservative views, strong religious influence and the resentment felt by those left behind provided the ideal fodder for populists waving the nationalist flag. It was, however, an interesting paradox: citizens voted for staunch nationalists to represent them while opinion polls showed high levels of public support for the EU. Hardly anybody seriously entertained the idea of leaving the Union; they were not that mad. They just wanted to do it their way – Frank Sinatra might have approved!

There is evidence to suggest that large income inequalities turn into a powerful political force when they merge with a regional identity. It then becomes 'the revenge of places that don't matter', in the words of the LSE professor Andrés Rodríguez-Pose.[22] This is surely not a phenomenon limited to countries of central and eastern Europe. It was manifest among 'Leavers' during the Brexit campaign and a key element of the Trump political bandwagon. The revenge of places and people that don't matter also appeared to be a driving force behind the political reaction of many *Ossis* in eastern Germany, the uprising of the *gilets jaunes* and the many votes cast for both the far right and the far left in French elections.

The strong winds unleashed by a more global world in an era of economic liberalism and rapid technological change were further reinforced in Europe by the continuous expansion of the integration project in terms of both numbers and functions. Member governments did not do enough to protect those more vulnerable and often tried to pass the blame to European institutions, which, however, had very few powers to deal with the problem. Meanwhile, there were more victims and more discontent. Nationalists and populists seized the opportunity and promised protection in national bunkers. This would of course mean a radical reversal of European integration.

In 2020, Luigi Zingales, an Italian professor at the Chicago Booth School of Business, wrote in the *Financial Times*:

> If you belong to the fortunate few, the EU has been a fantastic deal. Your savings are secure in a sound currency, you can travel without a passport, you can even send your kids to some of the best universities in the world at the lower fees offered to locals. But what about the workers of southern Europe, who have no savings, who cannot afford to travel abroad, whose kids barely finish school? What has the EU done for them?[23]

This is a stinging comment, with an element of simplification, of course. The distance between the fortunate few (in fact not so few) and workers in southern countries and elsewhere in Europe has grown wider over the years. *Cui bono*, for whose benefit, is the awkward question that political scientists often ask. Distributional issues have now reached the top of the political agenda in most countries. European institutions have always felt uncomfortable with distributional issues. They wanted to believe that European integration was a win–win game for all while social contracts remained mainly a matter for national governments. The win–win game is no longer, and European institutions are being forced to pay more attention to the distributional consequences of integration.

No representation without taxation

'No taxation without representation' was the slogan of American revolutionaries in the war of independence against British colonialism. 'No representation without taxation' should be today's European slogan, adapted to our times and the special conditions of the EU. The aim should be to allow Europe to act mostly as a facilitator for member countries to collect more taxes, especially from individuals and companies that now manage to slip through the net, while also laying the foundations for a limited European fiscal capacity side by side with the much more important fiscal powers of individual member states. The needs for public expenditure are growing. Inequalities, the greening of economies, the health crisis and now defence are the main driving forces. On the other hand, the borrowing capacity of governments is reaching a ceiling because the new age of 'magic money' cannot mean a free lunch forever. Governments will need to raise more taxes. And the Commission will need to repay the money it has borrowed in the name of the EU to finance the recovery programme.

Taxation is still subject to the unanimity rule in European councils, which renders decisions extremely difficult or well-nigh impossible. The so-called 'own resources' of the EU are limited to customs duties and agricultural levies on imports from the rest of the world, both declining over time because of international trade liberalization, plus a small percentage of VAT collected by member states on behalf of the EU. The common budget represents only about 1 per cent of GDP and the biggest part is financed through national contributions. The money goes mainly to agricultural subsidies and the Structural Funds, plus smaller sums for a whole range of other policies including the management of the single market, consumer protection, science and technology, border control and foreign aid. Small amounts are also provided for defence and security now that this last big taboo has been broken.

Although surely not insignificant, the EU budget is certainly not a proper budget when compared with those of member states. It is a hermaphrodite creature, the product of an economic and political entity in the making in which market integration has run far ahead of political integration. The big challenge facing the EU today is how to narrow the gap between the two.

A unified market and, even more so, a monetary union with high capital mobility, coupled with a virtual free-for-all on tax matters, makes no economic sense whatsoever. It is, however, the reality in Europe today, consistent with neoliberal globalization yet no less problematic for that. Competition among member states has led to lower corporate taxes and lower marginal rates on high incomes in most countries. Free movement of goods and especially of people and capital has thus acted as a major constraint on the ability of governments to tax. Libertarians may rejoice, but they do not care much about social cohesion or about the provision of public goods.

Lower taxes have gone hand in hand with more tax avoidance, which is legal if not necessarily ethical, and tax evasion, which is neither legal nor ethical. Many offshore tax havens offer ample opportunities for large companies and rich individuals to do one or both, while also providing refuge for proceeds from all kinds of illicit activities. It was reported in the *Financial Times*[24] that almost one-third of companies which received coronavirus loans from the Bank of England in 2020 were either registered or substantially owned by a resident in a tax haven. They do not pay taxes, but they receive subsidies: it sounds like a good definition of rigged capitalism.

Based on existing tax rates, the estimated annual revenue losses for the EU due to tax evasion by individuals amount to €46 billion. Add another €35 billion due to corporate tax avoidance and €50 billion because of cross-border tax fraud.[25] For the sake of comparison, the annual EU budget is about €170 billion. Surely, not every euro would be captured if member governments combined their efforts in cooperation with EU institutions; far from it. It would, however, constitute an important step which could pave the way for higher tax rates on corporate profits and higher marginal rates at the top end of the income and wealth ladder.

A much broader issue is here at stake. Combatting tax avoidance and tax evasion or fraud, as well as raising more taxes on internationally mobile capital and incomes, is about social justice. It is also about ensuring fair competition between and within countries of the EU. Small-sized companies catering mostly for the domestic market and individuals with modest incomes – in other words, those who have no ways of escaping the tax net – end up paying the most. Is it fair? On the other side of the Atlantic, Warren Buffett famously wondered in the past why he was paying a lower tax rate than his receptionist or cleaning person.[26] He never got an adequate answer from US politicians. Recent leaks from the IRS (Internal Revenue Service) revealed how little taxes the wealthiest Americans have been paying.[27] Is it not a political scandal?

Taxation looks like one of the last concessions to be made in the long hustle and tussle between national and European institutions. Richer EU countries in general have been reluctant to grant Europe more fiscal powers because they feared it would be like opening the Pandora's box of more transfers across borders. While a member, the UK used to lead the group of countries opposing any extension of EU fiscal powers, and tax harmonization more particularly. And when things got more difficult, the UK resorted to a different argument, namely that global cooperation was necessary for European tax agreements to be effective. But London did precious little to facilitate such international agreements. This was also the tacit approach in relation to any attempt to tax financial transactions, in trying to defend the interests of the City of London.

The UK exercises jurisdiction over many offshore tax havens. London is also 'host to a legal industry that has worked hard to make it possible for corrupt individuals from Russia, China, Nigeria, and many other countries to launder their money in England or to use London as the hub through which to launder it elsewhere'.[28] This is a quote from Branko Milanovic, former World Bank economist and an authority on economic inequalities. He is not the only one. The intelligence and security committee of the UK Parliament referred in a recent report to the 'London laundromat'.[29] All this reached the headlines when the UK government finally decided to act against Russian oligarchs following Russia's invasion of Ukraine.

Tax evasion and widespread corruption in developing countries – and in Russia – have been abetted for far too long by strong vested interests in many countries of the developed world. They include bankers and lawyers, real estate agents and developers, politicians, universities, non-governmental organizations and think tanks who all benefitted from efforts made by corrupt oligarchs to launder their money in the developed world. Speaking at the Summit for Democracy organized by the Biden administration in December 2021, Janet Yellen, Secretary of the US Treasury, admitted that 'the best place to hide ill-gotten gains is actually the United States'. She was remarkably frank.

Resistance to new EU powers on tax has also come from countries keen to preserve their right to use low and/or preferential taxes as a way of attracting foreign investment and international capital in general. The dividing line between the legitimate use of lower taxes as part of an economic development strategy by poorer countries and unashamed free-riding by others is not always clear. Ireland, for example, has long employed low and preferential taxation as a key part of a highly successful strategy to attract multinationals to invest in the country. But continuing to do so today when Irish incomes are already much above the EU average is difficult to justify. Central and eastern European countries have followed the Irish example with varying degrees of success. Meanwhile, the Commission has been trying for years to obtain an agreement on minimum tax rates on company profits, starting by harmonizing rules.

It is even more difficult to defend so-called sweetheart tax deals struck under cover between governments and multinationals that allow the latter to pay virtually no taxes. Various countries have indulged in such practices, including Luxembourg and the Netherlands, as well as Ireland. Poorer countries have done the same: Cyprus has been a popular tax haven for Russian oligarchs for a long time. The Commission has challenged such practices in recent years, although sometimes on shaky legal ground that has been exposed as such by European judges. The Commission had not been meant by the founders to play much of a role on tax issues. But the world has changed radically since the signing of the founding treaties. And this has led to surreal situations as, for example, when the Commission ordered Apple in 2016 to pay the Irish government €13 billion back in taxes, which the Irish government appealed against to the European Court and finally won the case. Irish magnanimity was surely much appreciated by Apple and other multi-nationals, which was after all the object of the exercise.

The Commission has long proposed a tax on digital multinationals based on turnover, to get around the problem of those companies paying minimal taxes by transferring profits across borders. Digital business models allow such firms to operate in different countries without a physical or even legal presence, and hence be able to declare profits where they will pay the least amount of taxes.[30] But the Commission had the support of only a minority among member governments. And the Trump administration treated any attempt by Europeans to levy new taxes on digital multinationals, most of which are of course American, as an attack on US interests. President Trump threatened retaliation, and those Europeans less keen on digital taxes found it convenient to argue that Europe should wait for an international agreement on the subject. Others thought it would be like waiting for Godot in the famous play written by Samuel Beckett: Godot never comes.

But they were proved wrong because Godot did unexpectedly turn up as an official representative of President Biden. The new US president proposed a rise in US corporate taxes and more importantly a minimum tax on global profits of US multinationals. It was soon extended to a more general proposal for a minimum tax rate of 15 per cent on global profits of multinationals, and the right to tax based on their sales in different countries, as a way of dealing with the problem of profit shifting. This US proposal finally succeeded in breaking a deadlock that had lasted for years in international negotiations under the OECD umbrella. We can only hope that implementation of this decision will not take as long.

The US thus turned from the ultimate veto player to a powerful driver for a new international corporate tax regime. Conscientious (or otherwise) objectors to minimum corporate taxes in Europe had been until then successful in resisting pressure from Brussels, Berlin and Paris. It proved, though, much more difficult to say no to Washington. It was of course a most welcome change, but it was also a reality crash test for true European believers. They were reminded once again of where real power lies.

Tax cooperation is one thing, granting the EU powers to tax is another. President Macron has repeatedly called for a Eurozone parliament, a common budget that would represent a few percentage points of GDP financed by European taxes, and a European finance minister in charge. A Eurozone budget would serve as an instrument for both stabilization and redistribution purposes. If ever adopted, such decisions would surely take the Eurozone, if not the whole of the EU, to a totally different stage of integration. Managing a common currency with a common budget and proper taxes is an economic game that true political adults play. An act of European sovereignty, in other words? The French president does not shy away from the forbidden word.

Others have been even more ambitious. For example, Piketty went further in a joint manifesto signed by prominent Europeans in 2018.[31] They proposed a common budget for the Eurozone amounting to 4 per cent of GDP, to be financed by taxes on the profits of large corporations, on top incomes and wealth, as well as on carbon emissions. The signatories wanted the money to be spent on European public goods. However, the idea that EU governments would be willing to transfer their power of internal redistribution through progressive taxation to European institutions verges today on daydreaming. It would require a level of political integration in Europe that looks unattainable at least for the foreseeable future.

New EU taxes have been on the agenda for several years. They include a tax on digital services, a financial transactions tax and carbon taxes. The Commission naturally wants a cut of new digital taxes to become part of EU 'own resources'. It has also been trying for years to obtain an agreement for a small new tax on international financial transactions. This is often referred to as the Tobin tax after the name of the US Nobel prize economist who first thought of it in 1978, mainly as a way of reducing instability and short-term speculation by throwing sand on the wheels of international finance, as Tobin put it.[32] Opposition to this tax has been strong and the negotiating power of the financial lobby even stronger. When the chips were down, only eleven EU countries were ready to proceed with such a tax, hence it was at least temporarily shelved waiting for an international agreement. Will President Biden help to break this deadlock as well? Whether it happens or not may also tell us which is the more powerful lobby in the US: Wall Street or Silicon Valley.

By far the most promising area for new EU taxes is climate policy.[33] It is largely a European policy, and the EU has been leading the way for the conclusion of international agreements in defence of a truly global public good. Carbon emission allowances are agreed in Brussels, and it would therefore make sense for at least part of carbon taxes linked to those allowances to flow back there. The money raised could then be used to finance Europe's green transformation and partly to pay back EU borrowing for the recovery programme. The same argument would apply, only more so, to future levies on imports from outside the EU based on their carbon footprint, following the example of customs duties on goods imported into the EU.

The Commission has been trying to sell the idea of the so-called carbon border adjustment mechanism for some time – and for good reason – to ensure that foreign producers will not enjoy an unfair advantage over their European competitors, who will have to incur ever-rising carbon taxes at home as part of the European policy to fight climate change. But it will be very difficult for Europe to proceed unilaterally without a World Trade Organization (WTO) agreement on this subject – an agreement with the US would surely help, wouldn't it? We shall return to this subject in the next chapter.

Primary responsibility for tax matters will of course remain with national governments for a long time to come. But the EU can make a real difference in two areas: first, by mobilizing its collective bargaining power vis-à-vis states and private actors in a highly asymmetrical world; and second, by effectively addressing the problem of unfair competition within its borders and beyond. Resistance is bound to be strong because foreign governments and big multinationals prefer to play one European country against another, and because the gains from tax avoidance and tax evasion are big both for direct beneficiaries in the private sector and for states that act as facilitators. The unanimity principle in matters of taxation is a relic of the past, yet a relic that some Europeans have been trying to preserve at all costs and hence block any attempt to reach a common policy in the name of sovereignty. Surely, worse crimes have been committed in the name of sovereignty, but the problem is there and it is a big one. Expect hard battles on taxes to be waged in European councils in the years to come.

Protect and empower

In times when social contracts are under serious challenge, the Union has a strong responsibility to protect and empower especially the weaker and more vulnerable members of our societies. Of course, this will be again a complementary role to that of national governments, with European institutions concentrating on things they can do more effectively. One recent and very important example was the joint response to the pandemic that included the large fiscal package, some common funding for health and unemployment plus a joint vaccination effort. It is, however, fair to add that joint European efforts are often characterized by laudable intentions that arrive short on delivery. The Brussels machine is slow moving and not always at its most efficient: the joint provision of vaccines coordinated by the European Commission was indeed a painful reminder.

The main responsibility for international trade deals and the completion of the European internal market lies with the Commission. The old liberalization zeal is bound to be increasingly tempered by regulatory, distributional and environmental concerns. Free trade, like European integration, has lost its political innocence, if it ever had one. In the years to come, trade and investment agreements with other countries will be a hard struggle for European negotiators trying to reconcile the benefits of economic interdependence with domestic economic and social constraints. In other words, democracy can be expected to reassert itself more at the expense of free markets in Rodrik's famous globalization trilemma. It would of course greatly help if the EU were to acquire more effective instruments to help adjustment to trade for those directly affected.

The weakening of the multilateral system will be an important additional factor. The WTO has not succeeded in providing a satisfactory framework for trade relations between state capitalist systems, notably the Chinese, and mixed market economies in the developed world. And it is unlikely to do so in the foreseeable future. Furthermore, the geopolitical tension between the United States and China inevitably spills over into trade and economic relations in general. Bilateral and/or regional deals have been for some time the new name of the international game.

On the internal European front, the everlasting effort to complete the internal market in the context of very diverse national political economies has become increasingly difficult. Structural Funds were meant as compensation (or bribe?) for the less developed economies of the EU. The Funds have certainly increased the visibility of the EU among the main beneficiaries. Inhabitants of less developed regions have certainly noticed the official signs commemorating the EU contribution to the building of new *autostradas*, airports and other infrastructural projects in their part of the world. Although most probably the situation would have been much worse without them, European funds have not succeeded in reducing regional disparities between and within member countries by much. Market forces have strong agglomeration effects and labour mobility has not solved the problem, while creating new ones. Of course, farmers have felt the European touch more concretely in their pockets through generous subsidies. But Europe's agricultural policy still benefits farmers with bigger properties and higher productivity much more than smaller farms. Is this really the object of the exercise?

No doubt there has been waste and corruption. The monitoring capacity of European institutions is limited, while on the receiving end of European solidarity we often find weak and malfunctioning institutions. There is indeed a close correlation between lower levels of economic development and bad governance;[34] it applies to Europe as well. Several local politicians and their cronies, who now point the finger at Brussels and wave the nationalist flag, have been direct beneficiaries of corrupt practices with EU funds.

Should European aid reward best behaviour and forget regions lagging consistently? Should European cohesion funds be spread to large numbers of beneficiaries, including relatively less developed regions in richer countries, or concentrate instead on those most in need? Economic efficiency needs to be reconciled with political expediency, which is particularly difficult in a multinational context with decentralized power, such as the EU. The acceleration of technological change through artificial intelligence and robotics is likely to intensify further the regional gap: areas hosting knowledge centres will be racing ahead, while others stagnate and lose their best and brightest. Those left behind will be easy prey to nationalists and populists. The regional problem is a key political issue with no easy solutions. European institutions and member states will therefore need to experiment with innovative ideas, and they will need more resources.

As with taxation, the main responsibility for social contracts[35] will continue to lie with national governments, which differ widely in terms of priorities and performance. The EU is a very broad church and can only act in a complementary and supporting role as regards social policy. Yet it can make a real difference so long as European institutions choose wisely their objectives and instruments. Until now, the Brussels bureaucracy has repeatedly tried to compensate for the shortage of policy instruments with lofty declarations. It has not always been a wise move. European pillars of social rights of one form or another can boomerang when the reality on the ground is so different from stated goals. Credibility is a delicate commodity, especially for European institutions that have no common history and symbols to fall back on when everything else fails.

Education and health are key policy areas to help reverse the trend towards growing inequalities.[36] They are also preserved domains of member states, and they will stay so. But here again the EU has a role to play. The Erasmus programme has enabled millions of young people to live and study for a few months in another European country, thus offering a formative experience which otherwise would have been limited to far fewer young people whose parents can afford it. Erasmus is thus a very good example of how Europe can make a difference for the many, and hopefully it will do so more in the future. The young generations should be an obvious priority for European institutions, especially in times when the intergenerational gap is growing. On the other hand, the coordinated effort to deal with the recent pandemic has opened new vistas for European institutions regarding health, while making it glaringly obvious that they lacked both powers and experience.

Different versions of a European unemployment reinsurance scheme have been on the agenda for years. The main purpose of such a scheme would be to provide funds to countries hit by an external shock and experiencing a sudden rise in unemployment. It would be meant more as a common instrument for macroeconomic stabilization than redistribution. But it would also provide an additional protective shield for those who lose their jobs in economic downturns. A useful addition to the European toolkit, no doubt; advocates of this scheme would, however, need to reassure countries who fear they will always find themselves on the giving side. Germans, Dutch and others see moral hazard. Therefore, such a European scheme would need to be accompanied by clearly defined conditions for the use of funds. The EU may not be too far from realizing this goal.

Minimum wages have been talked about for a long time and opinion among economists has become more favourable over the years. However, a single European minimum wage would make no sense because what is appropriate for Bulgaria means little in Denmark. Europe can therefore help to propagate the message although it cannot deliver the good. One could usefully start with the Brussels bureaucracy, where many hard-nosed economists still believe that further deregulation of labour markets is the right way to gain competitiveness, and forget about the rest.

Some people go much further: they talk of minimum income or universal basic income, meaning regular cash payments to all citizens with no strings attached. This remains a controversial proposal, to put it mildly, on both moral and economic grounds, hence a political long shot. It would certainly be very costly. A universal basic income across the EU as an integral part of European citizenship? This is today beyond the world of dreams, although it could be tried by individual EU members at home, at least by those who can afford it.

An advocate of basic income, Martin Sandbu writes that 'the real reason for introducing a basic income is to reshape power relations in the labour market and outside it ... [and] to eliminate disempowering insecurity and dependence that keep an economy of belonging out of reach'.[37] Sandbu makes a strong argument. The most important change during this latest era of liberal globalization has been the shift in the bargaining power between capital and labour. The elimination of economic borders has made the crucial difference because social contracts are premised on the capacity of national governments to control their borders. With a touch of simplification, we can say that capital has mobility as the main element of its bargaining power, while labour has the right to vote as the instrument of last resort and self-protection.

Economic interdependence pitted against the ballot box? If so, who will win? Politics is now gradually reasserting itself and crises play the role of catalyst. Growing inequalities and divided societies present a major political as well as ethical challenge. This is a challenge to be faced first and foremost by member states because politics remains essentially national. Some European countries will be able to cope much more effectively than others. But in a Europe without borders, effective cooperation among member states will be a necessary condition to help redress the imbalance between market and democracy. At the same time, European institutions are being forced to face up to the distributional consequences of their policies. Europe needs to strengthen its capacity to protect and empower.

Digital Laggard and Green Pioneer

The digital and green transformations of our economies are the most prominent examples of the new kind of challenges and policy choices faced by governments and societies today. They go far beyond narrow concerns about economic welfare and market efficiency. They raise broader issues about security and geopolitical rivalry, about social cohesion, democracy and individual freedoms, about the provision of public goods and the distribution of costs within and between generations – the survival of planet Earth being an existential challenge and the global public good par excellence. They inevitably present difficult trade-offs. The digital revolution and climate policy will radically change our way of life. They will also transform the European project and largely determine where Europe stands in the changing global order.

Hic sunt dracones

In our new digitalized world, we all enjoy the huge benefits that the fourth industrial revolution has to offer. We appreciated these benefits even more in conditions of lockdown during the pandemic when the digitization of our lives took another big turn. What would we have done without Zoom, invented by a Chinese American, and all the other digital platforms that enabled us to remain connected with each other around the globe? But while benefitting from the spectacular advances of technology and looking forward to new breakthroughs that will further revolutionize our lives, we have also become increasingly concerned about how such changes affect our individual freedoms, the social fabric and the functioning of our democracies. There are many good reasons to worry about the security of our personal data and the (mis)use of power that comes with access, not to mention control of such technologies and their products. Fears of hackers, terrorists and organized cyberwarfare mix with growing unease about public opinion manipulation and the emergence of new versions of Big Brother. It may not always be that obvious who is the most dangerous.

Social media have revolutionized our ability to connect with others. They are the great accelerator of change in our societies and a powerful instrument for mobilizing people in large numbers, for good and bad causes. By being able to spread news fast, they equally well spread fake news fast. For a long time, the owners of digital platforms stubbornly refused to assume any responsibility for distinguishing between news and fake news – or hate speech for that matter. And because algorithms learn fast our individual preferences, they feed us with information we apparently like, thus further strengthening our respective preferences and prejudices. This in turn helps to create polarized societies. There have been plenty of examples in recent years around the globe, the United States being perhaps the most prominent.

Thus, what first appeared as a democratic or libertarian revolution offering free and equal access to information for all has also come to be viewed as a mortal threat to democracy, if left unchecked. Who will regulate the provision and quality of information? The Chinese have their own way of dealing with this question, and it is surely not to every-body's liking. Silicon Valley libertarians on the other hand instinctively denounce any infringement of freedom – and they usually mean their own freedom to control the data. The arrival of the fifth-generation technology standard for broadband cellular networks (5G in its more popular use), as well as those known or still unknown revolutions in artificial intelligence, robotics and biogenetics among others, all carry with them mind-blowing promises. They also carry big threats. It all boils down to what use will be made of these new technologies, for whose benefit and under whose control.

Hic sunt dracones (Here be dragons)! This inscription was found on maps of the world beyond Europe in the medieval period, with illustrations of dragons and sea monsters as a warning to travellers that they would be entering unexplored territories. Writing about the digital revolution, Shoshana Zuboff of Harvard University has introduced the term 'surveillance capitalism'[1] in a book that served as a true wake-up call pointing to the abuse of power by those who control our personal data. How can we make the best use of the new opportunities created by new technologies while protecting ourselves from dragons lurking in the background?

New technologies bring radical change to our economies and the way we live and work. New, exciting jobs are being created while others are unceremoniously thrown into the dustbin of history. Schumpeter's force of creative destruction through innovation in capitalist systems is undoubtedly a force for the common good so long as it is accompanied by policies that make it compatible with inclusive societies. It does not come naturally through free markets. Some useful lessons should therefore be learned from the experience of recent decades, when technological change played a key role in structural transformations in the labour market and the rapid rise of economic inequalities in the developed world. This time, the force of creative destruction is likely to be even stronger and faster than ever before.

The globalized digital sector offers an extreme example of economic concentration linked to economies of scale and oligopolistic power: a winner-takes-all law seems to prevail. A few multinationals today control very large world market shares, and they have the habit of gobbling up, with an insatiable appetite, ambitious start-ups that might eventually challenge their dominant position. In 2020, the five largest US tech companies, namely Apple, Amazon, Microsoft, Facebook (now Meta) and Alphabet (which owns Google), represented roughly 25 per cent of the total capitalization of the 500 largest US companies in the stock market, and had already surpassed the total capitalization of all EU stock markets put together.[2] That was surely a confidence booster for Europeans! Between 2009 and 2019, the same five firms had made over 400 acquisitions globally,[3] and they continued writing cheques during the pandemic. So much for competitive markets. Chinese digital multinationals have been following their example, although more discreetly by concentrating on young start-ups. The biggest American and Chinese companies today control a very large part of all patents related to blockchain technologies, with a dominant share of the cloud computing market.

Now we understand much better how digital platforms make their large profits and pay little tax. They collect data on their billions of users through highly sophisticated algorithms and then target their advertising based on such individualized information. Users of Google and

Facebook, or platforms provided by Alibaba in China, obtain extremely valuable services for free. But in exchange, they (unknowingly?) provide zillions of data about themselves and their preferences through the use they make of these platforms. Hence, the source for large advertising profits for the service providers. 'If something is free, you are the product.' I am not sure who first coined the phrase, but they surely had a point. In the world of the internet, the user exchanges his or her private life for connectivity and access to information and fun. It looks increasingly like a Faustian pact. And little money ends up in public coffers through taxes, because of the capacity of digital platforms until now to shift their large profits to locations with the most favourable tax treatment.

European companies have lagged far behind their main competitors in the technological race. Among the top fifteen digital companies in the world today, not one is European owned. They are all American or Chinese. A similar picture emerges when we look at leading firms and start-ups in the field of artificial intelligence. But does it make any sense to talk about nationality for multinational companies, an innocent economist might ask. The answer is yes, because, when it comes to the crunch, multinational companies know very well who is their most significant Other in the world of states, in other words the government they can appeal to as their protector of last resort and the one that has the last word when security and national interest are at stake. This becomes all too obvious in a world where security and geopolitical concerns increasingly trump multilateral rules for international economic exchange. For Europe, being left behind in the technological race will have huge implications for development – the whole structure of the economy will be shaped by new technologies. It will also have a decisive impact on security and will largely determine Europe's position in the geopolitical balance of power. Technology today shapes geopolitics.[4]

Is Europe's failure to keep up with those leading the technological race due to unfair competition, because foreign companies enjoy privileged access to generous subsidies and/or the fruits of basic research and large defence programmes funded by foreign states? Is it because of Europe's still fragmented and relatively underdeveloped capital markets that do not provide sufficient funds for venture capital? Is it because of deeply ingrained risk aversion in European societies and an environment inimical to the kind of entrepreneurial spirit that characterizes the likes of Gates, Bezos or Zuckerberg? Or is it a combination of all the above, and much more?

Referees don't win (digital) games

The fear of Europe being left behind in the technological race is not really something new. I remember as a young student reading *The American Challenge*,[5] an international bestseller of the late 1960s written by Jean-Jacques Servan-Schreiber, a French editorialist and later politician. Servan-Schreiber highlighted the risk of Europe becoming an economic colony of the United States while the gap between the two became ever wider in terms of technology, management and marketing. It was a clarion call for European cooperation and independence. And as a good Frenchman, the author naturally saw his country leading the way while learning from the Americans. The main theme of that book is still topical today – you only need to adjust for new technologies and add the Chinese challenge.

The single market programme in the second half of the 1980s and early 1990s was meant to create the economic space for large European companies or champions that would be able to exploit large economies of scale and compete globally. The Lisbon strategy, adopted with much fanfare by European leaders in the year 2000, set a common target for the EU to become 'the most competitive and dynamic knowledge-based economy in the world' in ten years. Today, more than twenty years later, Europe is further away from that ambitious goal than it was back then.

The EU has a single market with 450 million consumers. The creation of a true single market is still an ongoing process, especially for the digital sector, where much still needs to be done to create a proper European market. The European Commission is in charge of the single market and competition policy. In recent years, it has been flexing its muscles with high-tech multinationals, mostly of US origin, trying to restrain their efforts to perpetuate and abuse their dominant position in the European market.

The Commission has imposed heavy fines on high-tech multinationals for violations of competition rules. But the process is slow and results are mixed at best. The Commission has been trying to deal with this problem by imposing a list of dos and don'ts with hefty quasi-automatic fines in case of breach. The Digital Markets Act and the Digital Services Act go much further than any other legislation in Europe and beyond. From their side, these multinationals mobilize armies of lawyers to challenge the Commission's decisions in the European Court. US high-tech companies have also been able to mobilize strong political support from Congress and/or the executive branch in Washington. The European Commission versus Google or Apple is as much a power battle as it is a legal one, although many lawyers will surely object in strong terms.

In a leading article,[6] the *Financial Times* compared the power that US large digital companies are wielding today with the monopoly power of Standard Oil in the energy sector about a hundred years ago, before it was broken up by US antitrust regulators. Strong evidence suggests that the European market has become more competitive than the US market, where economic concentration and lobby power have created a vicious circle.[7] Only politicians and regulators in the US can break it: a major challenge for the Biden administration.

Similar problems have been experienced on the other side of the Pacific, although the interplay between economic and political power differs in that part of the world, as might be expected. In 2020, the richest man in China, Jack Ma, and his Ant Group, which is an affiliate of the powerful Alibaba Group and Asia's financial digital giant, were reminded in no uncertain terms who is really the master of the game. Chinese political authorities stopped what was expected to be the largest initial public offering of shares (37 billion dollars) in its tracks. A hefty antitrust fine soon followed. It was all part of a strategy to break up the power of Chinese high-tech companies, and the Communist Party leadership seems determined to do so.

The EU has become a global regulatory power that often sets the standards for others. The General Data Protection Regulation, better known as GDPR, adopted in 2018, has been the European flagship in the battle to protect the privacy of users of digital platforms. Subsequent legislation is meant to enlarge the scope and strengthen the so-called Brussels effect. And in so doing, the Commission is acquiring ever more powers. But decentralized enforcement of EU legislation has already shown its limits: most national regulatory agencies are like David battling with Goliath – some are not so keen either to wage the battle.

In fact, EU institutions are engaged on two different fronts at the same time. Internally, they are struggling to keep member countries with often divergent interests together and get them to implement common rules, while trying to extend European regulatory powers in a world of foreign economic behemoths and growing geopolitical rivalry between the United States and China. The capacity to set standards and defend interests depends largely on European unity. But it also depends on whether Europeans can be more than just consumers in the digital world. Otherwise, their efforts will be like trying to referee games between foreign teams[8] in which players are not always ready to abide by the rules.

The internet was born out of research paid for by large space and defence programmes financed by US taxpayers. It all started with the so-called 'Sputnik moment' in the late 1950s when US political leaders decided to invest very large sums of money, realizing that the Soviet Union was getting ahead of them in the space race. The Defense Advanced Research Projects Agency (DARPA) has been largely responsible for the development of new technologies for use by the military in the US. DARPA-funded projects have led to major technological breakthroughs, from computer networking and the creation of the modern internet to graphical user interfaces in information technology, the GPS, drones and much more.

The booming success of Silicon Valley is surely a testimony to the entrepreneurial dynamism of US capitalism, no doubt about it. But dynamic entrepreneurs were also able to tap into top-notch research funded by US taxpayers and turn it into wider civilian use. This applies to other sectors of the economy such as pharmaceuticals as well. In China's version of capitalism, where the role of the developmental state is much stronger and more explicit, the link between the private and the public sector is of course much more pronounced. In fact, the boundaries between the private and the public are not easy to discern when it comes to big Chinese companies in high-tech sectors.

Neither model applies to Europe, which instead of being an effective regulator and referee risks becoming the turf on which American and Chinese high-tech elephants fight it out. This is not a comfortable future to look forward to. The case of the Chinese company Huawei is a good illustration of the awkward choices facing Europeans.[9] Huawei is the world's leading manufacturer and provider of 5G equipment, with an established position in 4G and 3G networks and the biggest market share in the telecoms sector globally. An official national champion of China with easy access to ample finance and government subsidies, Huawei outcompetes its rivals, although often accused by them in the past of violating intellectual property rights. Today, principally through Huawei, China is ahead of all other countries in terms of both standard setting and patents in 5G.

It is a disruptive technology, which will revolutionize not only the speed of exchanging information but also the capacity to 'digitalize' objects and activities that until now belonged to our familiar analogue world. We human beings live and communicate in an analogue world. Therefore, any company – and any government that may be behind it – that succeeds in acquiring a leading position in the new infrastructures and services related to 5G will have a major strategic advantage. The Trump administration decided that the US could simply not allow Huawei – and China – to obtain such a strategic advantage and hence resorted to every means available to stop it in its tracks. On this issue, US policy has not changed much with the arrival of President Biden.

The war against Huawei has included strong pressure on US allies to ban it from their domestic markets. Allowing Huawei access to or control of new 5G infrastructures in the Western world would indirectly open the door to the Chinese Communist Party, US officials have repeatedly pressed the point to their counterparts in Europe and beyond. It has also included attempts to cut the Chinese company off from its US and international supply chains, notably the purchase of microchips, of which a large part of world production is now concentrated in Taiwan and South Korea. If anything, US ambitions about the extraterritorial application of their laws and decisions seem to be almost boundless.

Is there enough hard evidence that telecoms equipment supplied by Huawei may be used for spying? In the words of a European Commission report, 'the absence of evidence of exploits does not constitute evidence of the absence of exploits'![10] Huawei in fact vehemently denies such allegations, while calling for all network equipment manufacturers to submit their products for inspection by a neutral, technically competent international standards body focusing on cybersecurity of telecommunications.

No doubt Chinese political leaders can force Huawei, or any other Chinese company for that matter, to share with them any sensitive information by invoking national security interests. And we know that China is ruled by the Communist Party. But such practices are not limited to totalitarian states. Forcing a digital company to share data with the intelligence services of the mother country can also happen in the best of democratic families. Unfortunately, we know from experience that democratic controls have not always been that effective in preventing abuse of such power in the United States or elsewhere. We are therefore talking about degrees of real or potential abuse, or more realistically whether the spying is done by our people or theirs.

When the chips were down, several European countries, the UK included, rushed to comply. But cutting Huawei off from domestic infrastructures entails considerable costs. Europe has neither the technological champions nor the hard power of the United States and now also China. The biggest part of European digital infrastructures today is controlled by multinationals subject to pressure from governments outside Europe. The same is true of data storage. In the words of José Ignacio Torreblanca, '[T]he US also dominates the world data centres and the use of bandwidth – giving it the opportunity to mine the data of other powers both openly and secretly (as Edward Snowden revealed).'[11] Gaia-X is another Franco-German initiative precisely to develop a European alternative to cloud storage services and hence ensure a degree of European autonomy.

In this new era of strategic rivalry, technological power is intermeshing more and more with political power. Our historian friend might be tempted to remind us that it has always been like this, and we are now only rediscovering old truths. However, the big difference today is that we are all so much more interconnected and new technologies are more pervasive than ever before. Will Europeans reconcile themselves to being the turf or should they simply delegate strategic decisions to their US ally? Looking for alternatives will inevitably lead Europe to new uncharted territory.

Learning new concepts and skills

Other developments have also helped to shake some Europeans at least out of their complacencies. One has to do with incoming foreign investment. They used to have a rather carefree approach until several takeovers of their companies by non-European firms made them think again. One such case was in 2016, when the German robotics firm Kuka was taken over by the Chinese company Midea, which has close ties to China's defence establishment. It set alarm bells ringing in Germany and elsewhere. Policy makers in Europe were thus reminded that openness to foreign investment has never been reciprocal, if such a reminder were ever needed. The pandemic served as another eye-opener. Everybody was then painfully reminded that security of supply, from ventilators to medicines and microchips, can easily turn into a strategic weapon. The weaponization of interdependence is already a familiar theme.[12]

European political discourse has begun to adjust as a result. Strategic autonomy and European sovereignty are relatively new concepts, often pronounced with a French accent. They have an economic dimension to start with but also a foreign and security policy dimension – and they are difficult to separate one from the other. Meanwhile, industrial policy has also been making a hesitant comeback from the land of the dead, to which it had been banished in the era of economic liberalism. Large economies of scale and winner-takes-all are key features of new disruptive technologies.

In 2019, the Commission angered the French and German governments when it decided against the mega merger of (German) Siemens and (French) Alstom that would have created a big European champion with a leading position globally in the rail industry. This helped to bring back to the surface the old discussion about industrial policy and European champions,[13] which often turns into an ideological debate between economic liberals, convinced of the wisdom of markets and fearful of government failure, and those who believe that some markets at least should be shaped by the public sector in the pursuit of broader societal goals. The former had gained by far the upper hand during the era ushered in by Reagan and Thatcher, and now the latter are trying to regain lost ground.

Mariana Mazzucato,[14] an innovative economic thinker, has used concrete examples from Silicon Valley and Big Pharma to argue that the state has played a central role in producing game-changing breakthroughs – even in the US, the paragon of free markets. The Apollo programme that landed the first human on the moon in 1969 should be 'a moonshot guide to change' for today's world, according to Mazzucato. She calls for 'mission-oriented policies' through which governments will try to mobilize different parts of society and shape markets in the direction of broader goals. The digital and green transformations of our economies, together with the necessary shift towards more inclusive societies, are precisely such goals. Could emissions-free vehicles be the Airbus of tomorrow, along with artificial intelligence and robotics as well? Governments should lead the way through strategic investments, large-scale risk taking, and coordinated action across different sectors in close private and public sector partnerships. This is her recipe for changing (and saving) capitalism in the twenty-first century. Nobody can accuse Mazzucato of thinking small!

The EU-27 are meant to spend two-thirds of the €750 billion recovery fund adopted in 2020 for the green and digital transformations of the European economy. Additional funds will be spent through the normal EU budget for structural policies directed mostly at less developed countries and regions of the EU, as well as for research and innovation policy largely through the Horizon programme. Things are indeed happening at the European level: significant amounts of money in the pursuit of such objectives. But in the highly decentralized structure of the EU, common priorities are then translated into twenty-seven national programmes, the quality of which is bound to differ widely – the quality of implementation even more so.

National perspectives also differ largely as a function of the position each country occupies in the international division of labour. The so-called 'headquarter economies',[15] which harbour R&D, innovation and the organization centre of large multinationals, have industrial strategies that extend beyond their national borders. They also have obvious candidates as potential European champions to promote. For the 'factory economies', on the other hand, which host subsidiaries of foreign multinationals attracted there mostly by lower labour costs and flexible standards, the key objective is to continue attracting foreign investment at home. Whether this investment is German, American or Chinese does not necessarily make much of a difference for them. In other words, the perspective of Slovakia, Hungary or Portugal is bound to be different from the way things are seen in Berlin, Paris or even Stockholm: it is not so much a matter of size as of the level of economic development.

New EU legislation for joint screening of investment from outside the EU became effective in 2020. It is meant to apply to cases in which security or public order are at stake or when such investment can undermine a project of common interest. But being choosy with foreign investment is not a luxury that all EU member countries can afford. Those with fewer choices may therefore need concrete incentives before they decide to join in a more restrictive European policy on inward foreign investment based on strategic considerations. There is usually a price to pay to keep everybody on board.

Divergence of interests among member countries is not the only constraint. European institutions have been programmed to think in terms of liberalization and competition policy, not in industrial strategy terms. They will therefore need to be socialized and reprogrammed before they are able to run an active industrial policy or mission-oriented policies à la Mazzucato. The Italian economist was in fact recruited as an adviser to help the Commission prepare the ground. Yet the mind may be willing, but the body is still weak. French and German officials have spoken in favour of the creation of a European DARPA. But how many Europeans share such ambitions? In the foreseeable future, the promotion of European industrial champions will be at best an affair for individual governments, or small groups of those willing and able, who will then have to negotiate their way through European competition policy.

In a study published by the European Council on Foreign Relations (ECFR) in 2019, the authors argued that 'the EU has the collective economic size and capacity to determine its own economic destiny, to set its own rules for economic life, to negotiate on an equal footing with partner economies, to tame would-be monopolies and even to set economic standards and regulations for the rest of the world'. And they continued: 'an economy of 450 million inhabitants ... can aim to master key generic technologies and infrastructures. The EU's aim should be to become a player in all fields that are vital for the resilience of the economic system.'[16] In fact, the stakes go far beyond the resilience of the European economic system. They also include individual freedoms, democracy and security; in other words, the capacity of Europeans to defend common interests and their way of life – assuming they can reach a minimum understanding as to what those common interests and the European way of life are all about.

The EU will need to find a compromise between economic interdependence and strategic autonomy. And in so doing, it will need a more diverse toolkit than the one presently available. In addition to multilateral, regional and bilateral economic agreements, competition policy and regulatory powers already available, the European toolkit will also need to include industrial strategies broadly defined and the screening of foreign investments, as well as targeted export controls and sanctions when necessary. Strategic autonomy will also require a more active use of the euro in the international financial system. To put it differently, the EU will need to learn new skills to better defend common interests. It will also need common institutions able to play such more demanding games.

Some Europeans will be tempted to interpret strategic autonomy as another form of protectionism, while others will continue to object to it in principle, fearing this may distance them from their main ally, the United States. Strategic autonomy and economic sovereignty have of course strong political and foreign policy connotations, even more so after Russia's invasion of Ukraine. It could not be otherwise. The EU today is much more than a single market. But is it ready to make the transition from a trade and regulatory power to a proper international actor who can think and act strategically in an era of disruptive technologies, high economic concentration and strategic rivalry? Europe's coming of age promises to be a difficult and sometimes traumatic experience. The language used by Europe's two protagonists is quite indicative of their different perspectives: the French talk of *l'Europe puissance* (Europe power), while the Germans usually prefer lower-key expressions such as *Handlungsfähigkeit* (capacity to act).[17] And others want things to remain the same, or simply do not think.

Saving their soul and planet Earth

Moving from digital to green, the challenge becomes truly of an existential nature. Climate change is the product of the biggest market failure ever experienced, and the protection of the environment is a global public good. According to overwhelming scientific evidence, greenhouse gas (GHG) emissions resulting from human activity are responsible for global warming which, if left unchecked, will have severe effects on the ecological balance, human life and biodiversity. Extreme weather phenomena such as floods, storms, fires and droughts, experienced with ever-growing frequency and scale in recent years, as well as the rapid melting of glaciers and ice caps, are a foretaste of much worse things to come, we are told by scientists.

The human and economic cost of extreme weather phenomena is rapidly rising. And there is no time to waste, if we believe the experts who warn us that a further increase in temperatures reaching 1.5–2° on the Celsius scale above pre-industrial levels will create irreversible effects on the global environment. The most reliable and generally recognized source on climate change is the periodic reports of the Intergovernmental Panel on Climate Change (IPCC) of the UN, which brings together leading scientists from different countries and provides policy makers with regular scientific assessments on climate change. Its 2018 report and the 2021 update[18] were both revealing and alarming in their predictions about the speed of climate change and their assessment of the big damage already done.

Unless we all drastically reduce our carbon footprint, global warming will have dramatic effects. They will include a rise in the sea level that will wash away areas where millions of people now live, turn other inhabited areas into deserts, and lead to many more floods, big fires, and other forms of punishment that Mother Nature applies for human greed and irresponsibility. It will be a cumulative process and many of these effects will be experienced during the twenty-first century. Such extremely bleak scenarios painted by scientists are, however, denied by those with an interest to defend and by a motley collection of believers in conspiracy theories that today find fertile ground in social media. They include former President Trump and a few more political leaders around the globe, mostly on the far right.

Climate protection is a global public good and will require a degree of global cooperation that has no precedent in history. Since China, the US and Europe combined and in this order are responsible today for approximately half of global carbon emissions, agreement among them on binding climate targets would be a minimum precondition and hopefully set the pace for others. Surely, it will not be an easy task, because moving to a carbon-neutral economy will require radical changes in what and how we produce and consume. It will also require a big change in lifestyles and very large amounts of public and private investment.

The distributional dimension of climate policies is a crucial factor. Developing countries ask for economic assistance from the developed world to cope with the costs of transition to carbon-free economies. They remind the economically more advanced countries of their disproportionately large share of responsibility for the accumulation of GHG emissions in the atmosphere over two centuries and more, and consequently argue that it is the developed world that should bear most of the cost today for the fight against global warming.[19] To complicate matters further, the Chinese still consider themselves as part of the developing world. The fact that poor people in less developed countries are the ones expected to suffer the most from climate change through the rise of sea level or desertification makes the political puzzle of global climate policies even more difficult.

The fight against climate change has a strong intergenerational dimension with broader distributional consequences within and between countries. It implies large and specific short-term costs associated with the transition to a carbon-neutral economy, while most benefits, although extremely important, are long-term, diffuse, and often hard to pin down by an unavoidably imprecise science. It is therefore the kind of problem that democratic systems more particularly are not very good at coping with, not to mention political entities with an extremely complex decision-making system such as the EU.

The contrast between the Fridays for Future movement of school students and the *gilets jaunes* revolt is quite typical. While students were skipping school on Fridays and demonstrating in the streets across Europe and beyond, inspired by Greta Thunberg, the emblematic young Swede, the *gilets jaunes* in France were demonstrating against higher taxes on petrol. Young students were trying to convince those in power to take the necessary decisions to save the habitat they will be inheriting from their parents. In contrast, one of the best-known slogans of the *gilets jaunes* was that 'the elites are talking about the end of the world and we are talking about the end of the month'. They meant that climate change is a long way away while poor people desperately try to make ends meet at the end of each month.

The revolt of the *gilets jaunes* was sparked by a new government tax in France in 2018 leading to the rise in petrol prices, which was in turn justified by environmental concerns. Those protesting came mostly from the suburbs and the countryside, because they depend on their cars and cheap petrol to go to work. They were unequally affected by this decision and felt strongly about their government's tax policies. Does this mean that policies to fight climate change are the kind of luxury good that only rich people can afford? Not really. Environmental sustainability and inclusive societies should go hand in hand. Failure to do so will mean the failure of climate policy.

Many Europeans have long referred to the EU as a normative power.[20] Whether a statement of fact, an aspiration or just wishful thinking, it has always been subject to debate. Environmental policy and the fight against climate change are in fact the best example of Europe's normative power. Faced with a problem that defies national boundaries, Europe has been trying to lead the way in terms of both international efforts and domestic policies. Europeans may risk losing the technological race, but they have at least done better than others in trying to save their soul – and planet Earth with it. Admittedly, with modest results so far although not for lack of trying. The words of Samuel Beckett are most appropriate in this context: 'Try again. Fail again. Fail better'[21] – and act fast, one may add.

The EU has been a leader[22] and policy shaper in international negotiations on climate change from the UN conference on environment and development in Rio in 1992 to the Kyoto Protocol in 1997 and the Paris Agreement in 2015. They are milestones linked to a series of multilateral negotiations held under the so-called Conference of the Parties (COP) of the UN Framework Convention on Climate Change (UNFCCC). COPs bring together representatives of more than 190 countries in different locations every year. COP26 took place in Glasgow in November 2021 and unfortunately produced more declarations of good intentions than concrete commitments.

The EU participates along with member states in these international negotiations, and European common targets are divided into 'Nationally Determined Contributions'. Europe has tried hard to build alliances and get its international partners to accept binding commitments for the reduction of GHG emissions. It has also been instrumental in raising the standards and setting an example for others to follow. For a long time, the most intractable problem was that the biggest polluter on a per capita basis, namely the United States, had refused to make any binding commitments. Former President Trump withdrew the US from the Paris Agreement and led the group of climate change deniers. Meanwhile, individual US states continued to adopt tough regulations to prevent global warming. These are indeed the joys of a federal system. And then, the Biden administration returned the US to the Paris Agreement and set out high ambitions with respect to climate policy. But President Biden faces strong resistance at home.

In successive treaty revisions, the EU has added new provisions to deal with environmental protection and climate change more specifically. In the legal jargon, the environment is a shared competence, which often makes for undignified jostling between European and national institutions: the joys of a pre-federal system! But it surely helps that many decisions can be taken by qualified majority while the Commission tries to make the most of what is legally feasible. In the process, the EU has developed the most comprehensive climate policy framework worldwide to deal with global warming. This rests on three main pillars: reduction of GHG emissions, increase in renewable energy sources as part of final energy consumption, and improvements in energy efficiency.

In 2005, the EU established the world's first major carbon market by adopting its emissions trading scheme (ETS), otherwise known in the jargon as a cap-and-trade market system, which is part of the Kyoto Protocol. The ETS set a cap on emissions and allowed participating economic agents to buy and sell emission allowances. And subsequently, EU countries succeeded in significantly reducing their carbon emissions (more than 20 per cent reduction since 1990), thus meeting the Kyoto targets, while global emissions continued to rise at an alarming pace. But since European emissions represent less than 10 per cent of the world total, Europe's efforts on their own could not have a decisive effect on the health of our planet.

Furthermore, Europe's success in reducing emissions was at least partly due to the long-term process of deindustrialization on the old continent. As part of a more general process of relocation within global supply chains, European companies have been shifting polluting production to the rest of the world where lower environmental standards prevail. Does this help the fight against climate change? Not much really, so long as Europeans continue with their consumption habits and simply substitute imported goods for those produced locally. Developing countries have denounced this practice as hypocrisy. In fact, the financial crisis, and even more so the pandemic, had a stronger effect on GHG emissions from Europe than any deliberate action to fight climate change.

The price of emission allowances distributed by the Commission remained low for many years,[23] although more recently it went up a lot and polluters began to feel the pinch. Furthermore, key sectors of economic activity with a strong polluting impact remained outside the trading scheme which covered only about 40 per cent of total GHG emissions from European territory. But their free licence is soon expiring. In other words, the reality of green transition is rapidly catching up with Europeans and the most difficult part of the job remains to be done.

The big new project

Upon taking office in December 2019, the new European Commission under Ursula von der Leyen announced the European Green Deal as its top priority for the next five years. It was endorsed exactly one year later by the European Council, which committed the EU-27 to a net domestic reduction of 55 per cent of gas emissions by 2030 compared to 1990 levels, and to a carbon-neutral Europe by 2050 in line with the objectives of the Paris Agreement. These are indeed ambitious targets.

The European Green Deal is meant to transform Europe's economy. In so doing, it will also radically transform the European project and change further the division of competences between the EU and its member states. We are still in the early stages, like before the introduction of the euro when the Maastricht treaty was signed, or even earlier. Nobody can safely predict how it will evolve. And we can only hope it will be better designed and executed than Europe's monetary union. It has been argued[24] that the provision of public goods will shape the next phase of European integration. For this to become true, difficult political battles will have to be waged and won within Europe and beyond.

The EU is like the long-distance runner in the first kilometres of an extremely demanding marathon race. The target of climate neutrality will need to be translated into European and national legislation, as well as effective policy instruments that deliver results. It will mean nothing less than the decoupling of economic growth from resource use and an almost complete decarbonization of energy production, the latter presently accounting for approximately three-quarters of total GHG emissions. It will also require radical changes in all means of transportation, as well as agriculture and the use of land resources; in other words, the way we all live, move around, produce and consume. And it will not be enough for Europe to make it to the end of this marathon race. The rest of the world should do so as well. It is a perfect example of what social scientists call a collective action problem.

European political leaders have committed more than 30 per cent of total funds under the pandemic recovery programme and the new seven-year budget of the EU to the green transformation of the European economy. This means around €600 billion for the period 2021–7: not a small sum by any standards, and the largest amount of public funds committed for the fight against global warming. They are meant to trigger more public and private investment, since the amounts required to meet the climate targets are a multiple of total EU funds already committed.

Faster decarbonization consistent with EU targets will require an extension of the ETS scheme to sectors not already included, a higher carbon price and higher taxes. They were all part of the ambitious proposals presented by the Commission in July 2021 under the name 'Fit for 55', referring to the target of a 55 per cent reduction in gas emissions by 2030. Commission proposals included among other things raising the renewable energy target to 40 per cent and cutting total energy consumption by 9 per cent. It was the most comprehensive plan ever to deal with climate change.

Transport will be a tough nut to crack: early reactions from the car, aviation and shipping industries among others were an indication of things to come. European consumers will also be directly affected. Alas, things were surely not made any easier by the big rise in the prices of oil and gas during the winter of 2021–2, which happened for a variety of reasons including low investment in fossil fuels in anticipation of the green transition. And then came the war in Ukraine, which, together with the human tragedy unfolding on the ground, also highlighted the energy dependence of EU countries on Putin's Russia, and Germany's dependence most notably. Europeans were thus forcefully reminded of the need for a common energy policy and the diversification of their energy supplies. The costs were rising high. Naturally, governments, producers and consumers alike were faced with other urgent priorities and their green ambitions risked being put for a (long?) while on the back burner. In any case, the temptation has always been there to follow religiously St Augustine's maxim: 'God give me virtue, but not today.'

It would of course greatly help if the Green Deal were to be a new form of Keynesian policy, combining the greening of economies with more growth. But this is probably too good to be true. More realistically perhaps, we will need to prepare ourselves for new ways of looking at growth and prosperity. Economists beware; you may need to rethink your analytical tools and ways to measure GDP among other things.[25] All in all, a true revolution in values and attitudes will be required for which our societies are not yet prepared. Younger generations may therefore have to take the lead. After all, they are the ones who will be around longer and hence forced to deal with the consequences of the success or failure of climate policy.

Climate policy, like most other European policies, is mainly the product of a continuous dialogue between the Commission and the Council. The latter takes the important decisions, while the former formulates new ideas and proposals and takes charge of the follow-up, chasing recalcitrant member states and economic agents during the implementation stage. With climate policy, the Commission is acquiring ever more powers, as with tech policy, while also being forced into the role of bad cop – not usually a popular role. From its side, the European Parliament struggles to assert itself and tends to adopt a maximalist stance on many issues: a kind of democratic lobby fighting for the good cause and for more European integration. Other EU institutions will need to be mobilized as well in the joint effort to fight climate change, notably the European Investment Bank (EIB), expected to turn increasingly into a green bank, and the ECB through its asset-purchasing programmes. Green bonds will be a useful tool to finance new investment.

Differences in terms of national priorities and administrative capacities will be more pronounced than usual when it comes to agreeing and implementing difficult decisions in relation to climate policy. In this respect, Europe's map is green in the north-west with pale shades of green turning in places to black (or brown) as we move eastwards and southwards. Luckily, Europe does not have that many climate change deniers, and environmental concerns rank high in the priorities of European citizens. And as in other parts of the world, far-right Eurosceptic parties also tend to be climate-sceptic. In contrast, most mainstream parties in Europe have endorsed the green agenda, although with varying degrees of commitment. Green parties are the flagbearers and they have been gaining ground in many parts of Europe in recent years. They are usually more European-minded than old mainstream parties, which makes perfect sense since their main concern lies with an issue that transcends national borders. This trend was confirmed in the 2019 European Parliament elections: Europe is greener than most of its constituent parts and trying to drag laggards along.

With a positive track record on environmental issues, Germany should be expected to continue playing a leading role on climate policy. The German green party has the longest history and government experience in Europe, and it is now a partner in the government coalition in Berlin. *Die Grünen* are therefore expected to make a real difference to German and European policies on climate change. The Merkel government had already decided to phase out nuclear power, unlike neighbouring France. In other words, European countries will continue doing it their own way under the broad EU umbrella. It is no problem, if they all end up with a carbon-neutral economy by 2050. This is of course the big bet. In the meantime, they will be loudly disagreeing among themselves as to what constitutes green energy during the long transition to a carbon-neutral economy.

The strongest resistance will come from countries in central and eastern Europe, Poland first and foremost, which are reluctant to commit to sizeable reductions in GHG emissions because they are still highly dependent on coal for their electricity. And they ask for generous compensation from EU funds as a precondition for committing themselves to ambitious green targets, the Just Transition Fund being a first EU step in this direction. On climate policy, as with cultural values, the main dividing line in Europe today runs east–west rather than north–south.

The green transition is bound to have a profound effect on the European project. It will be a green coming of age in a way and will force difficult political decisions. More specifically, higher carbon prices applying to all polluters will mean higher revenues. Should revenues from the sale of ETS allowances go to the EU, since they are after all the product of a common policy? Carbon emissions do not respect national borders, and imposing a price on them should be treated as part of a common European policy.

Giving EU institutions (partial?) ownership of revenues from the emissions trading scheme would help to repay the common debt raised for the €750 billion recovery fund. It would also be a strong testimony to member states' commitment to the big new project by providing European institutions with additional resources to facilitate adjustment. The Green Deal will be a reallocation policy on a very large scale that requires close partnership between the public and the private sector and large amounts of investment. Its success will largely depend on the capacity to compensate losers within and without Europe's borders. Can EU members collectively meet their ambitious climate targets without offering European institutions the means to do so? When it comes to the crunch, something must therefore give way: it will be either the ends or the means.

Imposing carbon taxes on EU's international trade through the so-called carbon adjustment mechanism will not be any easier. It is a key part of the 'Fit for 55' Commission package of measures. And it should complement the external tariff on imports from outside Europe's single market, which has long been part of EU's 'own resources'. The logic is clear, notably to prevent carbon leakage and create a level playing field between European producers and their foreign competitors, while also introducing incentives and sanctions for other countries to become equally ambitious in the green transformation of their own economies. Sure, calculating carbon input in traded goods will be a demanding task and getting major trade partners to agree to new WTO rules even more so. However, the EU has no other choice but to try and try again to build international alliances to this end.

Reaching a common understanding with the United States, and eventually also with China, will be a decisive factor in the global fight against climate change. It looked like an impossible task until the end of 2020. And then things began to change – and change fast. First, President Xi Jinping committed China to become carbon-neutral by 2060, and climate targets have been introduced in China's fourteenth five-year plan, although coal production continues to expand. Soon afterwards, upon assuming power President Biden set 2050 as the target for a carbon-neutral US. The Biden administration has since joined forces with Europeans in the fight against climate change and shows clear signs of wanting to take the lead, although not at all sure it can deliver at home. Other countries should be expected to join an international alliance to fight climate change, notably the UK as one of the pioneers all along, as well as countries such as Norway, Canada, Japan and South Korea. On the other hand, it may not be surprising that Russia and other members of the fossil fuel international lobby have been reluctant all along to commit themselves to binding targets.

William Nordhaus, the US economist who received the Nobel prize for his work on climate economics, has explained the failure so far of international agreements on climate change in terms of their uncoordinated and voluntary nature, which allowed room for the notorious free-riders.[26] Instead, Nordhaus proposed setting up a kind of international climate club in which participating countries would agree to undertake harmonized emission reductions designed to meet the climate objective. He proposed that participating countries should try to agree on an international target carbon price attached to GHG emissions while being able to choose between carbon taxes and Europe's ETS scheme. And they should then impose uniform penalty tariffs on imports from countries that choose to stay out: a variation of the European Commission's carbon border adjustment mechanism.

For such a climate club to be effective, or for that matter for any international climate agreement to deliver results, the world's biggest polluters will need to agree on the main principles and policy targets and be willing to apply them globally. In other words, a climate club would need a critical mass of participating countries and the right combination of incentives and sanctions. Continuing to play the role of pioneer and international facilitator in matters of climate policy, Europe should not have much difficulty in going along with such a scheme – it is after all close to what Europeans have been advocating for years. Europeans will first need to reach an agreement with the Biden administration, and then both the EU and the US should try to bring China along. It will be a crucial part of the success of the whole exercise. Will the many things that divide the West and China allow some room for cooperation in the fight against global warming? No harm in dreaming, practitioners of power politics may retort cynically. And given the enormously high stakes, dreamers will need to try harder and fail better next time – and fast.

The geopolitical implications of success (or failure) in the global fight against climate change will be simply enormous. Failure would imply, among many other things, large migratory movements away from places directly affected by the rise in sea level and desertification. For those who think that international migration is already creating an intolerable pressure on developed countries in Europe and North America, 'they ain't seen nothing yet'. Success, on the other hand, through the shift to a carbon-neutral economy and hence away from fossil fuels, will have huge implications for international economics and geopolitics.[27] In Europe's neighbourhood, Algeria, Libya and Azerbaijan, not to mention Saudi Arabia and the wider Middle East, will be heavily affected. In a carbon-neutral world, the Middle East as a region rich in fossil fuels and with a long history of foreign interference will lose much of its intrinsic interest for outside powers – for good or for bad.

Of course, the crucial relationship is with Russia, which has been the biggest energy supplier of Europe in terms of oil and gas. In the long term, Russia will be anyway a big loser from the green transition, although the long term had been expected to be long enough for all parties concerned to prepare themselves. The major shift away from oil – and especially gas as a transition fuel – had not been meant to happen before 2030 at the earliest. And the Nord Stream 2 gas pipeline had been constructed under the Baltic Sea to provide Russian gas directly to the biggest European customer, namely Germany, while causing much controversy within the Atlantic alliance and the EU. The US had strong views on security grounds and an economic interest as well because of its fast-growing exports of liquified natural gas (LNG). Countries in central and eastern Europe also had very strong objections. And then everything changed with the Russian invasion of Ukraine in 2022.

Relations with Putin's Russia are not expected to return to 'normal' for a long time to come. Meanwhile, Europeans will be trying to reduce drastically their energy dependence on Russia, while also considering the possibility of coordinated energy imports. The war in Ukraine has demolished any well-intentioned ideas that had existed before about economic interdependence with Putin's Russia. Germany particularly has found itself in an extremely uncomfortable position, with its energy policy in tatters. Gas may in fact never flow through Nord Stream 2. And Germans are subject to strong pressure from allies and partners to wean themselves quickly off their dependence on Russian oil and gas, while agonizing about the economic recession that would follow from such action. German political leaders had not hesitated that much when imposing economic austerity and recession on Eurozone sinners some years earlier. But surely, it is always easier to preach virtue to others!

Europe is a continent poor on resources. Its long history of imperialist drive was always closely linked with the desire to acquire control over critical resources, or at least secure access to them. The shift away from fossil fuels to renewables will imply for Europe a radical geographical shift of its dependence on other countries for the provision of energy and raw materials. Mediterranean countries and Africa are likely to become major providers of solar and wind energy – Africa of some critical raw materials as well. The same will be even truer of China, which is today the world's main exporter of critical raw materials, including rare earths and inputs for green technologies. China has invested large amounts in this area. It has established a lead in renewables technologies and is switching fast from fossil-fuel-powered to electricity-powered transportation. Relations with China will therefore acquire even greater importance than today. And diversification of supplies of key raw materials will be of the essence for Europe, together with substitution as far as possible of such critical materials and with increased recycling.

Getting the economics and politics right will be of course essential for success. But as we have been reminded only too recently with the pandemic, science may again have the last saving word. Major technological breakthroughs, including notably green hydrogen technologies, can make a huge difference. The responsibility of those in charge of public policy will therefore be to make wise choices and provide generous funding for research and innovation.

Defending Common Interests –
Against Whom?

Want to be a power?

In 2020, the EU-27 world share of GDP in current prices was 19 per cent, compared to 17 per cent for China and 25 per cent for the United States,[1] although the Chinese share was significantly bigger in terms of purchasing power and catching up fast. But the EU is more open to international economic exchange than the other two. In the same year, EU exports of goods and services to the rest of the world represented 22 per cent of EU GDP compared to 19 per cent for China and only 11 per cent for the US. The EU is the biggest trading partner in the world. It is also ahead of the other two in terms of foreign direct investment, both inward and outward. In simple words, the EU is a slightly more open economy than China and much more open than the US. This is of course much truer when we talk about individual European economies.

The negotiating strength of the EU-27 has been all along essentially a function of the large single market, the dynamism of European producers, and the common commercial policy which has allowed the Commission since the creation of the EEC to represent member states and negotiate on their behalf: strength in unity, it is called. The EU is also a large currency bloc that includes nineteen out of the twenty-seven member states. Despite its young age, the euro ranks second as an international currency, still a considerable distance behind the US dollar (roughly 20 per cent and 60 per cent respectively of world reserve currency shares), but far ahead of all other currencies. Members of the Eurozone have not yet decided what they want to be as they grow up in the world of adults, a world with a hegemonic currency, the US dollar, that comes with large privileges as well as responsibilities for the United States. Europeans were given a strong taste of how privileges can turn into abuse during the Trump administration, while more recently they joined forces with the Americans in imposing an unprecedented set of sanctions against Russia after the invasion of Ukraine. On the other hand, China's financial prowess is not yet commensurate with its increasing global economic presence, although probably not for very long.

Europe is therefore not yet a fully fledged economic power and much less a political power in the broader definition of the term. True, since 2011 the EU has been endowed with its own diplomatic service – the European External Action Service (EEAS) – headed by the 'High Representative', who is also a vice-president of the European Commission. He or she is a kind of rump foreign minister for the EU, yet with a weak mandate. The EEAS is meant to represent EU interests in individual countries around the globe, as well as in most international organizations. And the EU has its own seat alongside the bigger European countries in international gatherings of the select few, be they the G7 or the G20, which by the way adds to European over-representation in such forums – a remnant of history. All in all, these trappings of power are a misrepresentation of reality, because on many issues of traditional foreign policy the EU adds up to less than the sum of its parts. There is no common European foreign policy worth the name and internal divisions inevitably translate into reduced global influence.

European integration started as a peace project on a continent with a long history of bloody wars. It was in the early years of the Cold War and it took place on one side of the Iron Curtain under the protective umbrella of the United States. Regional economic integration was considered a means to European peace, and also a means to greater prosperity. But it was not the only option considered at the time by Europe's *illuminati*. In 1950, the French defence minister had proposed the creation of a European Defence Community, a proposal that was ditched by no other than the French only a few years later. Thus, responsibility for Europe's defence was delegated to NATO and indirectly to the United States. European history could have followed a very different course had this proposal been adopted back then.

As their inward-looking project gradually turned outwards, the founding members discovered that their trading bloc carried considerable negotiating power in international forums. And the British, always quick in recognizing power when they see it, quickly changed their mind about their own relationship with European regional integration. 'If you can't beat them, join them', they thought. This is precisely what they did in 1973, having been kept in the waiting room for years by General de Gaulle's veto.

With the end of the Cold War in 1989, former Soviet satellites turned from one day to the next into free countries, and they sought membership of both NATO and the EU as a natural reward for their newly gained independence. Those that acted fast were not refused. It was a triumph for the West, and also for European integration. Germany was reunified[2] after the fall of the Berlin Wall, and the European common currency was created as part of the new European package deal.

The international context also changed dramatically. The end of the Cold War ushered in the era of unipolar power – what many international experts refer to as the era of liberal hegemony of the United States.[3] It was hegemony for sure, neoliberal in economic terms and not always benign. US liberal hegemony led to foreign interventions and wars that cost much suffering and too many human lives; Afghanistan and Iraq are the most notable among them and big failures of US foreign policy. The terrorist attacks of 9/11 in 2001 were indeed a traumatic shock for Americans, but the war on terror they unleashed knew almost no bounds. Unconstrained power breeds hubris. More benign observers, however, prefer to see the US role of world policeman as a new version of the 'white man's burden'.[4] Be that as it may, the United States did not make the best use of the huge power it enjoyed having won the Cold War. And such power does not last forever.

The era of a unipolar, neoliberal and shrinking world, an era of revolutionary technological breakthroughs as well, contained the seeds of its own transformation. It allowed the emergence of China as a new global power and produced a political backlash in a deeply polarized and unequal society at home, which brought Donald Trump to the White House. It also created huge financial instability and more unequal societies across the developed world.

Alas, it is very unlikely that the unipolar moment[5] that lasted a few decades will be replaced any time soon by a multilateral order with strong international institutions and widely accepted rules, a global version of the European model, in other words, which is the stuff that Brussels dreams are made of. Instead, it will be most probably a world woefully short on global cooperation, with many conflicts and recurring violence, large asymmetries, and new Cold Wars waged on two fronts – Cold Wars that always risk turning dangerously hot. It would be wonderful if this were proven wrong. It will also be a world with a large concentration of economic power in a relatively small number of big multinationals.

Most Europeans have lost their imperialist drive and missionary zeal. They have today very little appetite for war, even less for out-of-border military missions. In 2019, Ivan Krastev[6] argued that Europeans should turn from missionaries to monks in a monastery, primarily concerned with protecting their own values and their common project in an increasingly unfriendly and illiberal world, which they no longer have any great urge to conquer or even try to change in their own fashion.

Whether Europeans can defend their monastery without outside help has always been the crucial question. Alas, the rest of the world does not only consist of peaceful monasteries, and Europe's close neighbourhood even less so. To the east and the south, this neighbourhood forms a long arc of instability. It includes a revisionist/revanchist Russia run by an autocrat who does not shy away from the use of brutal force; some semi-failed states in the Balkans and a potentially dangerous power vacuum in the region; the Middle East volcano in a constant state of eruption and Turkey as a rogue state; the Mediterranean with contested maritime zones and as a dangerous passage for large numbers of people seeking a European haven; and a big demographic bomb in Africa with a rich collection of semi-failed states and the rising threat from jihadis. This is certainly not a soft power's vision of fun, or the kind of world that secular monks can isolate themselves from.

Peace on the continent and in the wider neighbourhood is presumably the first priority for Europeans, together with the protection of their freedoms and their way of life. Most Europeans understand that their comparative advantage does not lie in the use of hard power. When weapons speak, the European voice cannot easily be heard. Europe's comparative advantage lies instead in a different perception of the world which largely draws from a successful internal model based on recon-ciliation and compromise, on patient negotiations and common rules. A new, bolder version of European soft power when the world most needs it, a kind of Switzerland writ large? Such a vision for Europe's international role would surely help to mobilize many Europeans, especially among the younger generations. But hard reality has also taught Europeans that soft power is certainly not enough in a world with bullies. President Putin for one has made sure they do not forget this lesson for long. Defence and security remain therefore the first priority for EU countries in their unsafe part of the world.

But Europeans also have highly open economies largely dependent on international exchange, with expensive welfare systems that need public funding. It is therefore in Europe's interest to promote international cooperation and multilateral rules[7] in relation to international economic interdependence, financial stability, the Internet of Things or the defence of global commons. However, in times of strategic rivalry, international economic issues become increasingly politicized and power asymmetries inevitably spill over into a wide range of policy areas.

Europeans should have learned this as well by now, be it about regulation and competition in high-tech sectors, taxation of multi-national companies, digital privacy or energy autonomy – or simply about protecting their companies from unilateral sanctions.[8] The dividing line between the 'low politics' of economic issues and the 'high politics' of traditional foreign policy and defence is getting increasingly blurred. The prime example today is high technology, which is geopolitics par excellence. Europeans surely have interests to defend also vis-à-vis their own allies.

In a world of large asymmetries and faltering multilateralism, individual European countries do not count for very much. This is not only true for Lithuania, Greece or Belgium. It is also increasingly true of countries of the size of France, Germany or the UK. Today, what is big in Europe is medium-small in global terms. Many Europeans, especially among the old members, have by now understood that if they do not hang together, they will hang separately. And the EU can no longer afford to behave as a 'fragmented power'[9] addressing sectoral policies one by one without drawing the links between them.

An ageing Europe with a declining population and a faster declining share of world GDP and trade will carry less weight in the future. New economic powers are fast catching up, especially in Asia. Almost two centuries of a Western-dominated world are now coming to an end. In an unstable and increasingly confrontational world, Europe's margin for manoeuvre will be further reduced in a big way. It is therefore time to begin to think strategically and learn to use the language of power. It will be like learning a foreign language for many inhabitants of the Brussels bubble. A European power project as a complement to, not a substitute for, the early peace project? This will be indeed the truest sign of Europe's coming of age. While the war was raging in Ukraine, the EU adopted its *Strategic Compass*.[10] Albeit not yet a European grand strategy, it marked nevertheless real progress towards a shared assessment of an increasingly hostile security environment. But the analysis still needs to be translated into joint concrete action.

The postmodern meets the post-imperial

Dealing with the Great Powers has been a continuous test of the EU as an autonomous and credible foreign policy actor, a test it has repeatedly failed until now. This used to be particularly true of relations with the large neighbour to the east during the post-1989 period, starting with hopes of 'Europeanizing' Russia and offering it a kind of associate status to be defined, later thinking of a strategic partnership between the two, and ending up with an outright adversarial relationship. The turning point was the crisis in Ukraine in 2014, which led to Russia's annexation of Crimea and the outbreak of war in the eastern provinces of the country with Russian involvement. The second and much bloodier act of the drama followed in 2022 when Russia launched a full-scale invasion of Ukraine. As a result, the European security scene changed dramatically, although this time Europe and the whole Atlantic alliance were united in dealing with Russian aggression.

When the Soviet empire collapsed, a historical opportunity was lost to lay solid foundations for peace in Europe that would include Russia and the whole former Soviet-controlled space extending all the way to Berlin. But opinions differ widely as to how to apportion blame between the key actors for this historical failure.

NATO successive enlargements and the way they happened were perceived in Moscow as encirclement by the West and in violation of promises apparently given to Russian leaders after the disintegration of the USSR.[11] Did the West lose Russia because of arrogance fed by outright victory in the Cold War? History teaches us that peace is often more difficult to win than war. George Kennan, the architect of the US policy of containment in the beginning of the old Cold War, called the decision to expand NATO to the former Soviet space 'the most fateful error of American policy in the entire post-Cold War era'. He was quoted[12] approvingly in the memoirs of William J. Burns, US ambassador to Moscow during the Yeltsin period and director of the CIA since 2021. Trying to put yourself even occasionally in the shoes of the Other could have helped. In the words of the Cambridge historian Mark Smith, 'no country is simultaneously so exotic and so ever-present'.[13] He wrote of Russia as (mis)seen by Europeans, not to mention Americans.

During the last twenty years or so, Western hawks led by the US have made an explosive match with Russian *siloviki*.[14] Of course, this is a much-disputed point of view. Many others have always been firmly convinced that the steady deterioration of relations between the West and Russia after Vladimir Putin succeeded Boris Yeltsin in the Kremlin was bound to happen, as soon as the inalienable right of newly liberated countries to decide their fate and choose their alliances hit against Russian insistence on spheres of influence. Admittedly, the latter point of view was given much more credence after Russia's invasion of Ukraine and Putin's claims of Russia's historical rights, which denied the existence of a Ukrainian nationhood: an autocrat unleashed. Or was it just another self-fulfilling prophecy? To be clear, no error committed by the West in the past could provide justification for the brutality of a full-scale war waged by the president of Russia against a sovereign, indeed 'brother', country.

Until then, the EU had often been divided, unable to devise a realistic strategy, and very much ill at ease with a neighbour who has a very different view of the world and few qualms about resorting to military force to defend its interests. From its side, Russia had in fact never taken the EU very seriously as a foreign policy actor and preferred to deal directly with individual countries. Russian leaders used to make a distinction between the EU and NATO, although progressively less so since they began to see both as instruments of Western encroachment on their 'near abroad', which includes former Soviet republics, many of them with large Russian or Russian-speaking minorities and considered crucial for Russia's security. The offer of an EU association agreement to Ukraine was treated by Moscow as a binary choice between the West and Russia, thus leaving Kyiv with very little margin for manoeuvre at the time, and the offer boomeranged.[15]

The EU and Russia make for a very strange couple indeed. The former is a postmodern political entity that has so far delegated the use of force to NATO and the United States, while trying to extend its power and influence by taking in new members and offering privileged agreements to others in the neighbourhood. And the latter is a post-imperial power, declining yet strong in military terms, with the world's biggest nuclear arsenal, fearful of being encircled, and yearning to be treated as an equal among the Great Powers of our times. It is a strange couple, yet forced to coexist because of geography and history. The EU and Russia have common borders through Kaliningrad, the Russian enclave squeezed between Poland and Lithuania, as well as through Finland, Estonia and Latvia.

Economic factors are also in favour of close interdependence between the EU and Russia, or so many people had thought for years, including notably German political leaders, until Putin did the unthinkable. Economic interdependence between the EU and Russia grew consid-erably after the fall of the Iron Curtain, yet it always remained highly asymmetrical: the EU was Russia's biggest trading partner all along while Russia ranked fifth – behind Switzerland – in importance for the EU in terms of trade in goods.

Russia has been a declining power yet rich in energy resources. For the period between 2015 and 2020, almost 30 per cent of EU oil imports and 40 per cent of gas imports came from Russia, which made the EU by far the single most important destination for Russian energy exports. In times of peace, for those who worried about excessive dependence on Russian oil and gas there were others who pointed to a relationship of symmetrical interdependence. Europeans depended on Russia for energy supplies and the Russian exchequer depended on European money. True, small countries close to Russia and heavily reliant on energy imports from Russia had on several occasions suffered from the whims of those who controlled the flow of oil and gas through the pipelines. But in general, Russia behaved as a responsible supplier and met its contract obligations. And we all knew all along that this energy dependence/interdependence would change with the gradual phasing out of hydrocarbons as part of the green transition, although the transition was meant to be rather long. German policy makers particularly used to operate on the assumption that Putin's Russia would continue to behave as a rational economic actor – and they apparently got it wrong.

After the dissolution of the USSR, Russia never became a proper democracy. The country has indeed a proud history and rich civilization, but democracy has never been one of its strong points. The transition to a market economy was not particularly successful either. In fact, it was nothing short of an economic and social disaster in the Yeltsin years, for which Western governments and advisers were not entirely blameless, having offered the wrong advice and precious little aid. Nor has Western moralizing always been entirely convincing, since large amounts of the ill-gotten gains of Russian oligarchs and corrupt officials were systematically laundered in the West until the day of reckoning arrived when President Putin decided to invade Ukraine

How does one deal with a heavily armed and trigger-happy neighbour who sets red lines for outsiders that attempt to enter his sphere of influence or 'near abroad', engages in tactics of bullying small neighbours, resorts to destabilization and disinformation campaigns abroad, shows little respect for human rights at home, and tries to assassinate 'enemies of the state' on foreign soil? Later, President Putin further upped the stakes by seeking to redraw the post-Cold War order. He wanted guarantees that NATO will not expand any further, notably to include Ukraine, and he also asked for the withdrawal of allied forces and missiles stationed close to Russian borders. The Biden administration tried to prevent a full-scale Russian invasion of Ukraine by employing the threat of sanctions, but without committing boots on the ground and always fearful of its Russia policy being treated as 'appeasement' by domestic and allied hawks. Meanwhile, French and German political leaders were desperately trying to find a respectable compromise that would avert the war – and failed. They knew full well it will be Europe that mostly suffers the consequences of a new war on its soil.

Putin's invasion of Ukraine is yet one more example of the law of unintended consequences. He succeeded in giving NATO a new lease of life, in uniting the West and the EU against him, while also contributing decisively to the consolidation of Ukrainian nationhood. No small achievement to be sure, yet at what price for the country he invaded, his own country suffering from sanctions that had never been experienced before, and the whole of Europe faced once again with the threat of war, large numbers of refugees, a new energy crisis and the possibility of a broader economic crisis to follow. Putin had planned for a relatively small-scale military operation, but he totally miscalculated the fighting capacity of Ukrainians and the strong response of a united West.

To be fair, post-1989 Russia had not always been a spoiler. In fact, there had been several instances of successful cooperation with Western countries, such as the early response to the 9/11 terrorist attacks and the beginning of the war in Afghanistan, as well as the conclusion of the nuclear deal with Iran, not to mention institutional relations with NATO and Russia's participation in the G8. But the mood in the Kremlin gradually changed and became ever darker with a succession of events that were perceived as further confirmation of Western arrogance and unilateralism. They included Western intervention in Yugoslavia, Iraq and Libya, which led to changes of regime and/or borders, the continuous expansion of NATO reaching Russia, and the colour revolutions in Georgia and Ukraine, largely attributed by Moscow to Western infiltration. Not surprisingly, Putin's Russia was also extremely wary of democratic experiments in its immediate neighbourhood.

It will take a long while before EU relations with Russia can return to anything like 'normal' between rivals (foes?) forced to live close to each other. At least as long as President Putin remains in power, Russia will continue to be perceived as a major security threat by other European countries and the Atlantic alliance in general. Close engagement and economic interdependence have given way to blocked communication channels and the spectre of war hanging again over the European continent. Needless to say, Europeans and the West have interests and values to defend, although they should have few illusions about being able to impose their values and views about democracy on Russia. And surely, they should have no interest whatsoever in throwing Russia into the arms of Xi Jinping's China. It will therefore be a particularly difficult course to steer: some might call it an exercise in realpolitik for highly skilled players.

A strong ally or weak protectorates?

Let us start with two quotes. The first is from a book published by a young US scholar in 1987:

Washington was ... forcing sovereign allied states and independent foreign companies to do what they perceived to be against their own national and business interests. The embargo was an intolerable affront to the Europeans, for, in their view, it brazenly asserted the United States' right to make trade and foreign policy for its allies – whether they liked it or not.[16]

It referred to the Siberian pipeline crisis and the attempt by the Reagan administration back then to impose its will on European allies. History often repeats itself: there were many parallels with the US sanctions imposed a few decades later in relation to the new Nord Stream 2 pipeline under the Baltic Sea, meant to provide Russian gas directly to Germany. Sure, this new pipeline had been all along a highly controversial project and US sanctions had the enthusiastic support of several European allies, especially in central and eastern Europe. But the idea of the US unilaterally deciding on the energy priorities of major allies and trying to impose this through sanctions stretched the limits of what constitutes an alliance among willing partners. When a compromise seemed to have been finally reached within the alliance, Russia invaded Ukraine and the pipeline remained shut. The US Secretary of State, Antony Blinken, naturally a key figure during this crisis, had been the author of the book quoted above more than thirty years earlier. History, indeed, plays strange games.

The second quote is from an interview published in the *Financial Times* in June 2021:

For my country, it is of the utmost importance that there are very limited or no situations where we have to judge whose arguments are better – the European Union's or [those of] the United States.[17]

It was the prime minister of Lithuania, Ingrida Šimonytė, who gave the interview. For the innocent reader, it may sound like a praiseworthy attempt to search for harmony between the EU and the United States and, when necessary, keep at an equal distance between the two. The trouble though is that Lithuania is not just a third country called upon to judge what may occasionally be different arguments (perhaps also different interests?) on the two sides of the Atlantic. Lithuania, to the best of our knowledge(!), is a member of the EU, and an ally of the

US. The two are of course not incompatible, on the contrary, but the question of where one's main loyalties lie was and still is pertinent.

For some Europeans, especially among the more recent members in central and eastern Europe, the goal of an autonomous European power risks splitting the Atlantic alliance and undermining the special relationship with the United States. And to be honest, they trust Washington more than Brussels, Berlin and Paris put together when it comes to matters of life and death, meaning the threat from Russia.

How Europe collectively defines its relationship with the United States will be the litmus test for Europe making the transition from a trade and currency bloc with an extended regulatory reach, which it is still today, into a proper international power able to defend the interests and values of a whole continent, a few countries perhaps still excepted. A more symmetrical relationship between the two sides of the Atlantic and a credible European defence capability within NATO are the essential prerequisites. Putin's Russia inevitably has a strong say in all of this, even though indirectly. The resurgence of Russian threat will inevitably rally the troops on the opposite side under US leadership. In other words, transatlantic relations crucially depend on perceptions of the threat from the east.

Europe as a proper international power able to define and defend common interests and values surely cannot happen from one day to the next. Ideally, Europe's transition to political adulthood should happen with the consent and support of the United States, which may finally decide it is in its long-term interest to have a stronger and more equal partner on the old continent, instead of a collection of weak protectorates that deliver relatively little for collective defence and occasionally make unpleasant noises. And who would be better placed to take such a historic decision than President Biden who throughout his long political career has been a true believer in a strong transatlantic relationship? Waiting for a new Trump to come to power in Washington DC and shake up European complacency would be a dangerous alternative for all concerned.

The Trump presidency was a big shock for most Europeans. Although popular with the likes of Orbán, Le Pen and Salvini, the former president made the Atlantic look much wider than ever before. During his term, negative views of the United States reached unprecedented record highs among Europeans, who ended up considering the US as a bigger threat to global peace than either Russia or China.[18] Shocked and rather powerless were most European political leaders faced with a US president who showed little respect for allies and international agreements, acted unilaterally and openly called for the disintegration of their Union. In the words of Robert Kagan, a neoconservative intellectual formerly on the Republican side, 'U.S. allies appeased and cajoled, bringing offerings to the angry volcano and waiting hopefully for better times.'[19]

The announcement of the Biden victory in the November 2020 elections was greeted with a big sigh of relief that was clearly audible across the European continent, with exceptions of course. But relief was combined with another shock as Europeans realized that 47 per cent of the US electorate had voted for Donald Trump after all that had happened during the previous four years. And the shock became even greater when they heard that the outgoing president refused to recognize the result and tried every possible means to reverse it, with most of the Republican Party rallying behind him. The assault on Capitol Hill was the climax.

To put it bluntly, for some years now the views expressed by leading Republican politicians make some of their far-right counterparts in Europe sound mainstream by comparison. And the practices they engage in, in several US states, are nothing less than an affront to democracy. US policy makers and academics have over the years regularly expressed their concern about the failures of democracy in other countries and called for action – mostly with the best of intentions. They now realize the danger is at home.[20]

In American history, isolationism has alternated with interventionism.[21] Following the demise of the USSR, US interventions and wars beyond the borders were waged in defence of the liberal global order, which was also meant to serve US interests. It was the fight of good against evil in a Manichean vision of the world consistent with the long tradition of political leaders, mostly from the Republican ranks, who genuinely believe in the exclusive (God-given?) right of the United States to define what is right for the rest of the world. In the land of the very good, the bad and the ugly,[22] Trump was indeed an extreme case. But American society remains very much polarized and there is no guarantee that the US political system will not produce any more Trumps in the foreseeable future. Several candidates are already grooming themselves for that role and Trump himself is threatening a comeback.

In a survey[23] conducted by ECFR, Europe's main foreign policy think tank, just after Biden's victory, a clear majority of those asked in eleven European countries believed the American political system was broken. They also believed that China will be more powerful than the US within a decade and would prefer their country to stay neutral in a future conflict between the two superpowers. Continuity in US foreign policy can no longer be taken for granted. Of course, such views turned into a kind of irrelevant luxury, or simply went underground, when Putin's Russia invaded Ukraine in 2022. War was back in Europe and the US successfully rallied the troops within the Atlantic alliance. In fact, cooperation between the two sides of the Atlantic in response to Russian aggression was quite remarkable. The question, though, is how long it can last, especially if or when different people come to power on the other side of the Atlantic.

NATO decisions are based on unanimity among its thirty members,[24] although nobody has ever been left with any doubt that the relationship between the United States and its European allies has been all along a relationship between leader and followers.[25] US annual military expenditure has for years very much exceeded that of all European allies put together, hence also the accusation levelled from Washington that Europeans are free-riders on collective defence. With less benign hegemons on the other side of the Atlantic, such accusations have been accompanied by outright bullying of European allies to toe the line on a wide range of issues. Former President Trump excelled in this sport in his own characteristic way, while high-level officials of the administration of George W. Bush had done so as well, and others before them.

American accusations of European free-riding on defence are largely justified, even though the US cannot be a standard of reference for others in terms of military expenditure. In 2020, US military expenditure accounted for as much as 39 per cent of the world total,[26] three times that of China, which ranked a poor second. The European countries with the biggest armies, namely France and the UK, each accounted for about 3 per cent of the world total. Successive US administrations have been exerting pressure on European allies to increase their defence expenditure to reach the NATO target of 2 per cent of GDP for each country, although such figures cannot be treated as an absolute measure of commitment. At the same time, US administrations have been consistently opposing any initiative leading towards a more unified EU defence effort, with the argument that such a development would lead to unnecessary duplication and undermine the unity of NATO. This argument is, however, only half of the true story.

The other half, usually unspoken, is the concern that a stronger and unified European defence might challenge American leadership of the Atlantic alliance. Obedient allies are usually preferable to allies with views of their own. Moreover, the interests of the US defence industry have always helped to shape official attitudes. Closer European defence cooperation would be expected to rely more on arms procurement from European manufacturers, hence the prospect of the US defence industry losing European contracts. Arms producers are a strong lobby in any country, not to mention the United States as the most heavily armed country in world history. For all the above reasons, the US has always opposed European initiatives aiming at closer European defence cooperation. And when necessary, the US resorted to good old divide-and-rule tactics. It has always been able to find willing partners.

This is not left-wing, anti-American propaganda. Such arguments, supported by documentation, were contained in a thoughtful and bold report[27] published in 2021 by an influential US think tank close to the Democratic Party and from which the Biden administration has drawn several recruits. In this report, the authors laid bare truths about European defence and the transatlantic relationship within NATO that Europeans dare speak only within closed circles. The bottom line of this long report was that members of the EU need to take greater responsibility for their own defence by creating a European army with its own command structure as part of the Atlantic alliance. Crucially, the authors argued that such a development would be in the interests of the US, Europe and NATO. While recognizing it would take time and should be up to Europeans to decide the pace, the authors strongly encouraged US political leaders to support Europe's transition to political adulthood. It was bold stuff indeed.

Defence no longer a taboo?

A former foreign minister of Belgium, Mark Eyskens, once described Europe as an economic giant, a political dwarf and a military worm. Different versions of this aphorism have been repeated over the years, and there is much truth in it.

Back in 1998 at St Malo, the British prime minister, Tony Blair, and the French president, Jacques Chirac, called for Europe to develop the capacity for autonomous action backed up by credible military forces, the means to decide and the readiness to use them. It was thought to be a turning point and Europe's common foreign and security policy was the product, on paper at least; PESCO followed later. The acronym stands for Permanent Structured Cooperation, which in simple words means the intention of EU members to proceed with closer cooperation and the creation of joint defence capabilities through specific projects. It is an optional, bottom-up approach relying on coalitions of willing and able countries. Twenty-five EU members have signed up. Nevertheless, its birth was followed by years of hibernation, which indicates that at least some of those present at its creation did not really mean it.

In 2017, former president of the Commission Jean-Claude Juncker referred to PESCO as the 'sleeping beauty' of European defence cooperation – Juncker always had a good sense of humour. But at long last, the sleeping beauty gave signs of waking up. It was Brexit, Trump and growing international tension that served as wake-up calls for Europeans. The EU Global Strategy document of 2016 also helped to concentrate minds.[28] The result was a growing number of defence projects covering a wide range of joint operations including missions to Africa, the Mediterranean and the coast of Somalia, as well as training facilities and cooperation on cyberwarfare and on space.[29] They all operate with different clusters of participating countries, always with one or more countries taking the lead. And a few billions of euros are available for collaborative defence projects and missions abroad since the creation of the European Defence Fund (EDF) in 2017.

Taboos were indeed broken, but reality on the ground did not change that much and not always in the right direction. Most PESCO projects were not the kind of strategic enablers that would pave the way for a common defence policy. True, Europe was no longer moving at the pace of the slowest because of the flexible approach adopted. But Europeans still lacked a common strategic vision, while military capabilities in several countries were in steady decline. Fragmentation, duplication and waste remained key features of the European defence scene. Furthermore, the wars in Libya and the Sahel had made it abundantly clear that Europeans were entirely dependent on the US for any significant deployment of forces beyond their borders. So much for European strategic autonomy. There is surely a difference between close cooperation within the Atlantic alliance, which is a good thing, and asymmetrical dependence, which may not be.

When it came to the crunch, many Europeans preferred to spend public money on welfare than defence, hoping that others would do the job for them, and even better if Uncle Sam did it from the other side of the Atlantic. Moreover, intra-European divergence had increased a great deal with the arrival of new members from central and eastern Europe. Apparently, some countries joined PESCO to make sure that not much actually happened there.

Defence capabilities vary enormously among European countries and so do their perceptions of external threat. Only France – and the UK – still have global ambitions and the capacity to engage in military operations beyond their borders. They are both nuclear powers with permanent seats on the UN Security Council. They both desperately hold on to those key features that still make a Great Power. From its side, France has long stretched the limits of divergence within the Atlantic alliance, although being less on its own in this role in the post-Cold War period. In contrast, its neighbour on the other side of the Channel has always concentrated its efforts on preserving the special relationship with the United States, hence relying more on borrowed power.

Brexit has undoubtedly weakened the credibility of an autonomous European defence pillar in the future. No surprise, therefore, that one among President Macron's many proposals relating to the future of Europe has been about the creation eventually of a European Security Council with the participation of the UK. In a future intergovernmental European security structure, the active engagement of the UK would make perfect sense. But it will have to wait at least for the dust to settle after Brexit.

France has been the leader all along in European defence efforts in terms of initiatives, money and personnel committed. And it is bound to continue being the leader, given French interests, the French army and the French nuclear deterrent. The key question is who will be ready to join France. Crucially, Paris and Berlin remained for years a long way apart on strategic vision, the main preoccupation of German political leaders being to protect the interests of Germany Inc.

A global economic power uncomfortable with the use of weapons for obvious historical reasons and with very limited capacity to operate beyond its borders, Germany tried, rather successfully until recently, to have the best of all worlds: relying on NATO and the United States for its security, while keeping privileged energy ties with Russia and being by far the biggest European exporter to China – almost half of EU exports to China are German exports. Germany was essentially trying to be a status quo power in a rapidly changing world, which required an increasingly difficult balancing act as tensions between Washington on the one hand, and Beijing and Moscow on the other, kept rising.

Russia's invasion of Ukraine was the breaker. It was a tragedy for Ukrainians, a big crisis for Europe and a severe blow for German policy. Western sanctions against Russia reached a new high and they included the new gas pipeline linking Russia with Germany, very probably for good. Furthermore, the government in Berlin announced a big increase in defence spending. It was a major turning point in German policy.

Defence spending had been low and the state of the German military left an enormous amount to be desired.[30] This is now meant to change. Germany in fact holds the key to closer European defence cooperation in the future. German readiness to join France and other European countries, engage more actively in European defence cooperation and invest in money, soldiers and military equipment through joint arms procurement would make a huge difference. Taking an active role in the creation of a European army as an integral part of the Atlantic alliance would also be more acceptable to German public opinion than asking for more money to spend simply on national defence.

In fact, opinion polls have consistently produced large majorities among Europeans in favour of European collective defence. On this issue, European citizens seem to be ahead of their political leaders. Even before the war in Ukraine, a proper debate among experts had already begun on whether Europe can actually defend itself.[31] No agreement for sure, yet it was a good sign that things had begun to move at long last. The war in Ukraine has surely shattered the post-Cold War order in Europe and has given a new lease of life to NATO. Whether it will have a similar effect on European defence cooperation as part of the Atlantic alliance is still a question waiting for an answer.

Currency, borders and army are the key attributes of sovereignty. Europe already has both the currency and the borders, although not all EU members are part of common arrangements that have gone through difficult trials in recent years. Some Europeans have begun to discuss the army again. At this stage, it honestly looks like a long shot. But think of the fall of the Berlin Wall, the financial crisis and more recently the pandemic: unexpected events that acted as great accelerators of change leading to a more unified Europe. Trump while in office succeeded in dividing Europeans on matters of high politics, although in this respect the longer-term effect of his presidency may go in exactly the opposite direction. What about the Putin effect? Putin as Europe's great unifier or the one who sets European ambitions for strategic autonomy back many years? If I were to put it provocatively, US elections may in the long term serve as a stronger catalyst for European unity than Russian aggression.

Currency and army could form the two key elements of a new and bigger version of the Franco-German grand bargain, extended to other countries and paving the way for the next stage of European integration: Europe turning into a true political adult. The Germans sacrificed the Deutschemark for the creation of the euro, and they have been ever since the undisputed leader of the Eurozone. The French have the nuclear deterrent and a UN Security Council seat to offer to a future European foreign and security policy. They would naturally expect to play a leading role in a common European defence effort. But surely, a European rapid deployment force of 5,000 soldiers as envisaged in the EU *Strategic Compass* would hardly be an adequate answer to the new threat from Russia. That can only be the NATO deterrent. Europeans will therefore need to gradually find ways to reconcile membership of NATO with their own defence cooperation ambitions.

In recent years, further integration has increasingly relied on coalitions of willing and able countries who decide to move faster than the rest while keeping the door open for others to follow later, if they so wished. It is difficult if not impossible to imagine any serious progress towards a common European foreign and defence policy with all EU-27 members on board, including Orbán's Hungary, for example, and based on unanimity. It will therefore have to be a core group that leads the way. And US support would surely make a huge difference.

Who needs more enemies?

Is China a partner, a competitor or a rival? Perhaps 'all of the above' is the correct European answer. China is very different from Russia. With a population of 1.4 billion, China has truly performed an economic miracle during the last forty years or so. The Chinese economy is expected to overtake the US economy in absolute size by 2040 at the latest. And in purchasing-power terms, it is already bigger, although the Chinese per capita income is still only about one-third of the per capita income in the US. China is today the biggest exporter to the EU and third in terms of imports behind the US and the UK, with a large trade surplus that has persisted for a long time.

The Chinese economic miracle has been performed through a very unorthodox mix of a capitalist economy under the heavy guiding hand of the Communist Party, which in 2020 celebrated its 100th anniversary. I remember a conversation I had in Beijing more than twenty years ago with a high-ranking official and intellectual of the Communist Party who had a PhD from Harvard. He expressed then his concern about rising inequalities in China and the effect they might have on political and social stability in his country. By the way, President Xi Jinping has recently launched a big campaign to reduce inequalities at home. My interlocutor at the time also added that the market forms part of the Chinese DNA. For a communist, it was a rather surprising statement and made in a totally unabashed manner.

This is arguably where the big difference lies between China and Russia. It has to do with a multiplicity of factors that include a long tradition of Chinese merchants operating throughout East Asia and beyond; large numbers of people with PhDs from Harvard and other top universities at home and abroad, in a country where education is given the highest priority; and a strong will among the population to escape from two centuries of underdevelopment. Factors also include an authoritarian political system that keeps things under tight control and is totally ruthless when deemed necessary – remember the Tiananmen Square massacre in 1989?

Of course, the authoritarian political system does much more than just keeping tight control. Through the state apparatus, the Chinese Communist Party has used the market as a tool for economic development: shockingly pragmatic, often wise and gradualist in its approach.[32] We are now told that one important reason for the Chinese economic success was that the country managed to escape from the neoliberal shock therapy inflicted on Russians and others in the early stages of the market transition, opting instead for gradual reforms.[33] The Chinese do learn from the West but apply those lessons selectively.

The Chinese economic miracle is an integral part of globalization. No country has benefitted more from it than China. The economy was gradually opened, initially relying on low wages and export-led growth. It became an integral part of global supply chains, benefitting from large foreign investments, and made a remarkably quick transition from a low-wage economy to a technological leader in many sectors. A huge savings rate sustained double-digit rates of growth for almost four decades, while generous state subsidies helped to finance industrial champions that can also rely on a very large and fast-growing domestic market.

Meanwhile, the world's biggest and ever-growing stock of foreign reserves, itself the product of large trade surpluses over the years, has allowed the Chinese state degrees of freedom that most other countries simply cannot imagine. It has also provided the means to finance China's fast-growing economic presence across the globe. The Belt and Road Initiative (BRI), the most ambitious project of investment in infrastructure worldwide, otherwise known as the new Silk Road, is expected to cost more than one trillion euros. All in all, it's a big first: from rags to economic superpower in less than forty years.

Sure, China has taken advantage of the rules of the game as set by Western countries – unfair advantage in many cases. Currency manipulation helped to keep the Chinese currency undervalued for a long time, while domestic producers enjoyed protection from foreign competition and often large subsidies. The long list of complaints now directed against China by its economic competitors also includes alleged theft of industrial secrets and technology patents. Complaints became ever louder and more aggressive as Chinese economic prowess grew fast and competition from Chinese companies intensified. In the early years, large profits for managers and shareholders of multinationals that invested in China and made it part of their global supply chains, highly lucrative deals for Western financiers and cheap imports for domestic consumers kept many people happy in the West. The losers did not have much of a voice. But this could not last forever.

The scene has changed radically in recent years and economic competition has morphed into geopolitical rivalry. A fast-rising economic power with a lead in several high-tech sectors, including 5G and artificial intelligence, with an increasingly assertive foreign policy, rising military expenditure and lots of money to spend abroad, with a communist leadership and a huge population is now being perceived as a strategic threat in many places, Washington DC most notably. In the highly polarized US political system, one of the few things that commands broad consensus today is the China threat.

President Biden has given an ideological spin to his call to arms addressed to friends and allies: a battle between democracies and autocracies.[34] American political leaders often have this penchant for Manichean views of the world. Does China truly constitute a security threat for the US and its allies in the region, including Japan, which is rightly considered as a strategic partner of the EU? And does mainland China have plans to invade Taiwan? Nobody has clear-cut answers, but let us not forget that perceptions sometimes create their own realities leading to vicious circles of policies and counter-policies. American academics have rediscovered the ancient Greek historian Thucydides and his insightful analysis of the factors that had led to the war between Athens and Sparta in the fifth century BC. Graham Allison from Harvard, who earlier wrote an authoritative book on the Cuban crisis in the 1960s, has now coined the term 'Thucydides' trap'[35] to describe situations in which an emerging power is challenging the hegemonic power, a situation that has often led to war in History. Allison has China and the US in mind today.

A new Cold War to face the Chinese challenge and unite Western democracies would be a dangerous prospect in a globalized and heavily armed world facing existential challenges, including notably climate change. Sure, there are many things to rethink and change regarding the rules of the economic game. For starters, it is now clear that WTO rules are inadequate to deal with a market economy under the heavy guiding hand of the state, such as the economy of China, which became a member of the WTO in 2001. Unfair competition, strategic autonomy in key sectors, and the link between high technology and security are legitimate concerns that need to be addressed. The rules of the game of economic globalization more generally need to be revisited, and not only because of unfair competition from China.

On the other hand, engaging China more actively in the management of global interdependence and the global commons, as well as giving it the place it deserves in international institutions, could be much more productive than China-bashing. And properly addressing the problems of global capitalism and big inequalities at home would surely do more to strengthen democracies in the West than engaging in an ideological war against capitalist/communist China that really has no ideology to export – nationalism, of which there is plenty in China today, is not an exportable ideology. Western democracies should not need foreign enemies to unite against.

For sure, the West has security interests in Asia and the Pacific and should also have clear red lines. But if the United States persists in treating China as a strategic threat and tries to get everybody else to follow, Europeans will find themselves in a very awkward position. They already have the experience of Huawei and US pressures to ban it from their digital infrastructures. Similar pressures have been experienced in other policy areas too. Many Europeans are less convinced this is the right way to deal with China's rising power – geography of course makes a big difference, although less so in a digital world.

Europe depends much more on international trade than the United States. And Berlin most of all would not like to take many risks with German exports to and investment in China. How much does loyalty to your senior ally weigh against your economic interests – and your better judgement as well? It will surely not be the first time that Europeans are faced with such a dilemma, and it would be important for all concerned that they collectively try to exert some moderating influence on America's missionary zeal while also exerting collective pressure on China to deliver and not to follow Putin down the road to Armageddon.

The relationship with China is bound to remain essentially transactional. Trying to export Western views and values about democracy and human rights will not take us very far. So long as the one-party regime in China continues to deliver high rates of growth and material benefits for the large majority among Chinese people, the regime may not have that much to fear internally. European and American pleas for democracy and human rights are therefore unlikely to gain much traction with the political leadership in Beijing. And to put it bluntly, those with a colonialist past and a bad historical record in China may also need to be a bit humbler when delivering lectures on human rights. The Chinese and other Asians have long memories, while Europeans sometimes find it convenient to have selective ones. Last but not least, Europe and the West in general have a strong interest in preventing the formation of an alliance 'with no limits' between China and Russia directed against them.

The BRI has been presented by President Xi as the project of the century. It is meant to reunite the Eurasian continent through large infrastructural projects, thus providing faster and better access for Chinese exports to wealthy European markets while also extending Chinese influence on the way. The so-called 17+1 initiative is directly linked to it. It brings together China and now, since Lithuania left, sixteen central and eastern European countries, including eleven EU members and five countries in the western Balkans whose appetites have been whetted by the prospect of large Chinese investments.

In response to the obvious objections raised by Brussels and strong political pressures from Washington, Chinese officials reply *sotto voce* that this is the only way for smaller European countries to get their voice and interests heard in Beijing. Otherwise, channels of communication tend to be monopolized by the bigger EU countries, the Chinese add rather undiplomatically. Can the EU offer its inner periphery and close neighbours a concrete alternative to BRI? This is the key question; the rest is just words. It is also interesting to note that China has shown more sensitivity to the interests of Russia than the EU in the wider region. Countries where Russia has claimed a special interest such as Belarus, Moldova and Ukraine, as well as countries in the Caucasus, have been left out.[36] It is quite telling as to who counts more in Beijing, and it may be more so in the foreseeable future.

Impossible choices

For some issues in foreign policy, realistic choices are extremely narrow, if not practically impossible. For the EU, further enlargement and migration come close to fitting the bill. Both present major challenges to the EU, with no obvious solutions at hand and widely diverging opinions internally. Caught in the middle, the hapless policy maker in Brussels can usually do no better than resort to the time-honoured method of fudging or simply kicking the can down the road.

The export of *Pax Europaea* to more unstable and less developed parts of the continent by taking in new members in the EU has been tried several times until now. Membership of the EU was meant to consolidate and further accelerate the process of democratization, modernization and economic development. In economic terms, it has worked in most cases; in political terms, less so. Compare, for example, the rather impressive transformation of Spain and Portugal with the more qualified experience of several countries in central and eastern Europe where the functioning of democracy and the rule of law today leaves much to be desired, and where national populism and corruption also thrive. Perhaps the scars that communist rule leaves behind are much more difficult to heal.

Successive rounds of enlargement of the EU have been described as its most successful foreign policy. With some qualifications, this may indeed be true. For those in doubt or (rightly) exasperated with the antics of Orbán and other new-born 'illiberal democrats', it is worth trying to imagine what central and eastern Europe would have looked like today without the EU. The experience of Moldova and Belarus, not to mention Ukraine, may offer an interesting input to this mental exercise. However, exporting *Pax Europaea* through enlargement has come at a considerable price. An ever-expanding and highly diverse empire with a weak centre and an extremely cumbersome method of decision making risks morphing into Europe's postmodern version of dysfunctionality.

Europe's borders to the east remain conveniently undefined, hence also the number of countries that may eventually become eligible for EU membership. Being European, democratic, with a functioning market economy and able to apply the huge body of EU legislation are the key preconditions for eligibility. But as we know from experience, they are all subject to interpretation that may differ depending on circumstances and interests. More countries have applied to become members and others are eagerly waiting for the green light from Brussels to do so. Some are already flying European flags on their government buildings.

For most candidates, EU membership appears to be an existential issue: their political and economic viability hinges on it, as well as peace in the wider region. This is true, for example, of the six small countries in the western Balkans that are more advanced on the long march towards EU membership. In this rather unhappy region of Europe, peace remains fragile and democracy in short supply. Poverty goes together with bad governance and widespread corruption. Strongmen are in power, several areas have turned into ganglands and borders are contested. Under such conditions, it is hardly surprising that the best and the brightest want to leave – many more are expected to do so once the EU makes it easier for people to emigrate.

It would be unfair to accuse the EU of not trying to improve the situation in the region.[37] With peacekeeping missions in Bosnia and Hercegovina, a key role in negotiations between Serbia and Kosovo, economic and technical aid with conditionality to all countries, and different kinds of agreements to help prepare them for membership, Brussels has surely been trying for years, although with poor results. Montenegro and Serbia began accession negotiations with the EU some years back, but progress has been extremely slow. Albania and North Macedonia are still waiting for the green light to open negotiations, while Bosnia and Hercegovina, together with Kosovo, are even further behind as potential candidates. While the EU pretends to negotiate to let them all in, they pretend to reform. This is the bitter truth. Meanwhile, as the prospect of EU membership fades into the distant future, Russia, China and Turkey buy influence in the region on the cheap.

EU institutions still have great difficulty in handling cases of member countries where democracy and the rule of law do not function properly. If it is difficult with Hungary, Poland, Bulgaria and others, do we honestly believe it will be easier with Albania or Montenegro? Since Cyprus remains a divided island almost twenty years after joining the EU, will it be easier to turn Bosnia and Hercegovina into a functional entity? And how many more weak members can the EU take before it is completely gridlocked? On the other hand, allowing a black hole to develop inside Europe would not only be terrible for those who live there but also dangerous for peace and stability on the continent. If the EU fails in its own backyard, can it have much credibility as an international actor?

Similar arguments apply to Ukraine's application for membership lodged in the midst of Russia's invasion in 2022, followed by similar applications from Georgia and Moldova. Through their heroic resistance and enormous suffering, Ukrainians have earned the admiration of other Europeans and much of the rest of the world. And they surely deserve all the support they can get from the EU, as do other countries in the region as well. But a quick ticket to entry as full member is simply not a realistic option for any of them.

The answer for the ever-increasing number of candidate countries, including Ukraine, may instead lie with a stronger European centre, more funds and a more differentiated approach to membership. A stronger centre will be needed to manage a highly diverse and ever-expanding Union. More funds will be needed to help prepare candidate countries in a graduated approach to membership with conditions attached. At present, pre-accession aid is truly peanuts compared with transfers to those who are already members. In other words, the long wait in the pre-accession room should become more meaningful and more productive instead of being just a deeply frustrating experience. And Brussels may need to go further by devising more gradual and differentiated forms of integration to cater for the enormous diversity on the European continent. Easier said than done, for sure. But wishful thinking has never been a good substitute for policy.

Accession negotiations with Turkey have an even longer history. They began in 2005, building on an association agreement that went back to 1963. Too big and too different: this is the way Turkey has been traditionally seen in many European capitals that never took very seriously the prospect of Turkey becoming a full member. In recent years, Erdoğan's Turkey has developed into a revisionist power making its presence strongly felt in the wider region, from Syria and Libya to the Balkans, the Caucasus and the Mediterranean, increasingly nationalistic and often reminiscing about its Ottoman imperial past, and with an authoritarian regime that shows little respect for human rights.

Under such conditions, Turkey's EU membership has completely disappeared from the radar as a realistic possibility, at least so long as

President Erdoğan remains in power and most probably beyond. The question, however, remains for Brussels and EU national capitals about the right mix of engagement and containment in EU policy towards Turkey.[38] With a geostrategic role, a big army and a large market, Turkey is also an important host country and a key transit point on the global migration trail. Especially today, this counts a great deal for policy makers in Europe.

Migration is the other big issue that presents Europe with almost impossible choices. The facts on the ground make for a very difficult political puzzle to solve.[39] Much of Europe's neighbourhood to the east and the south – and further out – includes war zones, bad governance and poor economic conditions. Europe is a true paradise by comparison. Income levels of EU countries on the northern side of the Mediterranean, not among the richest in Europe, are a multiple of those in north Africa. Many more people now know how those on the other side live and they are often desperate enough to risk their lives to get there. Moreover, people smuggling has become a big business: it provides an organized system and usually false hopes for those trying to escape from awful conditions at home. If anything, the push factors for mobility from the south and the east to the north are expected to increase further in the future because of demographics and climate change.

On the receiving end, Europe has an ageing and declining population. A century ago, Europe's population was about 20 per cent of the world total. By 2030, it is expected to be around 8.5 per cent, with the highest median age compared to other parts of the world. Europe will need to attract skilled people as part of the global competition for talent to join a shrinking labour force and others to do many of the jobs that Europeans are increasingly reluctant to do. These include jobs in hospitals and taking care of ageing Europeans. Legal immigrants will also be contributing to social security systems under stress because of European demographics.

Of course, Europeans would like to be able to choose who comes in, ideally through the regular channels. But they will also want to stem the flow because politics at home is unlikely to allow room for large numbers of immigrants in the foreseeable future, whether one likes it or not. European societies do not seem ready for large additional inflows, and anti-immigration parties will be making sure it stays so. They have a strong presence in many European countries and influence attitudes among the more mainstream parties. When xenophobia has reached the shores of a country such as Sweden, with a long tradition of social democratic values and a remarkable openness to the outside world, we know the problem is real and big.

In other words, a growing mismatch between supply and demand for immigrants is likely to develop in the years to come, as well as a mismatch between economic needs and political feasibility at home. It risks becoming even bigger and turning explosive each time there is a war or a big crisis in Europe's neighbourhood and further afield. European leaders will then be called upon to try and reconcile not just supply with demand but also humanitarian values with political reality at home. And it will not be at all easy. The signs have been there for some time. As a result, European countries have been taking measures to discourage large immigration inflows by building a Fortress Europe and pulling up the drawbridges.

These measures include pushbacks of irregular migrants on land and sea that are not admitted in public, incentives to neighbouring countries to stop people from trying to come to Europe and to take back those whose asylum applications have not been accepted, even outsourcing the management of migration to third countries, as well as a more effective control of Europe's external borders. Such measures are hardly consistent with values that Europeans purport to cherish.

One important side effect of Europe trying to 'take back control' of borders – the slogan that helped Brexiteers win the 2016 referendum – has been to strengthen Frontex, the European Border and Coast Guard Agency: more integration through stealth or necessity? Who could have guessed a few decades ago that Dutch and German officers would be patrolling the waters between Greek islands and the Turkish coast, together with their Greek colleagues? A similar thing was happening on the border between Lithuania and Belarus, where Lukashenko's dictatorship used foreign migrants to exert pressure on his neighbours and the EU in general.

Geography makes some EU members more directly exposed to immigration pressures than others. They are the ones who seek solidarity through an EU system of relocation of asylum seekers. For years, the Mediterranean had been the main transit route for immigration, and countries in central and eastern Europe were most adamant in their opposition to any reallocation of people reaching the European shores. They did not want immigrants, especially those from outside Europe, who were perceived as a threat to their national and Christian identity. Things changed, though, when they began to receive large numbers of refugees fleeing the war in Ukraine in 2022. They were fellow Europeans and Christians and therefore welcome. The contrast with the way governments and local populations had reacted to refugees fleeing the war in Syria a few years earlier was indeed stark.

The Commission is called upon to try and make a common policy out of all this. Its new pact on migration and asylum was presented in 2020. It included partnerships with countries outside the EU to stem migrant inflows, more effective control of the external borders, and flexible forms of intra-European solidarity. In the words of an expert on migration, 'Europe looks inward and promotes deterrence cloaked in humanitarian discourse.'[40] Or is it simply trying to make the best of a bad job?

In recent years, wars in Syria, Iraq, Afghanistan and now Ukraine have accounted for most refugees or immigrants in Europe. It may not, however, continue to be so in the future. Long-term trends point more towards Africa as the biggest source of migration to Europe. Africa has a demographic explosion and its population is expected to exceed two billion people before 2040. It will be mostly young people on a continent with many wars, bad governance, low living standards and high unemployment – a continent that missed, with few exceptions, the opportunities provided by the latest era of globalization. Climate change can only be expected to add further to pressure for human mobility, because more and more people in Africa will be forced to flee desertification.

Africa should attract more European attention in the years to come.[41] Security and migration will be at the top of the agenda. China has already entered the scene in a big way by providing large amounts of investment and development aid in return for access to resources and political influence. Many people in Europe and the West in general argue that China offers Africa a poisoned chalice. It may be true, but words will not be enough. Europeans have so far not been able even by a long distance to match China's offerings in money and human presence. Will they do so with vaccines? Europeans have a historical and moral responsibility, especially those with a colonial past. It would help a great deal if more of their political leaders begin to acknowledge this responsibility and act accordingly.

The general message is that in a rapidly changing and highly unstable world characterized by growing strategic rivalry and large asymmetries, Europe can no longer withdraw inside the cocoon of US protection and only talk about trade, regulation and multilateral rules. Europe needs to think strategically and project collective power as the only way to defend common interests and values. To do so, it will need to break with the unanimity rule in most foreign policy decisions and gradually develop a credible common defence capability, which, admittedly, will come at a cost. A more symmetrical transatlantic relationship in terms of rights and obligations should also be an integral part of the new European grand bargain. It will very much depend on the perception of external threat from the east. Europe's relations with the United States and Russia, protector and main source of threat respectively, have always been inextricably linked together.

It is surely a tall order and not everybody will be ready to face up to it. Some countries will therefore have to take the lead and create coalitions of the willing and able. Today, this is the only realistic option. Failure to do so would unavoidably lead to Europe's marginalization and all that it stands for in times when so much is at stake.

Delivering the Goods:
Elites and Democracy

An elitist project in anti-elite times

European integration began as an elitist project: a benign conspiracy by a small number of Europe's *illuminati* a few years after the end of the Second World War. It has grown remarkably since then and it is now much more than a common market but still far short of the United States of Europe, the (usually) unspoken dream of some of the conspirators all along.

Regional integration has been closely tied to peace, prosperity and democracy on the European continent. Party leaderships from the centre right to the centre left quickly bought into the cause, thus ensuring a broad political consensus on European integration. This consensus was matched with wide albeit passive support from European citizens – experts called it permissive consensus. In other words, citizens of member countries allowed their political leaders a wide margin of manoeuvre for decisions associated with the general direction of European integration, which was perceived as part of foreign policy where the big choices are always made at the top. And for a long time, it delivered the goods.

Political scientists developed sophisticated theories about the internal cumulative logic of integration.[1] At the risk of oversimplification, it means that each step of integration – the economic part of it more particularly – creates the need for going further and deeper. You start by eliminating tariffs on trade, some producers later begin to complain about unfair competition, and then you are forced to tackle domestic regulations and subsidies, and eventually taxes. Next thing, you look for ways to compensate losers – and so on and so forth, leading to ever more integration.

No doubt, functional spill-over has been important. Arguably, integration through law has been even more so, with the European Court of Justice playing a determining role.[2] Having said that, events do not always follow a logical sequence and it is precisely the unexpected that has shaped European integration more than anything else. After all, it was the fall of the Iron Curtain and German unification that led to the creation of the euro, more than functional spill-over from the single market. It was later the pandemic that brought about the issuing of debt in the name of the EU, and it is a rapidly changing international environment, notably the threat from Putin's Russia, that now acts as a catalyst for more European unity.

The continuous expansion of European integration has been the result of a multiplicity of factors, both internal and external: no automatic process and no irreversibility either. As the stakes grew higher, national presidents, chancellors and prime ministers came to occupy the centre stage. These twenty-seven national leaders are the masters of the European universe. They take initiatives, respond to crises and reach compromises whenever possible. They are of course assisted by a complex set of institutions among which the Commission is by far the most important.

National leaders are the ones with whom the European buck stops. This is particularly true of the more politically sensitive areas such as the management of the common currency, home affairs, migration, foreign policy and security policy, which have been added to the European agenda in recent years, while the old Community method still applies for the management of the single market. Among the older generations of devoted Europeans, many are deeply unhappy with this intergovernmental development of the Union, while others recognize it as the inevitable price to pay for the remarkable expansion of the integration project.

For a long time, European integration became the epitome of consensual politics at the very top, a slow and cumbersome process in search of compromise in which some national leaders are always more equal than others. For a good many years, the liberalization of markets and the management of the euro were the best examples of an ideological convergence within and across national borders. These were the times when economic liberalism ruled OK and key political decisions were taken in the name of TINA, Thatcher's slogan that stands for 'There Is No Alternative.'

Under such conditions, it was only natural that much of the everyday running would be left to technocrats, notably Commission experts and central bankers.³ There was thus not much room left for democracy. Political leaders took the big decisions and experts were responsible for everyday management. In similar fashion, consensual politics characterized the workings of the European Parliament: a broad pro-integration church extending from centre right to centre left, including liberals and greens. Dissenters were treated as weirdoes at best. They were, however, more numerous on the touchy issue of immigration from the beginning.

It was, still, a fragile consensus. The constant addition of new members to the EU added to the diversity of interests and opinions, hence rendering decisions more difficult in European councils. Meanwhile, new EU functions reached the core of sovereignty by directly affecting the everyday life and welfare of European citizens, who were thus less inclined to delegate decisions to their political leaders with no questions asked. Even worse, a growing number among them found themselves on the wrong side of the integration project and liberal policies in general. With time, the economic environment became less favourable and the European project less inclusive – at the peak of the euro crisis, the Brussels machine was more dysfunctional than ever.

Thus, Euroscepticism grew and took a more organized form with the rise of anti-systemic movements. Dissenters were branded as populists, which they usually were in adopting simplistic divisions between 'corrupt elites' and 'pure people' while offering ever simpler solutions to complex problems. Yet branding dissenters as populists hardly helped to solve the problem. Populism was the symptom, not the cause, of deep discontent among significant sections of the population.

In the words of Cas Mudde, one of the leading experts on the subject, 'populism is essentially an illiberal democratic response to undemocratic liberalism'.⁴ He cites three main examples of 'undemocratic liberalism' where broad consensus among mainstream parties at the top had excluded for years any real debate within European countries. His examples are EU integration, immigration and neoliberal economic policies. In fact, all three were closely interconnected as part of the broad liberal consensus until populists challenged the consensus at the top, riding on the bandwagons of successive crises.

Furthermore, ideological convergence between mainstream parties on some of the big issues was combined with the growing constraints imposed on national policies through the opening of borders. The combination of the two left little space for democratic choices,[5] hence the notorious TINA. And adding insult to injury, this ideological convergence failed to deliver the goods. Growing inequalities and big crises followed, while populists were only too willing to channel public discontent and profit from it – why shouldn't they? They mounted a challenge against elites, as well as against political correctness as expressed by the now faltering liberal consensus. It was during the euro and immigration crises when the anti-elite campaign reached its peak in the early and mid-2010s. It came mostly from the right but also from the left of the political spectrum. It was then that the permissive consensus turned into constraining dissensus.[6]

Admittedly, even in good times, European integration offers an easy target for all kinds of populists. Decisions affecting our lives taken mostly by foreigners in grey Brussels, complicated compromises that are difficult to understand while the supporting cast often speaks in technocratic gibberish. It is an easy story to tell and so easy to place the EU in a conspiratorial context, especially in times of crisis and addressing those who feel left behind by the 'system'. They were in fact many. British tabloids led by the Murdoch press long excelled in this sport. They reached their apotheosis during the 2016 referendum campaign in a deeply divided and increasingly unequal society in which – to be honest – there was not much love lost for Europe anyway.

The main reason no other country followed the UK to the exit was not so much love for the European project as fear of the alternative and large amounts of EU transfers for the poorer countries. The EU in crisis was perceived by many people to be part and parcel of the 'system' in crisis, of course more strongly so in countries such as Greece, Italy and Spain than in Germany or Finland. But no single European country was completely spared the rise of anti-elite anger when the 'system' ceased to deliver the goods for many people. No country in the West was spared either the much broader crisis of globalized capitalism and of representative democracy. Globalized capitalism constrained political choices and produced highly unequal effects, while democracy with no choices has little meaning. Meanwhile, party politics, which had been all along the living part of representative democracy, was ceding its place to unmediated politics through the social networks.

Subsequent developments pointed to a partial reversal of the anti-systemic tide. In the 2019 European Parliament (EP) elections, nationalist parties received about 25 per cent of the total vote. It was a good result for pro-Europeans, and it was greeted as such. Nationalists were indeed a minority with a very diverse collection of parties. But is it right to brand all nationalists and Eurosceptics as populists? Not really, and it does not help much either, although admittedly there is considerable overlap between them.

Some countries had more than their fair share of nationalists and populists. Greece, for example, was ruled by a coalition of radical left and nationalist right between 2015 and 2019: a rather unorthodox combination which the country survived, but only just. Far-right parties are now everywhere and they are particularly strong in Italy and France. On the eastern side of the former European divide, Hungary and Poland have been ruled for years by right-wing nationalists/populists, and their political fellow travellers are strong in other countries of central and eastern Europe as well. In fact, switching from communism all the way to far-right nationalism (or fascism) does not seem to be all that difficult nowadays.

Many of these far-right nationalists constitute a real threat to the political order in Europe and a threat to democracy. The EU has tried to create a kind of political quarantine for countries such as Hungary and Poland. It had first done so for Austria when a party of the far right joined the government coalition in Vienna at the turn of the century. But can the EU do the same if the wrong people were to come to power in Italy or France? The spectre of Salvini, Le Pen and friends has been haunting many Europeans, and for good reasons. Democracy is indeed a fragile system in the best of countries, the European construction even more so.

Having learned from its own mistakes, the EU has handled the pandemic very differently from earlier crises. An unprecedented common recovery programme through the so-called Next Generation EU and a joint vaccination effort have helped to avoid the worst. It is difficult to imagine how the EU would have survived yet one more and much bigger crisis. However, EU institutions and national governments could not entirely avoid the rising anger of the disaffected or the spread of new conspiracy theories. Vaccines and lockdowns provided the new fodder.

Conspiracy theories flourish in the anonymity of the social media, often pumped by dark forces of misinformation. Elites, experts and the 'system' are their favourite targets. The genie has been out of the bottle for some time now and in no way can it be squeezed back in. Welcome once again to our Brave New World.

European democracy, of a kind

The EU democratic deficit has a long history. Of course, it is a non-problem if you think of European integration as an essentially intergovernmental project run by national presidents, chancellors and prime ministers together with their respective ministers.[7] They all draw legitimacy from their national political systems and reach European decisions by consensus – or just about – so the argument goes. From a different perspective, though, it looks more like the triumph of the executive branch over parliament in all member countries, part of a more general trend made even stronger by European integration. It becomes, however, increasingly problematic as the scope of integration enters new and more sensitive areas of decision making. And since consensus does not always work, it sometimes turns explosive when the legitimacy of one national leader clashes with the legitimacy of another. At the peak of the euro crisis, the legitimacy of Chancellor Merkel and her finance minister Schäuble usually prevailed over the legitimacy of others.

Direct elections to the EP every five years are meant to be the big feast of European democracy. In some ways, they are indeed: citizens from twenty-seven countries electing their representatives to a parliament that keeps acquiring more powers. Yet the European political system in the making remains centred on the rule of the executive, while European elections continue to be essentially national affairs run by national parties. The turnout is still modest by European standards and shockingly low in some countries of central and eastern Europe.

Is the glass half full or half empty? European elections have surely helped to raise public awareness of European issues and choices. They have contributed to the gradual creation of a European public space, yet a space mostly inhabited by a minority of the European-minded and the experts. Jürgen Habermas, a leading philosopher from Germany and strong advocate for the creation of such a public space, admitted back in 2013 that although the EP had been meant as a bridge between European and national arenas, 'this bridge is almost devoid of traffic'.[8] Traffic has increased since then, although not dramatically. On the other hand, information and awareness of public issues cross-cutting intra-European borders has been growing fast. Today, gay rights in Poland or the abortion law in Malta are matters for which interest is certainly not confined within the countries directly concerned. More and more non-nationals intervene in national debates across Europe, and nationalists hate it.

The EP has been flexing its muscles in the continuous power game between European institutions. It plays an increasingly important role in European legislation, although hardly perceived as doing so by most European citizens. The EP has now made a habit of rejecting some of the new Commissioners nominated by national governments every five years, having first subjected all of them to demanding examinations in public hearings. Sure, this is much more than can be said of what national parliaments do with their respective national ministers. The EP has also tried to have the final say with the selection of the president of the Commission, through the system of leading candidates adopted by each of the broad party confederations participating in European elections. This system is better known in the jargon by the German term *Spitzenkandidaten*. It did not, however, succeed for long, because the conclave of national presidents, chancellors and prime ministers meeting as the European Council decided otherwise in 2019.

Can European democracy exist without a European *demos*, or is it like trying to put the cart before the horse? Those who raise this question tend to forget that in most European countries the state had come before the nation or the *demos* and that nation building was a long process lasting a few centuries. After all, is there a single *demos* today in Spain, the UK or Belgium, not to mention Baltic countries with large Russian minorities?

In a world of ever-growing interdependence through international trade, global supply chains and large movements of capital and people, as well as in terms of health, cyberspace and the environment, any attempt to deal collectively with global problems hits against the constraints imposed by the multitude of sovereign nation states, sovereign albeit ever less autonomous. No surprise we now speak of 'governance' rather than 'government' to indicate not only the diversity of actors within and beyond national borders but also the increased fuzziness of the process.

The EU constitutes by far the most advanced attempt in trying to reconcile these two different realities. It is still a very imperfect answer to Rodrik's trilemma between global markets, sovereignty and national democracy,[9] still producing far more policies than politics, yet better than anything tried anywhere else until now. Kalypso Nicolaïdis has coined the term *demoi-cracy*[10] to describe the split reality of the European political entity consisting of twenty-seven national democracies – *demoi* is the plural of *demos* in Greek. We might also call it a confederation, which is an older and more familiar term among the experts. But call it whatever you like, the problem will be the same: how to extend democracy beyond the national borders. It is bound to be a long, difficult and often frustrating exercise.

The attempt to engage national parliaments in European decision making, hence to try and draw legitimacy directly from its national source, is not an easy path to follow either. In a European system that relies largely on consensus and unanimity, it could produce eternal gridlock. It is slow and cumbersome enough as it is today. Still, the main reason most national parliaments are not so much involved in European decision making is that power has steadily shifted from the legislative to the executive. The Danish parliament is an exception, having acquired for itself an active role in European decision making by keeping national ministers going to Brussels on a short lease. Other national parliaments also play a role on special occasions, and the German Bundestag more frequently so because some animals are more equal than others in the European zoo!

Since EU representative democracy is still rather weak, how about direct democracy? Would it not help to bring citizens closer to European decision making? Alas, referendums are a double-edged sword. They offer citizens the opportunity to register their preferences in an unmediated fashion, but experience suggests they can also be easily hijacked by demagogues. No surprise German politicians are dead against, given the use made of referendums during the Nazi period. In fact, except for the Swiss, no other European country had much experience in the post-war period until referendums made their entry into the democratic process mainly via EU integration. Referendums took place in a few countries and then the habit spread.

People have been asked in referendums whether they wanted their country to join the EU, which is arguably close to an existential question given the importance that EU accession has for national sovereignty. Except for Norwegians, who said 'no' twice in the past and stayed out, all other national referendums on accession have produced a positive answer until now. The British were asked twice whether they wanted to stay or leave once they were already members. In 1975, they answered 'yes', and the second time in 2016 they opted for divorce after more than forty years of European marriage.

Several governments have also asked their people to pronounce on major revisions of European treaties, notably the Maastricht treaty of 1992 that led to the creation of monetary union, and the constitutional treaty that followed a decade later. In some cases, the answer they got was 'no', which produced big political tremors both at home and in the EU. Those treaty revisions would have sailed through national parliaments because of wide cross-party consensus on European integration. Popular majorities thus turned out to be very different from parliamentary majorities.

People against political elites? European referendums have often produced unusual coalitions that cut across the old divide between right and left, apparently because the old divide was no longer relevant for many people. And in so doing, these unusual coalitions raised a direct challenge against the broad ideological consensus prevailing until then, of which European integration was a key part. Cosmopolitans versus nationalists, *Somewheres* versus *Anywheres*, the division between city and countryside: they have all acquired a new political importance. It happened in France and the Netherlands in the 2005 referendums on the European constitutional treaty. It happened with a much bigger bang with the Brexit referendum in 2016.

Sure, demagogues played a big role in all those cases. Sure also, it is easier to gather a coalition against something – whatever? – rather than get people to vote in favour of a concrete proposal, especially when many people are unhappy with the state of the country and their own condition. And to top it all up, it is surely much easier to say 'no' to

European treaty revisions which only experts really understand. After all, how many people care about the division of powers between the Council and the Commission, except for those paid to do so?

The European political system today requires unanimity among members when it comes to treaty revisions and other big decisions. It had been difficult enough to reach compromises in intergovernmental conferences and secure ratifications by so many national parliaments. Adding referendums in individual member countries and hoping to get a positive answer in all of them was really stretching European luck too far. It was rather a recipe for political disaster.

How, then, did European political leaders attempt to deal with the problem of growing dissensus and negative results in referendums? Not in the most democratic of ways, it has to be said. Having struggled hard to reach compromises on complex legal texts that set the key objectives for the next stage of European integration and the framework for the functioning of European institutions, those at the top simply refused to take no for an answer. Instead, they tried to bypass negative popular verdicts in individual country referendums by engaging in dangerous political and legal acrobatics. And they decided to do so consensually within the European Council, although the most difficult part of the balancing over the void was left to those governments that had to deal with negative popular verdicts at home.

When the Irish people made the 'wrong decision' with respect to the Nice treaty and later the Lisbon treaty, they were asked to vote again after some changes in the legal texts. For their part, people in France and the Netherlands thought they had struck a deadly blow to the constitutional treaty by voting against it in the 2005 referendums, only to discover that the core of the text reappeared a few years later as the Lisbon treaty. Adding insult to popular injury, the new treaty was then ratified by national parliaments to avoid more accidents with referendums. The only exception were the Irish, who could not escape one because of their constitution, and they were forced to vote twice to get the answer right. In 2015, the Greeks voted with a large majority against the economic package offered to them by their Eurozone partners. Only a few days later, they were forced to accept even more punishing terms. Admittedly, the government in Athens had made a complete mess out of an admittedly very difficult economic situation.

In all those cases, democracy suffered badly and so did the European project. Never again was the conclusion reached by most of Europe's political leaders, meaning no more revisions of European treaties and no more referendums. Better stay within the straitjacket of our existing treaties for as long as it takes and hopefully our good lawyers will continue to provide us with creative interpretations of these treaties, so they thought. The alternative would be courting another political disaster in a very diverse Europe, and in difficult times when political elites no longer command much respect from their citizens. But what if the straitjacket becomes too tight? This is the key question that may require a political answer sooner rather than later.

On this point, it would be fair to recognize that the British political class apparently takes democracy more seriously than at least some of its former European partners. Notwithstanding the fact that most MPs in Westminster were strongly against Brexit, they bit their lips and went along with the popular decision. Many Europeans were rather surprised. They had thought a way could be found to circumvent the 52 per cent majority in the Brexit referendum. But in a democracy the sovereign people have the right to make mistakes and eventually pay for them. It was arguably a big mistake the British people have made with Brexit. Let History be the ultimate judge.

Strongmen and autocrats

Nationalists and populists succeeded in coming to power in some European countries and then began to take measures that challenged the very fundamentals of liberal democracy, namely the rule of law, institutional checks and balances, and individual freedoms. They saw themselves as the embodiment of the people's will, with a distorted view of Rousseau's *volonté générale*.

In Hungary, 'illiberal democracy' was proudly proclaimed by Viktor Orbán and his Fidesz Party.[11] In his many years in power, Orbán introduced measures against the independence of the judiciary, took direct control of much of the mass media and tried to muffle the rest, extended state control over previously independent educational institutions, manipulated the electoral law in his favour, restricted gay rights and launched anti-Semitic attacks, while always stoking the fires of nationalism and presenting himself as the true defender of family and Christian values. According to Freedom House, which monitors the quality of democracy and human rights in many countries around the world, Hungary is now the only country in the EU that qualifies as partly free.[12] Even if Orbán were to lose an election in the future, it would be extremely difficult for any successor to dismantle the power structure he has set up.

Orbán did not go about the business of seizing control over Hungarian institutions and society at large in a quiet fashion. On the contrary, he proudly and loudly elaborated his views on 'illiberal democracy' and made a big fuss denouncing the dictatorship of Brussels and the decadence of elites in western Europe. He clearly enjoyed acting as agent provocateur – many of his voters presumably enjoyed it too. He played with popular fears about a shrinking population at home and the loss of national identity, and he invested in Hungarian irredentism. Many Hungarians who were unhappy with the state of their country took advantage of the freedom of movement in the EU and emigrated, which made life easier for Orbán at home. They were a living proof of Krastev's pithy comment that today in Europe it is easier to change country than change the government.

Orbán often sounded like Putin, with whom he apparently enjoyed mutual respect and admiration. His virulent criticism of Brussels, however, never stopped him from enjoying the blessings that come with large amounts of EU funds, while his political cronies were accused of directly benefitting from these transfers. Not surprisingly, he showed no intention of following the UK to the exit. In simple words, the Hungarian leader managed very skilfully for years to get away with murder while most members of the European family watched with embarrassment and seemingly powerless.

Orbán was not the only one. His example was followed in neighbouring Poland, when the PiS (Law and Justice) Party under the leadership of Jarosław Kaczyński, an admirer of Orbán, returned to power in 2015.[13] They then began to take measures that interfered with the independence of the judiciary and mass media, while also introducing restrictive legislation on individual rights, including abortion and sexual orientation. On the same lines, several regions and provincial towns in Poland declared themselves LGBTQ-free zones! Under growing criticism and closer investigation from Brussels, the governments in both countries then challenged in no uncertain terms the right of EU institutions to interfere in their domestic affairs. In 2021, the Polish Constitutional Tribunal went much further by challenging the primacy of EU law and the right of the EU to interfere with the Polish justice system. By the standards of the EU, it was like declaring nuclear war.

Hungarian and Polish nationalists treated the EU essentially as a common market and a milk cow for funds, but also as a threat to national sovereignty and national identity. They found allies in other countries, mostly in central and eastern Europe. On cultural and identity issues, there is today an east–west divide in Europe, which has much to do with history and demography. Of course, it is not an absolute divide. Orbán in Hungary and Kaczyński in Poland have many things in common with the likes of Matteo Salvini and Giorgia Meloni in Italy, Marine Le Pen in France and others across Europe, not to mention the most powerful of friends on the other side of the Atlantic, namely Donald Trump and company.

Brussels institutions are never comfortable dealing with identity and cultural issues. After all, they had not been programmed for such tasks. On the other hand, the link between European integration and the rule of law in member countries is more straightforward, because the EU as a legal construct depends entirely on the equal application of common rules and regulations by national institutions and courts in each member. Thus, when countries with relatively weak democratic traditions began to join, EU membership became directly linked to democratization and the strengthening of the rule of law in the new members. The Commission was then entrusted with the role of policeman. In fact, the accession of both Bulgaria and Romania was delayed by a few years precisely because they were not deemed to fulfil the requirements for proper rule of law. But Brussels was soon to discover that its powers became much less effective the moment a candidate country joined the EU and gained a seat around the Council table.

The EU has legal and economic instruments to fight against violations of democracy and the rule of law in its members. But such instruments are not easy to use – and for a long time the political will was not there either.[14] In a club where there is continuous and close interaction among members and where many decisions are taken by consensus, national political leaders try hard not to step too much on each other's toes. The way each one handles their domestic politics is sensitive territory not to be trespassed on by others, that is until rogue behaviour goes beyond the limit of collective tolerance. At some point, both the Fidesz government in Hungary and the PiS government in Poland crossed this limit. But it took them years to do so.

Article 2 of the Treaty on European Union, otherwise known as the Lisbon treaty, states that the Union is 'founded on the values of respect for human dignity, freedom, democracy, equality, the rule of law and respect for human rights, including the rights of persons belonging to minorities'. The punishment for 'serious and persistent breach by a Member State' will be suspension of voting rights in the Council, according to Article 7 of the same treaty. Since there is no provision in the treaty for expelling a member, the suspension of voting rights therefore constitutes the ultimate form of punishment, to be used only when everything else has failed.

EU institutions are required by treaty to go through a long examination before they reach the final stage in a continuous back-and-forth between the Commission, the Parliament and the Council, a process that requires large majorities in both Parliament and Council. At the final stage, the Council can only decide to deliver punishment by unanimity without counting the country that sits in the dock. Both governments in Hungary and Poland have made it abundantly clear they would protect each other assuming their case ever reached the final stage.

Much ado about nothing? Surely the treaty does not make it easy to take measures against countries that may violate fundamental European values. Those who drafted the treaty recognized the delicate balance between a highly decentralized Union and its member states. But can politics then take over from law? As late as 2021, Fidesz MEPs continued to sit together with their colleagues from the European People's Party, a confederation of centre-right parties which also happens to be the biggest political group in the European Parliament. They were allowed because numbers make a big difference in the Parliament in terms of the distribution of funds, presidencies and memberships of committees, and influence more generally. Numbers of MEPs had also determined who would be appointed president of the Commission, until the European Council decided otherwise in 2019.

For years, Fidesz members were treated as a kind of misfits, yet tolerated within the broader family of Christian democrats. The role of German Christian Democrats under the leadership of Angela Merkel was crucial in keeping Orbán inside the big tent. Merkel's strong sense of compromise conveniently combined with large German investments in Hungary, notably those of the auto industry. No surprise that European institutions were so slow and hesitant for years in tackling flagrant violations of democracy and the rule of law in Hungary.

Another example was Boyko Borisov, who ruled Bulgaria with a heavy hand for years, former bodyguard of a former king who had also been elected prime minister. Such things can happen when people get desperate. Borisov enjoyed political protection within the broad family of the European centre right by being a loyal ally and keeping a low profile outside his national borders. This gave him considerable freedom to engage in – shall we say? – unconventional (and undemocratic) political practices at home. In contrast, Polish nationalists never experienced the same degree of benign treatment from the European centre right. Early enough, they had chosen a different political camp together with British Conservatives, and as a result they were left with fewer European allies.

More recently, EU institutions have tightened the grip on wayward members. The European Court of Justice also joined the battle by deciding in 2021 that attempts by the Polish government to interfere with the independence of the judicial system were incompatible with EU law, and its Polish counterpart retorted it was none of its business. It became a big political issue and a test of credibility for European institutions, which were steadily upping the stakes. After all, if the EU cannot defend democracy and the rule of law within its own borders, how can it be taken seriously when trying to export those same values to countries outside? The cynical observer might, however, remind us that the US has been doing the same with messianic fervour for many decades while tolerating various kinds of undemocratic practices in individual US states at home. Alas, values and foreign policy have never made an easy match and Europe may be no exception, uncomfortable though this truth may be.

Economic instruments were also marshalled by EU institutions in exerting pressure on political misfits within the European borders. EU members with blatant violations of the rule of law and large-scale political corruption had been for years on the receiving end of large amounts of EU funds. The release of such funds is now linked to the rule of law through a conditionality clause which has been given the seal of approval by the ECJ. This can serve as a powerful weapon given the importance of EU transfers for many members. At long last, the Commission seems therefore prepared to make good use of the economic weapon, with political support from enough members in the Council. Is this one more manifestation of Europe turning into a political adult, albeit slowly and with much trepidation?

EU pressure could in the end prove to be the most effective by sending a clear message to citizens in the countries concerned and rallying domestic resistance against undemocratic practices – 'the ultimate safeguard against their own demons', in the words of Rupnik.[15] So long as large majorities are keen on remaining in the EU, common institutions will have strong weapons in their hands for the defence of democracy and the rule of law in member countries. It has not, however, worked in Hungary, where Orbán was re-elected to power with a large majority in 2022.

There are different kinds of misfits and different kinds of democracy in Europe. EU institutions have a difficult task in ensuring that minimum common standards are respected by all members. They are employing ever more instruments to achieve results. For example, the European Public Prosecutor's Office (EPPO) that started its operations in 2021 is meant to investigate and prosecute fraud in relation to the use of EU funds. It will form part of a collective effort to deal with the much bigger problem of political corruption. The EPPO is also one more example of 'enhanced cooperation' in the EU, meaning that some countries decide to go further with integration than others. At the time of writing, twenty-two EU countries were part of the EPPO.

Coalitions of the willing and able

European integration has gone through a rapid acceleration phase during the last more than three decades. But not everybody always got on board. Some EU countries decided to proceed further with integration while others stayed behind, either by choice or because they could not meet the criteria for joining – such criteria were also a new thing. The result has been a much less uniform EU, while different legal instruments have been used to make it kosher.

The provision for the so-called 'enhanced cooperation' in the European treaty allows for a minimum of nine EU members to establish more advanced forms of integration or cooperation with access to common EU institutions in a policy area already within the treaty framework. It is distinct from legal opt-outs that allow individual members to be excluded from common policies. These are all devices within the EU legal framework meant to provide some flexibility and allow some countries to move faster than the rest, albeit subject to constraints. And when these constraints proved too tight for those keen to move faster, they sometimes resorted to less conventional methods. They signed intergovernmental agreements outside the EU legal framework that only bound the signatory parties. The main advantage of such agreements was that outsiders had no right of veto, hence no leverage on the signatories.

An important precedent was set by the Schengen treaty, signed in a small town in Luxembourg in 1985 by just five EU members. It was a strictly intergovernmental agreement outside the EU treaty framework, and it was meant to extend the freedom of movement of people by eliminating internal border controls among signatory countries. It has grown exponentially since then in terms of both membership and scope. Today, twenty-six European countries are members of Schengen, including non-EU members such as Iceland, Norway and Switzerland, thus blurring the dividing line between membership and non-membership of the European club. The same also applies to the so-called European Economic Area, which allows non-EU members access to the single European market, with no voting rights but with a participation fee that takes the form of financial contributions to EU common policies.

Schengen now forms an integral part of EU law. It is administered by EU institutions, although it includes non-EU countries. All members have a common visa policy for citizens of countries outside the area. There is an opt-out for the Republic of Ireland to enable the latter to keep an open border with Northern Ireland, as well as criteria of eligibility that allow Norway to be in while Bulgaria, Romania, Croatia and Cyprus are still out. The rules of Schengen were, however, repeatedly suspended during Europe's never-ending crises of recent years when individual countries reintroduced border checks to keep non-EU immigrants and later Covid suspects out of their national territory. Nothing ever comes with the seal of permanence, and even less so in Europe's fragile construction.

The Maastricht treaty of 1992 followed the more conventional legal path. Unlike Schengen in its original version, Maastricht was an EU treaty that led to the creation of monetary union, with formal opt-outs for Denmark and the UK as the only realistic way to overcome the threat of veto. The authors of the Maastricht treaty also set strict economic criteria to be fulfilled before a country can adopt the euro – as with Schengen, a few countries are still today in the waiting room. Thus, employing different legal instruments in the beginning, both Schengen and Maastricht have opened the way for coalitions of willing and able countries to move faster than the rest, and they have set a pattern.

It has been called differentiated integration, multiple speeds, variable geometry. Academics have written learned articles and books on the fine nuances and several political leaders have come up with their own ideas.[16] Cooperation in justice and home affairs, defence through PESCO and, most important of all, the Eurozone are the obvious examples. Coalitions of willing and able countries have invariably included France and Germany in a leading role, while Denmark and the UK, when the latter was still a member, made the richest collection of opt-outs.

From the very beginning, the most important and advanced form of differentiated integration has been the Eurozone. Sharing a common currency and gradually integrating ever more areas of macroeconomic policy to make monetary union functional is of course a totally different ball game from managing a single market. Membership of the Eurozone has expanded from eleven to nineteen today, by itself a strong vote of confidence for the euro project in times of crisis, but also a confirmation that the doors remain open for those able to fulfil the criteria. So far at least, differentiated integration has not implied the creation of an exclusive club for the privileged few.

In trying to manage the euro crisis, members of the Eurozone were forced by events to take bolder steps. These included the signing of new intergovernmental treaties outside the EU legal framework for the so-called Fiscal Compact and the European Stability Mechanism (ESM), which came together as a package. The former consisted of a set of strict fiscal rules as a precondition for the creation of the ESM as a lender of last resort, since the authors of the Maastricht treaty had not made any provision for a European monetary fund to be used in emergencies. It was the Germans who insisted on the link between the Fiscal Compact and the ESM. And because they were in a rush – a big crisis to handle, remember? – they helped to break yet one more taboo in EU affairs.

A provision was included in these intergovernmental agreements allowing them to take effect without having to wait for all signatories to ratify them. Instead, it was decided that a super majority would do by adding the weighted votes of signatory countries. To put it bluntly, this provision was meant to take care of one or more possible last-minute doubters among the smaller countries while the big ones kept for themselves a blocking vote. It was intended as an additional means of pressure to accelerate the process of ratification. But it was also an important step away from the erstwhile sacrosanct rule of unanimity. The same happened again with another intergovernmental agreement that led to the creation of the Single Resolution Fund at the peak of the euro crisis.

In an ever-enlarging and diverse Union faced with big challenges, the answer so far has been more Europe and a more differentiated Europe. In many ways, it has also been a less supranational Europe. This is most likely the way to follow in the years ahead. Given the fundamentally different visions among EU members about the future of the European project and the role of Europe in a rapidly changing world, coalitions of willing and able countries are today the only realistic option available. They should proceed with further integration while leaving the door open for others to join later.

Some Europeans are content with regional integration essentially as an economic project – a minority in fact resent any interference from Brussels in the way they run their affairs at home – while others allow themselves the luxury of dreaming of a European political union and Europe as an international power.[17] Such differences have always been there. They have, however, become much starker because of successive enlargements and a rapidly changing economic and political environment. For sure there are federalists in Poland, perhaps also in Lithuania, and many nationalists in France, although arguably fewer in Germany. Yet national majorities differ considerably and so do prevailing visions of Europe.

The Eurozone is already the prime example of differentiated Europe and it will continue being so in the foreseeable future. A minority of EU members will remain outside for economic or political reasons or both, while those inside will by necessity become gradually more integrated as the only way to make their economic and monetary union more functional and resilient. Theories of spill-over are particularly relevant in this case. Differentiated integration is a fact of life, but it may also be a fact that the gap between members and non-members of the Eurozone will grow further in the years to come. This is bound to have broader political implications for the European project, no point in pretending otherwise.

With foreign policy and defence policy, Europeans are still at an early stage. Experience tells us that the search for a common denominator for all twenty-seven members with strict observance of the unanimity rule will continue to be a highly frustrating exercise with precious little result. In a modest way, PESCO has already shown the way. Doing away with the unanimity rule is a basic precondition – the coalition government in Berlin has already taken a clear stance in favour. But it may not be enough. Any real progress in terms of foreign and defence policy cooperation will most probably have to rely on coalitions of willing and able countries in which France and Germany, as well as Italy, Spain, the Netherlands and others, take the lead. Would members of the Eurozone be the natural candidates for closer cooperation in foreign and defence policy? After all, they are already members of the upper tier of integration. However, the answer needs to be qualified. Strategic visions and priorities of individual Eurozone members are still far apart. It may therefore have to be a smaller group in the beginning.

Differentiated integration and the further blurring of the dividing line between membership and non-membership of the EU could also provide the answer for new enlargements. Politicians and lawyers should be able to invent formulas of partial or graduated EU membership that include more generosity in development aid, tied to conditionality, as a much better alternative to candidate countries waiting for ever in the antechamber. Europe's complex reality requires more thinking outside the box.

On the other hand, differentiated integration cannot solve all problems.[18] To start with, it cannot bring about a radical reform of EU institutions and the common decision-making process. It cannot also deal effectively with distributional issues. When 'frugal' countries, for example, insist on a small EU budget into which they would like to pay as little as possible, the problem cannot be solved by leaving them out of any new common arrangement. The same applies, only more so, when countries resort to unfair competition on matters of taxation. It is no different either when it comes to solidarity among countries regarding the allocation of refugees and irregular immigrants coming to Europe. A smaller group among the twenty-seven deciding to go further with a common European policy on immigration and political asylum would not solve the seemingly impossible equation of fair burden sharing.

In other words, on all issues with a strong distributional dimension, free-riders, unfair competitors and all kinds of conscientious objectors need to be brought inside the tent one way or the other. Nothing is gained by leaving them out. The same equally applies to fundamental values enshrined in EU treaties. Autocrats and 'illiberal democrats' would simply love being offered the choice to be excluded from common provisions regarding the rule of law. The latter should therefore remain part of the common denominator for all.

Ready for revolution?

Ahead of the EP elections in spring 2019, President Macron, in an open letter addressed to all European citizens, came up with the idea of a Conference for Europe to 'propose all the changes our political project needs, with an open mind, even to amending the treaties'. It was typical Macron in terms of the scale of ambition and political courage – some might call it audacity – to address citizens of member countries above the heads of their political leaders. Following the European elections, which produced a big pro-European majority of MEPs with a higher turnout of votes than in previous elections, the new leaders of EU institutions took up Macron's proposal. And a joint non-paper of the French and German governments soon followed as the, by now, almost inevitable next step. However, the idea was later caught up in long squabbles of EU institutions about who would be in charge, and how, as often happens when bold ideas are being translated into political acts. The arrival of the pandemic only made things worse.

The Conference on the Future of Europe was finally launched in March 2021. It included an innovative, bottom-up exercise with citizens' assemblies at both national and European level. Organizing large European panels on a long list of topics with citizens randomly selected from twenty-seven countries to represent the wide diversity of the European continent was by itself a mind-boggling exercise, involving numerous facilitators, experts and interpreters to enable communication in Europe's Babel of languages. It was also a highly ambitious and innovative exercise the impact of which can only be judged on delivery.

All these citizens' panels were meant to provide a valuable input to the Conference Plenary, which in turn is meant to report by consensus. Good luck to those entrusted with the drafting of the report. The task of reaching such a consensus in today's EU-27 looks truly awesome, which also means that the risk of the European mountain once again giving birth to a mouse is a very real one. If it were to happen, it would be good neither for democracy nor for the European project.

Earlier, the Council had poured cold water on the ambitions of ardent Europeans by stating that it did not expect the Conference to trigger a new treaty revision. Many national governments were dead against such a prospect because they had either little appetite for ambitious reforms or simply no desire to get involved in another painful exercise likely to lead to a political disaster, as with the constitutional treaty almost twenty years ago. The requirement for unanimity for any treaty revision under Article 48 of the existing treaty, combined with the wide divergence inside the EU-27 and the prospect of national referendums, scares the living daylights out of European political leaders – and they are right.

The only way to break out of this legal and political dead end would be a decision to work outside the existing EU legal framework.[19] A group of countries may decide to set up a convention to draft a European Constitution (or any other name they choose to give it) which will bind only those countries that sign and ratify it, thus doing away with the threat of veto. It may require large majorities before it is put into effect, but certainly no unanimity, which remains the biggest obstacle to Europe's coming of political age. Those not ready for this bold move can therefore stay out, but they would not be able to stop others from going ahead.

Once the rule of unanimity is lifted, national referendums would no longer be a threat. On the contrary, they may be highly desirable as the means to provide direct legitimacy for such an important political project. Citizens of individual countries would then be presented with a clear choice: do they want to be part of a European political union or not? If they choose to vote no, which would be a perfectly legitimate decision to make, it would be a decision that binds only their country and not others.

It would be a political revolution and the initiative can only come from the top. And it would surely be difficult and messy. Lawyers would have a big task trying to find a legal modus vivendi between the new political entity and the existing EU, or what is left of it. The main trade-off of such a bold decision to proceed with a European political union consisting of a smaller group of countries is obvious, whichever way one may try to dress it up. It is between a stronger and more integrated European political entity better able to face up to the big challenges of the world today, on the one hand, and more divisions inside Europe, on the other. It would be by no means an easy political choice to make between the two. But judging from the experience with the euro and other major European initiatives in the past, once a group of countries, including both France and Germany as a minimum, decide to move ahead, it works like a rallying point for others. Not that many European countries can really afford to stay out in the long run.

Such a revolution is not for tomorrow – perhaps not in our lifetime or the next, hard realists would argue most emphatically. There is little appetite for bold moves among today's embattled political leaders, although they might be pleasantly surprised to discover that many European citizens are receptive to them – if we are to believe opinion polls. Europe needs big crises to mature as a political entity. It remains to be seen whether a full-scale war on its soil, namely the war in Ukraine, becomes the required catalyst.

Who Needs Europe, and What For?

Times of transition

We live in times of transition, when so many things are changing around us. It looks more like the end of an era, although it is impossible to predict what may follow. We can discern trends, perhaps even identify fragile equilibriums in political, economic or social terms that no longer look sustainable. But nobody can predict events that will eventually shape outcomes. And we know from History that events have a logic of their own, and I surely do not mean fate.

Putin's Russia was always extremely unhappy with the order imposed by the winners of the Cold War in the former Soviet space and beyond. The Russian president challenged this order repeatedly and upped the stakes much further by launching a horrific war against Ukraine, the kind of war Europe had not experienced for decades. At the time of writing, we do not know how and when the war would end, but what we do know for sure is that there can be no return to the post-Cold War order. Peace is often more difficult to win than war. We are repeatedly reminded of this wise saying as we look back at the opportunities lost to create the conditions for a long-lasting peace on the European continent after the dismantling of the Soviet empire. Ukraine is now paying a huge price and the broader dire consequences of the war will be felt throughout Europe. A new Cold War on two fronts, with Russia and China coming closer together, is hardly a prospect to relish – and cold wars always risk going out of control.

The geopolitical tectonic plates are shifting fast. For the United States, the 'unipolar moment' after the end of the Cold War has lasted for more than three decades and is gradually coming to an end. The rapid rise of China is challenging US hegemony and Washington is in no mood to accept it as an inescapable fact. Mobilizing available resources and rallying allies to the new cause constitutes one of the few things that unite Americans today in an otherwise deeply divided society. However, arresting the rise of China and/or trying to disentangle the United States – and the West – from Asia's rapidly rising power in an already highly interdependent world will not be at all easy. It would also be extremely costly for all concerned. Global supply chains cannot be broken with a simple order. And China is already too big a market for Western multinationals to ignore. Nobody can vouchsafe that the old and the new superpower will not be eventually caught in Thucydides' trap: world peace is at stake.

With a greater dispersion of power at the global level, many unresolved conflicts, international cooperation in short supply and no world policeman any longer ready or able to impose order, as the United States so often did in many places in the past, we are entering a more Hobbesian phase of international relations, the anarchical society[1] with little order and too many weapons around. These are indeed dangerous times. I am not arguing here that the United States always did a good job with the power it had; far from it. Think of Iraq and Afghanistan, think of Latin America, as characteristic examples of the abuse of US power and/or policy failure. But many people would argue with conviction that anarchy is much worse than even a flawed order. Of course, it all depends on which side of the fence you stand, or rather whether you are the offender or the victim, the winner or the loser.

Climate change is an existential threat for all humankind. This frightening reality is rapidly dawning upon us and the warning signs are there for all to see. Extreme weather phenomena are already happening with alarming frequency. But fighting climate change requires global cooperation, which is far from evident, and even less so in times of growing rivalry between the Great Powers. Fighting against climate change raises major distributional questions between and within countries. The intergenerational distribution is arguably the most difficult of all.

Those in charge today are being called upon to engineer a massive economic transition that requires very large investments and implies considerable costs by raising the price of polluting goods and activities during the long transition period. The benefits will be mostly felt by our children and grandchildren. If we collectively fail, other issues will become almost irrelevant, including the geopolitical power struggle on an increasingly unliveable planet. But how many political leaders can afford today to think beyond the ephemeral? The recent pandemic has, if anything, painfully reminded us how difficult it is to deliver global public goods, in this case global public health, in a decentralized yet highly interconnected world of nation states.

Technological change is revolutionizing the world and our lives. And it is happening at a mind-boggling pace. There are virtually no limits to what the human mind can invent, and most people look forward – and rightly so – to the new opportunities created by artificial intelligence, for example, in a meta-universe where (almost) everything will be possible. And yet there are good reasons to worry about the capacity of our societies to harness new technologies for the common good, to empower rather than alienate people, to serve the many and avoid an excess of power in the hands of the few, to promote social cohesion and strengthen democracy. Virtual reality could end up as a nightmare if not handled wisely; somebody should tell Mr Zuckerberg among others and do something about it urgently. On the other hand, incorporating artificial intelligence into weapons can produce a much worse nightmare for humankind. The key question always is what use we make of technological progress.

Capitalism has triumphed: it has turned global and ruling communist parties have been converted to it. The Chinese Communist Party is the most prominent example, in its own way of course. Yet at the same time, the legitimacy of the capitalist system has suffered, mostly in the developed world. Societies have become more unequal and more divided – those in the English-speaking world even more so arguably because they took the (neo)liberal revolution more seriously than others.

Growing inequalities have gone hand in hand with a widespread feeling of unfairness in Western societies. Global oligopolies, especially in high-technology sectors, defy competition rules and enjoy excessive power over those who use their services. The financial system appropriates exorbitant profits and bonuses while being bailed out by the state with taxpayers' money when things go wrong. Tax evasion is widespread particularly among the super-rich. Meanwhile, the creative destruction of global markets has left numerous victims. Wages have long failed to catch up with productivity, and insecurity has grown dramatically for those on the lower ranks of the labour and income ladder. Weak social contracts and badly squeezed middle classes make for a very fragile political equilibrium at home.

Indeed, our political systems have become much more fragmented and our states less governable. Trust in liberal democratic institutions has declined, while younger generations whose life chances are significantly worse than those of their parents are keeping their distance from democratic party politics. Although the populist tide has been partially reversed in some countries, social discontent is almost palpable. The pandemic has only made things worse. Admittedly, it could have turned into an almighty disaster if our governments had not learned some lessons from the financial crisis a few years earlier. But still, things are not good.

During the pandemic, the anti-systemic revolt took a new turn. Those in search of conspiracies everywhere and with zero trust in state institutions, elites, science and the 'system' in general reached the conclusion that vaccines and lockdowns were the new forms of oppression by the forces of evil. These people constitute a sizeable and dangerous minority. Alas, in today's fractured societies, such reactions may no longer be treated as an aberration.

Nationalism has grown in many places. It is partly a reaction to the constraints imposed by international interdependence on the capacity of individual countries to decide for themselves. The space for democracy has become much narrower. Nationalism is also a kind of refuge for more vulnerable members of society who fear rapid change. And it has been further reinforced by increasing numbers of immigrants in developed countries. Those who feel they got a raw deal out of the liberal version of globalization have reacted more strongly than others, although not always in a rational fashion. Turning to demagogues has not been the best way to defend their interests. Nationalisms tend to cancel each other out, although most often at a heavy price for peace and prosperity. And when international cooperation and multilateral rules fail, it is the strong who take what they may and the weak who suffer what they must: Thucydides again. Those countries on the lower ranks of the power ladder should have learned this lesson the hard way.

It is not at all difficult to paint a bleak picture of today's world: geopolitical instability, rising tension among the Great Powers, polarized societies and the resurgence of nationalism combined with an existential threat for all the world's inhabitants in the form of climate change. You add a pandemic, an energy crisis and a food crisis and you could end up with a perfect storm. And then you start looking for wise leaders to protect you from the storm – and there are not that many around.

How does Europe fit into this rather bleak picture? This small, very diverse and densely populated continent with old civilizations and a rich history replete with wars, including imperialist wars fought in faraway places, has been on the dependence end of the stick for several decades. Western Europe relied on the United States as its protector and saviour of last resort throughout the Cold War, which had placed the whole of Europe at the centre of rivalry between the West and the East. The West won the Cold War with the United States as its leader. Large parts of Europe thus gained freedom and peace, although not all. But Europe also lost its centrality. Alas, the price for Europe regaining centre stage seems to be the return of the spectre of war on the European continent.

Most Europeans enjoy relatively high levels of prosperity. Europe is ageing and slowly shrinking in numbers. This is because of a combination of long life expectancies and very low birth rates. Europe's share of world trade and GDP is declining as well, while less developed parts of the world are gradually catching up. It should have been expected and there is nothing wrong with it. But Europe is also lagging in several cutting-edge technologies, which risks creating excessive dependence on decisions made by others, with broader negative implications for the security, welfare and individual freedoms of European citizens. Technological dependence is thus being added to the military dependence which has been a fact of life for many decades.

In a world characterized by big global challenges, growing strategic rivalry and large asymmetries, relative decline for Europe risks going together with marginalization. Europeans have long lost the desire to run the world – or the illusion they could do so. But they may end up having little say and even less ability to defend their fundamental interests and values, including their freedom and security.

Resilient, but ready for change?

Most Europeans share the use of a sturdy vehicle which has been tried on very difficult terrain for many years. It is called the EU: a strange vehicle indeed, unlike any other on the roads of the world, surely not a flashy vehicle, rather slow and not easy to drive either. However, it has been able to accommodate ever-increasing numbers of passengers and covered a remarkably long distance, often in adverse conditions and with accidents on the way. Resilience is the key word.

Only one passenger, the UK, has so far decided to leave the communal vehicle and look for its own independent means of transportation at a juncture where the road gets much rougher. All other passengers have stayed on, although bickering most of the time about the direction they take and the speed they travel while jostling with each other for access to the wheel and the best seats. They are all meant to have equal rights. In practice everybody knows that some passengers have more rights than others – they are after all so much bigger in size. And those usually confined to the back seats know only too well it is still much better than having to walk by themselves. It is not always fun – sometimes it gets ugly inside the bus – but strangely enough the bus keeps moving on, and outsiders marvel how.

The large European single market still constitutes the cornerstone of European integration. It is a great achievement that allows for the free movement of goods, services, people and capital across a very large space with no national borders – almost no borders, to be precise, because they tend to reappear in times of crisis. The single market contributes significantly to economic prosperity and ensures free choice for European citizens in terms of where they want to live and work, and how to spend their money. All twenty-seven EU members are part of the single market while several countries outside, including now the UK, are linked through all kinds of custom-made agreements.

The existence of a common trade policy has turned the large single market into a powerful negotiating weapon in the hands of the EU. No outside country and no foreign company, however big they are, can be relaxed about losing access to a market of 450 million relatively prosperous consumers. This makes the EU a trade superpower. It has also become a regulatory superpower with high standards for the protection of the worker, the consumer and the environment, usually among the highest in the world. But it is a continuous uphill struggle against free market zealots and powerful organized interests, not to mention institutional failures in a highly decentralized system. Naturally, it also leads to excesses. Opponents of European integration concentrate on the latter.

The European single market is also underpinned by structural policies mostly directed towards the less developed parts of the Union. Thus, the free movement of goods, services, people and capital inside the EU is tied to development and redistribution policies through the common budget. This is still a mild version of what happens inside most European countries, where redistribution and social protection operate on a much larger scale through the welfare state. Social policy remains today mostly in the hands of national governments.

European integration as a convergence machine reducing the economic gap between more and less developed parts of the Union has worked less well in recent years. Regional disparities remain; in some parts of Europe, they have become worse. Those in the forgotten regions protest with their votes, albeit diminishing in numbers as more and more people leave in search of better prospects, usually outside their national borders.

The freedom to leave one's country has become a key attraction of EU membership for new and prospective members. If in doubt, ask people in the western Balkans who are desperate to join the EU and emigrate. They want to follow the example of many others who have already left their countries in search of better opportunities in the more developed parts of the Union. Join and leave: it may sound like an oxymoron. Free movement of people has turned at best into a mixed blessing for both home and host countries inside the Union. It may not be politically correct to say so because it challenges the official mantra about the fundamental freedoms of the EU. And yet it is an undisputable fact that also serves as fodder for nationalist and populist movements in several countries.

Free markets and technological change combined have strong agglomeration effects. If anything, such effects have been accentuated during the recent phase of globalization. Corrective action is therefore needed unless our societies are prepared to live with ever larger urban concentrations, wide regional disparities and more deserted areas in the hinterland. Or will the problem be at least partially solved through digitalization and teleworking? There are idyllic places with very few inhabitants in many parts of Europe. The digital revolution could turn them into small paradises for people who enjoy the luxury of distance working.

The EU and its member states have developed instruments to deal with large regional disparities, but resources and administration are inadequate. A European single market needs an appropriate mix of liberalization measures and accompanying policy instruments to make it a positive-sum game for the large majority among European citizens. This is, after all, what the European model of mixed economy and welfare state with its different national variations has always been all about. It was challenged by the (neo)liberal revolution and now the pendulum is swinging back.

Politics remains mostly national while markets have become increasingly European and global. This creates an inherent asymmetry. In a half-baked political system trying to catch up with market integration, which is the case of the EU and unique in the world, there is an inherent liberal bias in economic terms, hence the initial scepticism of many social democrats and socialists vis-à-vis the European project. But is political ideology the key factor in European politics? An economic liberal from Greece is still much more likely to support EU structural policies and transfers than a German social democrat. Guess why!

This inherent liberal bias of European integration has been increasingly challenged by changing facts on the ground. They include greater inequalities between and within countries, the financial crisis and its aftershocks, Europe's technological dependence and the climate crisis. As a result, the emphasis has gradually shifted away from liberalization towards empowerment policies and the provision of public goods. It has also shifted from austerity to macroeconomic expansion. EU institutions have been trying to adjust to this new reality by fits and starts and most often in response to crises. The latest example was the pandemic, which brought about a true game changer in the form of an ambitious recovery programme with a strong redistributive bias between members and the issue of common debt. It also brought about a coordinated effort in public health, in which the EU had very little competence before. Such developments would have been simply unthinkable only a few years earlier.

One of the big questions for the future will be whether the recovery programme serves as precedent for more joint borrowing to finance large investment programmes or whether it remains a one-off response to an extraordinary crisis. And the answer will depend to a large extent on the use made of these new resources by member states and the kind of domestic reforms they help to bring about. Can the EU drag along laggards within its borders with the use of common rules, financial incentives and conditionality? The record has been mixed so far. To achieve better results, it will need more power at the centre and more money.

Demands on the public purse have been constantly rising. Where will the money come from? Borrowing at close to zero interest rates has reached its limits and debt levels are already too high for comfort in several countries. New and better taxes are needed. A more effective, environmentally friendly and socially fairer system of taxation would go a long way in restoring legitimacy and trust in our democratic systems.

Unconstrained national sovereignty in tax matters no longer makes any sense in an economic space where capital particularly is very mobile and can easily arbitrage between different national tax regimes. Multinational digital platforms have been very active in this game and made large gains. The EU has the size and collective bargaining power that individual countries do not have. It could therefore provide the right framework for tax cooperation among member states. It could also selectively raise common taxes to finance common policies. The fight against climate change is the most obvious example. Taxation has a political and symbolic value as well. If this battle is waged successfully, it would help a great deal to bolster the legitimacy of the European project among broader sections of society. They may not include, though, nationalists, tax evaders and free-riders all fighting in the name of (what else?) national sovereignty.

Most EU members share a common currency, a common monetary policy, and a common framework for fiscal policy which remains in the hands of national governments. Members of the Eurozone belong to the most advanced tier of integration. They have committed themselves to sharing the main levers of economic policy. But European monetary union has had anything but a smooth ride, which may suggest that the project had been flawed from the beginning or that some members had not been ready for it – most probably both.

Be that as it may, almost everybody now agrees there is no way back. No possibility of divorce in other words – never say never? – even when this polygamous arrangement looked at its most unhappy. Being left with no realistic alternative, members of the Eurozone have endeavoured to strengthen the common arrangement and make it more liveable for all concerned. And in so doing, integration has gone further and deeper. The apotheosis of functionalist theories or the conspiracy of the *illuminati*?

The European monetary union is still a highly imperfect construction. It is also asymmetrical, with Germany as the leader who wields strong veto power and occasionally makes concessions having previously exhausted all other alternatives. Moreover, the euro remains today the most extreme manifestation of the gap between economic and political integration in Europe. Some of its architects had thought of monetary union as the most effective lever for political union. But in times of big crisis, it became a hugely divisive factor that threatened to blow apart the whole European construction.

Once the pandemic is over and its aftershocks begin to fade away, we may expect a partial return to the old 'normal', albeit only partial because other causes of the overall policy shift are unlikely to go away as well. Urgent issues include the completion of the banking union and the reform of fiscal rules to make them more flexible and allow more room for public investment in times when it will be most needed. A small common budget, mostly for stabilization purposes, could also be part of required reforms. European economies are entering the post-pandemic era, having previously suspended most rules, and now with much more debt and greater need for private and public investment. The ECB and national treasuries will have to steer a hazardous course between stagnation and inflation. And let us not forget that the euro can serve as a powerful instrument to strengthen Europe's strategic autonomy.

The Green Deal is Europe's big new project. It is a long-term project with a target date almost thirty years from now for the decarbonization of the economy. EU institutions are trying to set guidelines, coordinate action between member states, adopt common rules and policy instruments and provide a large part of the finance required. If the Commission had not existed, it would have had to be invented if only to help with the green transformation of European economies. The EU is also a key player in international negotiations. If successful, the Green Deal will radically transform not only the economy but also the politics of Europe. The good news is that Europe is trying better and harder than most of its international partners. The sobering news, though, is that we are still at the early stages and implementation will be rendered ever more difficult by high energy costs and a confrontational international environment.

But we simply cannot afford to go slow on climate policy. It is a matter of survival.

Looking back to what happened during the last decade and more, it has been a truly transformational change of the domestic economic agenda in Europe. Agendas shape policies, and policies eventually transform institutions – or is it the other way round? Many European political leaders may not have yet fully digested the nature and scale of change.

The world outside

The EU has the experience and the capacity in managing the ever-growing interdependence between its members through a mix of liberalization, regulation, stabilization and redistribution policies. It is surely far from perfect, but still much better than anything else in today's world. In contrast, the prospects for global cooperation do not look promising and multilateral rules are too often ignored. WTO rules proved too weak in the past to ensure conditions of fair trade and led to justified complaints that China, as the foremost example, has exploited loopholes to the full.

Moreover, security considerations increasingly take precedence over economic objectives. If anything, this tendency was reinforced by the pandemic and will be even more so with war returning to Europe and the unprecedented sanctions levied against Russia after the invasion of Ukraine. While the process of global interdependence slows down, if it does not altogether shift into reverse gear, which looks like a plausible scenario today, the forces pushing for further integration in Europe are likely to persist. European integration and globalization are parting ways.

As one of the big economic blocs in the world, the EU is faced with the hard task of reconciling the benefits of international interdependence with its own economic and social priorities. To put it bluntly, the EU and its member states will need to reconcile economic openness with social justice and the ballot box, an exercise that has become increasingly difficult with time as the number of losers at home has grown. Economic liberals will call such talk protectionism, but they will first have to explain what went wrong with globalization before. Attempts to draw a clear line of division between free trade and protectionism by squeezing everything under one or the other category have little relevance for the world today. They are political slogans rather than fact-based analysis.

A major task of the EU in the years to come will be to help member governments find a better modus vivendi between global markets and domestic social contracts. This is absolutely crucial although not widely understood. Economic interdependence can and should proceed faster between countries with compatible economic structures and priorities. But given Europe's close integration into the world economic system, it would make little sense for Europeans to turn economic interdependence into a weapon to be used in a political and ideological war with China. Europeans will have good reasons to view their relations with China differently from the United States.

The competition and regulatory arms of the European Commission regarding new technologies have been put to good use. But the key question remains whether European companies will be able to play global championship games in the future, instead of the Commission just trying to referee games played by others. Continued technological dependence on companies, and indirectly also on governments, beyond Europe's borders would severely reduce the capacity of Europeans to define independently their interests and defend their freedoms and way of life. To avoid this, Europe will need to complement an effective competition policy with industrial strategies fit for purpose in the new technological era, and try to reconcile the two. The key priority for Europeans should be to think strategically and collectively. They should invest in a big way in innovation and help mobilize large amounts of resources. They will also need institutions that think outside the box.

Because of its long-accumulated experience of cooperation and compromise, Europe would be ideally suited to trying to inject a healthy dose of reason and moderation into the management of global interdependence. This could apply to the design of new and better multilateral rules and institutions to govern international economic exchange. It could also apply to the greening of the global economy, with Europe playing a leading role in the creation of an international climate club that will combine incentives and sanctions to achieve this crucial goal for humankind. The European model has indeed valuable things to export to the rest of the world. Instead of imperial conquests in which they specialized in the past, Europeans might try instead to export the logic of cooperation and the defence of global commons. It would be a most welcome change.

Such arguments should apply even more to broader issues of peace and security. In a world in transition, with growing strategic rivalry and rising nationalism, Europe can be the quiet power that does not think and act in Manichean terms, is patient with negotiations, acts in moderation and seeks compromise solutions. But let us have no illusions. The force of persuasion of a European Venus will depend not only on her beauty and the intrinsic value of her arguments. It will also crucially depend on the kind of power she can project. Such power will need to include trade instruments, economic sanctions, and military weapons as the ultimate means of persuasion. Europe needs credible means to defend its interests and values.

It is high time Europeans begin to face up to some fundamental questions. Can matters of European security and relations with a revisionist/revanchist Russia be decided in their absence, and if not, how should they handle an aggrieved and aggressive neighbour, a declining power yet heavily armed? There must surely be a better way of handling relations with Russia than what was tried and failed in the last thirty years or so. And should European countries continue to free-ride on US security protection? Objections to free-riding can come as a matter of principle. But there are also legitimate questions about how reliable such protection may be in the future and at what price it may come.

The long history of isolationism and exceptionalism in US foreign policy, the US pivot to Asia, the painful experience with the Trump administration, and the extreme views aired by several US politicians today should make Europeans think about what may be in store for them in the future. They may also not forget the almost unlimited urge in Capitol Hill to apply US laws extraterritorially through a dollar-based international financial system. Sometimes, Europeans too find themselves on the wrong side of US extraterritoriality.

The alliance with the United States of course remains crucial for the security of Europe, especially when faced with a revisionist and trigger-happy Russia. But Europeans need to take greater responsibility for their collective security inside the Atlantic alliance and face up to the costs. Excessive dependence on an external protector, even though usually benign, is not a healthy state of affairs. Taking more collective responsibility for their security would also give Europeans less excuse to blame others when things go wrong. It is all about becoming a political adult.

Many people believe Europe will never make this transition from an economic to a political power, from soft to hard power. They are probably the same who in earlier times were entirely convinced that a common European currency was a pipe dream and preparations for it a kind of tribal rain dance. They were the same who later predicted that the European project would never make it through the financial crisis, the migration crisis and more recently the pandemic. Admittedly, this new transition required of Europe today will be even more difficult.

Big events and big crises have indeed been the catalysts for major new initiatives in European integration. Should Europeans wait for Trump or his new incarnations to return to the White House? Should they wait for a major new conflagration in the Balkans, the Middle East or Africa, or for China's resurgent nationalism and malign use of new technologies, before they begin to forge a common foreign and security policy worth the name? And most important of all, has Putin's Russia given them a loud enough wake-up call? Even unintentionally, Putin may have rendered a great service to European unity. The radical change in German policy could help to usher in a new era in European defence cooperation.

Europe is essentially a regional bloc with limited global ambitions, albeit sometimes pretending otherwise. Its neighbourhood broadly defined is neither stable nor peaceful. Soft power is not enough when it comes to wars in the Middle East or Africa which directly impact on European security. And the choice between engagement and containment is never easy when dealing with bullies outside. Those inclined to a more muscular approach to foreign policy are usually tempted to dismiss most forms of engagement as appeasement.

Finding the right mix between engagement and containment is one thing; recognizing that the right mix should be defined at European rather than national level is another. A divided Europe can hardly play an effective and stabilizing role in its neighbourhood, or anywhere else for that matter. It becomes an object rather than a subject of international diplomacy as outside powers play one European country against another.

Even France, Germany and the UK should have learned this lesson from experience.

An advanced form of engagement has been the well-tried method of Europeanization. Bringing countries of the European periphery into the EU fold has been indeed the most powerful tool of common foreign policy. But we now know it has limits. How many more new and weak members can the EU take before the Brussels machine grinds to a halt? Enlargement fatigue is unlikely to change any time soon. The stabilization role of the EU in its immediate neighbourhood, including notably the western Balkans – now also Ukraine and other countries in the former Soviet space – will require a stronger and more political European centre, more money, and ways to associate countries much more closely with the European project but still short of full membership. It could all be part of a more united yet more differentiated Europe in the making. If you think this is a contradiction in terms, you may need to delve more into the history of European integration.

Many people from nearby countries and further afield want to come and settle in Europe. It is a paradise of peace and prosperity compared to conditions they experience at home. With a declining and ageing population, Europe indeed needs immigrants. But not in the form of large unregulated inflows which provoke a political backlash on the receiving end. Europe's humanitarian values – and international conventions created under very different conditions years back – have been repeatedly sacrificed for the sake of political stability and social peace at home. Let us admit it will be difficult to reconcile supply with demand for immigrants in the years to come and even more difficult to reconcile humanitarian values with political realities. It would greatly help, though, if European countries can agree on the essentials for a common migration policy and try to better integrate immigrants who are already in.

What next?

Let us look at the bigger picture. For many years, the EU has kept acquiring more functions and members. Good old functionalists point with glee to the inherent expansive logic of economic integration and the reduced capacity of member states to handle problems on their own. On the other hand, those who believe in the primacy of politics stress the importance of big political events such as the fall of dictatorships in southern Europe, German unification and the dismantling of the Soviet empire as key factors that have shaped the course of European integration – the war in Ukraine being the next one? Meanwhile, fans of conspiracy theories keep denouncing the role of the *illuminati* and the Brussels cabal in this everlasting plot against proud European nation states fighting to protect their sovereignty.

Believe what you want: the simple truth is that the EU has been constantly growing albeit not in a linear fashion. Brexit constitutes the main exception to the rule. Slowly but surely, the EU has been acquiring more functions, some of which are normally associated with a federal state, notably the common currency, while new members have added considerably to internal diversity. Trying to reconcile the two, the EU has relied more on differentiated integration among its members and less on common institution building. The latter requires treaty revisions and treaty revisions require unanimity, which is more than one can hope for in today's political context. The rule of unanimity for all big decisions in the EU has morphed into the tyranny of minorities.

The result has also been more intergovernmental cooperation and more ad hoc arrangements. It is extremely messy for sure, but this is not all. Responsibilities grow but the capacity to deliver does not follow suit. The widening gap between expectations and capabilities[2] leads to disappointment and weakens the legitimacy of the European project. EU institutions are being constantly judged on delivery. They have a much smaller reservoir of legitimacy to draw from than national institutions. As new functions are being constantly added in a bigger and more diverse EU, European treaties become like a legal straitjacket. It is often difficult for common institutions to breathe in it and hence deliver what is expected from them.

At some stage, hopefully sooner than later, member governments will need to face up to the challenge of a new treaty revision, or a new treaty altogether to be signed and ratified by countries willing and able to proceed further with integration. Alexander the Great allegedly cut the Gordian knot with his sword. All twenty-seven members trying to untie the EU's Gordian knot and succeeding today looks like an impossible dream. After all, some of the twenty-seven dreams are so different from the rest.

Those not allergic to the forbidden 'f' word, where 'f' stands for federal, will need to take the initiative. Experience tells us that when a core group of countries that includes both France and Germany decide to move ahead, others join. Admittedly, it did not always work in the past, but in response to big crises it sometimes did. Today, Europe is faced with big crises and challenges which go beyond the capacity of the existing EU structure to deal with effectively. Taxation and inclusive societies, the green transformation, foreign and defence policy are the most prominent examples.

A more federal-like political entity in Europe unshackled from the unanimity straitjacket should also be better able to address the democratic deficit, which, in part at least, is the result of political integration lagging far behind market integration. Democratic choices in member states have become much narrower because of growing interdependence. European integration should therefore be seen as the way to help restore collectively what has been lost by Europe's proud yet increasingly frustrated nation states. To put it differently, the relationship between the EU and its member states should be seen as a positive-sum, not a zero-sum, game. And sovereignty is not something you either have or do not have, as so many nationalists pretend.

Of course, the crisis of democracy today goes deeper and wider. Trying to mobilize citizens to the cause of a more democratic and united Europe will surely not be an easy affair. Those bold enough to take it up will need to fight against resurgent nationalism and many demagogues. They will also need to fight against long-established, popular views of European integration as a boring, bureaucratic affair with interminable negotiations and special privileges for those who run it – not entirely unjustified, it should be said.

Vision combined with realism will be necessary to make an exciting political project out of European integration – not just an elitist project. A former German chancellor, Helmut Schmidt, once famously said that those who have visions should go and see a doctor. But with all due respect to the memory of one of the best German chancellors, hard realism without vision – and a healthy dose of idealism – has never been enough to change the world for the better. Europeans will need both realism and vision to make their continent safer, more democratic and prosperous, while not forgetting that Europe is only a small part of a shrinking yet highly unstable world on a planet in mortal danger.

Waiting for a new treaty, a core group of countries will urgently need to move faster towards a common foreign and defence policy. A rapidly deteriorating external environment is pushing them in this direction. Others may follow later. Even the UK could be persuaded eventually that a common European security policy is a good investment for all, a strong complement to, not a substitute for, the Atlantic alliance.

Europeans need to take the next big step after a long, chequered but ultimately successful experiment in integration, open borders and sharing of sovereignty. If they succeed, it will be indeed Europe's coming of age as a political entity. But if they fail, they may end up as frustrated spectators watching History pass them by – or even worse, because peace, democracy and their fundamental freedoms are at stake.

Notes

Chapter 1

1 Loukas Tsoukalis, *The Politics and Economics of European Monetary Integration* (Allen & Unwin, 1977), reprinted with the same title (Routledge, 2017).

2 Leon L. Lindberg and Stuart A. Scheingold, *Europe's Would-Be Polity: Patterns of Change in the European Community* (Prentice Hall, 1970), 62.

3 'This is the way the world ends / Not with a bang but a whimper.' Extract from *The Hollow Men*, a poem by T. S. Elliot (1925).

4 For a vivid, personal account of the transition in central and eastern Europe and the power politics of the 1990s, see Timothy Garton-Ash, *History of the Present*: *Essays, Sketches, and Dispatches from Europe in the 1990s* (Random House, 1999).

5 Among the best books on the earlier history of European monetary integration, the reader may consult Tommaso Padoa-Schioppa, *The Road to Monetary Union in Europe: The Emperor, the King, and the Genies* (Oxford University Press, 1994); Kenneth Dyson and Kevin Featherstone, *The Road to Maastricht: Negotiating Economic and Monetary Union* (Oxford University Press, 1999).

Chapter 2

1 Loukas Tsoukalis, *The New European Economy: The Politics and Economics of Integration* (Oxford University Press, 1991) and subsequent editions.

2 Edward Mortimer, 'Identity to cling on to: in a world of dissolving states, nations matter more than ever', *Financial Times*, 6 April 1994.

3 See Anthony Giddens, *The Third Way: The Renewal of Social Democracy* (Polity, 1998). The author, a leading British sociologist and former Director of LSE, was the main guru of the 'Third Way'.

4 Francis Fukuyama, *The End of History and the Last Man* (Penguin, 1992).

5 Jacques Rupnik, 'Explaining eastern Europe: the crisis of liberalism', *Journal of Democracy*, 29/3 (2018), 24–38, https://journalofdemocracy.org/articles/ explaining-eastern-europe-the-crisis-of-liberalism

6 Misha Glenny, 'How the east was lost: the triumph and tragedy of 1989', *Financial Times*, 25 October 2019, https://www.ft.com/content/f167612e-f4

cd-11e9-b018-3ef8794b17c6. For a beautifully written personal account of an extreme case of transition, namely in Albania, see Lea Ypi, *Free: Coming of Age at the End of History* (Allen Lane, 2021).

7 See Sarah Hobolt and Sylvain Brouard, 'Contesting the European Union? Why the Dutch and the French rejected the European Constitution', *Political Research Quarterly*, 64/2 (2011), 309–22, https://journals.sagepub.com/doi/pdf/10.1177/1065912909355713

8 For Europe's mismanagement of the financial crisis, see among others Adam Tooze, *Crashed: How a Decade of Financial Crises Changed the World* (Penguin, 2018), part III; Ashoka Mody, *Euro Tragedy: A Drama in Nine Acts* (Oxford University Press, 2018); Martin Sandbu, *Europe's Orphan: The Future of the Euro and the Politics of Debt* (Princeton University Press, 2015).

9 See also the memoirs of former President Obama who offers a fascinating personal account of how his administration handled the aftershocks of the financial crisis and his frustration with European governments. Barack Obama, *The Promised Land* (Penguin, 2020).

10 Varoufakis caused much damage to his country during his short tenure of office. But he ended up writing several bestsellers and acquired an international reputation in the process. In one of his books, he claims to have used information drawn from Eurogroup meetings which he had secretly taped: Yanis Varoufakis, *Adults in the Room: My Battle with Europe's Deep Establishment* (Farrar, Straus and Giroux, 2017).

11 See Josip Glaurdic, *Hour of Europe: Western Powers and the Breakup of Yugoslavia* (Yale University Press, 2011); Jonathan Eyal, *Europe and Yugoslavia: Lessons from a Failure* (RUSI, 1993).

12 See Philip H. Gordon and Jeremy Shapiro, *Allies at War: America, Europe, and the Crisis over Iraq* (Brookings, 2004).

13 Robert Kagan, *Of Paradise and Power: America and Europe in the New World Order* (A. Knopf, 2003).

14 See Henry Kissinger, 'To settle the Ukraine crisis, start at the end', *The Washington Post*, 5 March 2014. https://www.washingtonpost.com/opinions/henry-kissinger-to-settle-the-ukraine-crisis-start-at-the-end/2014/03/05/46dad868-a496-11e3-8466-d34c451760b9_story.html. For two different readings of what happened in 2013–14 in Ukraine, see John S. Mearsheimer, 'Why the Ukraine crisis is the West's fault', *Foreign Affairs*, https://www.foreignaffairs.com/articles/russia-fsu/2014-08-18/why-ukraine-crisis-west-s-fault; Piotr Buras et al., 'Ten global consequences of the Ukraine crisis', *European Council on Foreign Relations*, 16 June 2014, https://ecfr.eu/article/commentary_ten_global_consequences_of_ukraine272

15 For two authoritative yet contrasting analyses of the rise of populist movements and parties, see Barry Eichengreen, *The Populist Temptation: Economic Grievance and Political Reaction in the Modern Era* (Oxford University Press, 2018); Pippa Norris and Ronald Inglehart, *Cultural Backlash: Trump, Brexit, and Authoritarian Populism* (Cambridge University Press, 2019). See also Cas Mudde and Cristóbal Rovira Kaltwasser, *Populism: A Very Short Introduction* (Oxford University Press, 2017).

16 Patrick Diamond (ed.), *The Crisis of Globalization: Democracy, Capitalism, and Inequality in the Twenty-First Century* (I.B. Tauris, 2019).

17 *From Max Weber: Essays in Sociology* (Oxford University Press, 1946). See also Luuk van Middelaar, *Alarums & Excursions: Improvising Politics on the European Stage* (Agenda, 2019), 91–114, for a fascinating account of how Europe tried to manage the refugee crisis and turned more intergovernmental in the process.

Chapter 3

1 See Helen Wallace, 'JCMS Annual Review Lecture: in the name of Europe', *The JCMS Annual Review of the European Union in 2016* (Wiley, 2017), 8–18. For an eloquent story of Britain's troubled relationship with Europe, see Hugo Young, *The Blessed Plot: Britain and Europe from Churchill to Blair* (Macmillan, 1998); and Roger Liddle, *The Europe Dilemma: Britain and the Drama of EU Integration* (I.B. Tauris/Policy Network, 2014).

2 The quotation is from an article penned by Winston Churchill in the *Saturday Evening Post* on 15 February 1930.

3 Loukas Tsoukalis, 'Alcuin Lecture 2013: is there a future for the European Union – and with Britain in it?', *Cambridge Review of International Affairs*, 28/4 (2015), 589–98.

4 It was reported by Anthony Gardner, a former student from Oxford who served as the US Ambassador to the EU during the Obama administration. See Anthony Luzzato Gardner, *Stars with Stripes: The Essential Partnership between the European Union and the United States* (Palgrave Macmillan, 2020).

5 The French term for the whole body of EU legislation.

6 David Goodhart, *The Road to Somewhere: The Populist Revolt and the Future of Politics* (C. Hurst, 2017).

7 See William Drozdiak, *The Last President of Europe* (Public Affairs, 2020); Helen Drake and Sophie Meunier, 'Is France back (again)? European governance for a global world', in Helen Drake et al., *Developments in French Politics* (Palgrave, 2020).

8   See Sylvia Kritzinger et al., *Assessing the 2019 European Parliament Elections* (Routledge, 2020).

9   For a collection of views, the reader may consult Richard Baldwin and Francesco Giavazzi (eds.), *How to Fix Europe's Monetary Union: Views of Leading Economists* (CEPR, 2016), https://voxeu.org/content/how-fix-europe-s-moneta ry-union-views-leading-economists

10 See Fareed Zakaria, *Ten Lessons for a Post-Pandemic World* (Norton, 2020); and Adam Tooze, *Shutdown: How Covid Shook the World's Economy* (Penguin, 2021).

11 See for example the joint report by European think tanks, *Re-Energising Europe: A Package Deal for the EU27*, Third Report, New Pact for Europe, 2017, https://www.newpactforeurope.eu/documents/new_pact_for_europe_3rd_ report.pdf

12 Helen Wallace, Nikos Koutsiaras and George Pagoulatos (eds.), *Europe's Transformations: Essays in Honour of Loukas Tsoukalis* (Oxford University Press, 2021).

Chapter 4

1   See Barry Eichengreen, *The European Economy Since 1945* (Princeton University Press, 2007).

2   One of the most cited works on this subject is Marc J. Melitz, 'The impact of trade on intra-industry reallocations and aggregate industry productivity', *Econometrica*, 71/6 (2003), 1695–1725, https://scholar.harvard.edu/files/melitz /files/aggprod_ecma.pdf

3   Friedrich Hayek, an Austrian-British economist and philosopher born just before the end of the nineteenth century in Vienna, was one of the key defenders of classical liberal thought. Milton Friedman, born a few years later, was an intellectual leader of the early Chicago school of economics and became known mostly for his work on monetary theory. Both Hayek and Friedman extolled the virtues of the free market system.

4   The Levellers were a political movement during the English civil war in the seventeenth century that fought for popular sovereignty, extended suffrage and equality. For an interesting comparison with popular demands today, see Michael O' Sullivan, *The Levelling: What's Next After Globalization* (Public Affairs, 2019).

5   Robert Gordon, *The Rise and Fall of American Growth* (Princeton University Press, 2016).

6   Theories of secular stagnation were initially introduced by Alvin Hansen in the

1930s and more recently revived by Harvard economist Lawrence Summers, a prolific writer with rich experience in policy making. See Lawrence H. Summers, 'Accepting the reality of secular stagnation', *Finance & Development* (International Monetary Fund), 57/1 (2020), 17–19, https://www.imf.org/external/pubs/ft/fandd/2020/03/pdf/larry-summers-on-secular-stagnation.pdf

7 See Peter Hall and David Soskice, *Varieties of Capitalism: The Institutional Foundations of Comparative Advantage* (Oxford University Press, 2001).

8 Marcel Fratzscher, *The Germany Illusion: Between Economic Euphoria and Despair* (Oxford University Press, 2018), 11.

9 Claire Busse et al., 'EU Coalition Explorer', *European Council on Foreign Relations*, July 2020, https://ecfr.eu/special/eucoalitionexplorer

10 See, among others, Ulrich Krotz and Joachim Schild, *Shaping Europe: France, Germany, and Embedded Bilateralism from the Elysée Treaty to Twenty-First Century Politics* (Oxford University Press, 2012).

11 See Erik Jones and Gianfranco Pasquino (eds.), *The Oxford Handbook on Italian Politics* (Oxford University Press, 2015); Andrea Lorenzo Capussela, *The Political Economy of Italy's Decline* (Oxford University Press, 2018).

12 Named after a small town in Hungary where the first meeting of the group of the four central European countries took place in 1991.

13 For a vivid account of European Council meetings in times of crisis, see Luuk van Middelaar, *Alarums & Excursions: Improvising Politics on the European Stage* (Agenda, 2019).

14 Hubert Védrine, *Les Mondes de François Mitterrand* (Fayard, 1996), 298.

15 Peter Mair, *Ruling the Void: The Hollowing of Western Democracy* (Verso, 2013).

16 Thomas L. Friedman, *The Lexus and the Olive Tree: Understanding Globalization* (Farrar, Straus and Giroux, 1999).

17 See also Christopher J. Bickerton, Dermot Hodgson and Uwe Puetter (eds.), *The New Intergovernmentalism: States and Supranational Actors in the Post-Maastricht Era* (Oxford University Press, 2015).

18 I borrow this phrase from Vivien A. Schmidt, *Europe's Crisis of Legitimacy: Governing by Rules and Ruling by Numbers in the Eurozone* (Oxford University Press, 2020).

19 A phrase attributed to Lord Ismay, who was the first secretary general of NATO between 1952 and 1957.

20 In an interview President Macron gave to *The Economist*, 7 November 2019, https://www.economist.com/europe/2019/11/07/emmanuel-macron-in-his-own-words-english

21 See also Stephen Szabo, *Parting Ways: The Crisis in German–American Relations* (Brookings, 2008).

22 'When the facts change, I change my mind. What do you do, sir?' This is a famous quote attributed to John Maynard Keynes.

Chapter 5

1 His collected writings can be found in Antonio Gramsci, *Prison Notebooks*, vols. 1–3 (Columbia University Press, 2011).

2 For the earlier history of European monetary integration, the reader may consult Tommaso Padoa-Schioppa, *The Road to Monetary Union in Europe: The Emperor, the King, and the Genies* (Oxford University Press, 1994); Loukas Tsoukalis, *The Politics and Economics of European Monetary Integration* (Allen & Unwin, 1977), reprinted with the same title (Routledge, 2017); Kenneth Dyson and Kevin Featherstone, *The Road to Maastricht: Negotiating Economic and Monetary Union* (Oxford University Press, 1999). For a historical account, see Markus K. Brunnermeier, Harold James and Jean-Pierre Landau, *The Euro and the Battle of Ideas* (Princeton University Press, 2016).

3 See Jean Monnet, *Memoirs* (New York: Doubleday, 1978).

4 Quoted in *The Economist*, 25 September 1993.

5 See, for example, Paul Krugman: 'The euro crisis will end with something "impossible" happening', *Insider*, 12 July 2012, https://www.businessinsider.com/paul-krugman-on-the-euro-crisis-2012-7. Another US economist and Nobel prize winner wrote a passionate book denouncing austerity policies and the mismanagement of the euro crisis: Joseph E. Stiglitz, *The Euro and Its Threat to the Future of Europe* (Allen Lane, 2016). See also Ashoka Mody, *Euro Tragedy: A Drama in Nine Acts* (Oxford University Press, 2018), in which the sharp economic analysis by the Indian former IMF economist is not matched by an equally accurate assessment of Europe's political dynamics.

6 The term 'exorbitant privilege' is first attributed to Valéry Giscard d'Estaing, finance minister in the 1960s before becoming President of the French Republic. See also Barry Eichengreen, *Exorbitant Privilege: The Rise and Fall of the Dollar and the Future of the International Monetary System* (Oxford University Press, 2010).

7 See also George Pagoulatos, 'Integrating through crises: revisiting the Eurozone's reform conundrum', in Helen Wallace, Nikos Koutsiaras and George Pagoulatos (eds.), *Europe's Transformations: Essays in Honour of Loukas Tsoukalis* (Oxford University Press, 2021).

8 Loukas Tsoukalis, *What Kind of Europe?*, 2nd edition (Oxford University Press, 2005), 142–66.

9 Jean Pisani-Ferry, *The Euro Crisis and Its Aftermath* (Oxford University Press, 2011), 33–7.

10 See Olivier J. Blanchard and Daniel Michael Leigh, 'Growth forecast errors and fiscal multipliers', *IMF Working Papers*, January 2013, https://www.imf.org/external/pubs/ft/wp/2013/wp1301.pdf

11 A concept introduced by the US economist Robert Mundell, which won him a Nobel prize in 1999. See his classic article 'A theory of optimum currency areas', *American Economic Review*, 51/4 (1961), 657–65.

12 The term was used by Karl Schiller, German minister of finance at the time of the first EMU negotiations back in 1970, quoted in Tsoukalis, *The Politics and Economics of European Monetary Integration*, 99.

13 One of the few people who saw very early on the likely consequences of financial deregulation and mobile capital was Susan Strange, a leading scholar of international political economy and, I am proud to say, my mentor. See her *Casino Capitalism* (Blackwell, 1986).

14 See Agnès Bénassy-Quéré et al., 'Reconciling risk sharing with market discipline: a constructive approach to euro area reform', *Centre for Economic Policy Research*, Policy Insight 91, January 2018, https://cepr.org/sites/default/files/policy_insights/PolicyInsight91.pdf. For a different view from Italy, see also Marcello Messori and Stefano Micossi, 'Counterproductive proposals on euro area reform by French and German economists', *CEPS Policy Insights*, February 2018, No. 2018/04, https://www.ceps.eu/wp-content/uploads/2018/02/PI2018_04_MMandSM_PI91.pdf

15 For a strong critique of this decision, see the article by a German constitutional lawyer, Franz C. Mayer, 'To boldly go where no court has gone before: the German Federal Constitutional Court's *ultra vires* decision of May 5, 2020', *German Law Journal*, 21/5 (2020), 1116–27, https://www.cambridge.org/core/journals/german-law-journal/article/to-boldly-go-where-no-court-has-gone-before-the-german-federal-constitutional-courts-ultra-vires-decision-of-may-5-2020/7A837C355A29F52CAE46F8CEBB1AE4E7

16 For a reprint of the classic book, see Milton Friedman, *The Optimum Quantity of Money* (Routledge, 2017); and for a more recent collection of views on the subject, see Richard Baldwin, 'Helicopter money: views of leading economists', *VoxEU*, 13 April 2016, https://voxeu.org/article/helicopter-money-views-leading-economists

17 See Sebastian Mallaby, 'The age of magic money: can endless spending prevent economic calamity?', *Foreign Affairs*, 99/4 (2020), 65–77, https://www.foreignaffairs.com/articles/united-states/2020-05-29/pandemic-financial-crisis

18 Olivier Blanchard, 'Public debt and low interest rates', *American Economic Review*, 109/4 (2019), 1197–1229, https://www.aeaweb.org/articles?id=10.12 57/aer.109.4.1197

19 See Stephanie Kelton, *The Deficit Myth: Modern Monetary Theory and the Birth of the People's Economy* (Public Affairs, 2020).

20 For an excellent history of debt, of booms and busts across eight centuries, see Carmen M. Reinhart and Kenneth S. Rogoff, *This Time Is Different: Eight Centuries of Financial Folly* (Princeton University Press, 2009).

21 Benjamin J. Cohen, *Currency Power: Understanding Monetary Rivalry* (Princeton University Press, 2015). The author has strong doubts whether the euro, or the yuan, will be able to challenge the supremacy of the dollar for a long while, and he is not the only one.

Chapter 6

1 Anand Menon, 'Uniting the United Kingdom: what comes after Brexit', *Foreign Affairs*, 6 July 2016, https://www.foreignaffairs.com/articles/united-kingdom/2016-07-06/uniting-united-kingdom

2 One of the best historical accounts of the European economy since the end of the Second World War can be found in Barry Eichengreen, *The European Economy Since 1945* (Princeton University Press, 2007).

3 Christoph Lakner and Branko Milanovic, 'Global income distribution: from the fall of the Berlin Wall to the Great Recession', *World Bank Economic Review*, 30/2016, 203–32, https://openknowledge.worldbank.org/handle/109 86/16935

4 For the latest report, see Lucas Chancel et al., *World Inequality Report 2022* (Paris: World Inequality Lab, 2021), https://wir2022.wid.world/www-site /uploads/2021/12/WorldInequalityReport2022_Full_Report.pdf

5 *Growing Unequal?* (2008); *Divided We Stand* (2011); *In It Together: Why Less Inequality Benefits All* (2015); *A Broken Social Elevator? How to Promote Social Mobility* (2018); *Under Pressure: The Squeezed Middle Class* (2019).

6 Philip Barrett and Sophia Chen, 'Social repercussions of pandemics', *IMF Working Paper*, January 2021, https://www.imf.org/-/media/Files/Publications /WP/2021/English/wpiea2021021-print-pdf.ashx

7 For a broad overview of the unequal effects of the recent liberal globalization era, see Branko Milanovic, *Capitalism, Alone: The Future of the System That Rules the World* (Harvard University Press, 2019); Martin Sandbu, *The Economics of Belonging: A Radical Plan to Win Back the Left Behind and Achieve Prosperity for All* (Princeton University Press, 2020); Anthony B. Atkinson, *Inequality: What*

Can Be Done? (Harvard University Press, 2015); and Joseph E. Stiglitz, *The Price of Inequality: How Today's Divided Society Endangers the Future* (Norton, 2012).

8 See Emmanuel Saez and Gabriel Zucman, *The Triumph of Injustice: How the Rich Dodge Taxes and How to Make Them Pay* (Norton, 2019).

9 See Thomas Philippon, *The Great Reversal: How America Gave Up on Free Markets* (Harvard University Press, 2019).

10 Thomas L. Friedman, *The Lexus and the Olive Tree: Understanding Globalization* (Farrar, Straus and Giroux, 1999).

11 Dani Rodrik, *The Globalization Paradox: Why Global Markets, States and Democracy Can't Coexist* (Oxford University Press, 2011).

12 For one of the classic works, see Daron Acemoglu, 'Technical change, inequality, and the labor market', *Journal of Economic Literature*, 40/1 (2002), 772.

13 Thomas Piketty, *Capital and Ideology* (Harvard University Press, 2020), 7.

14 See the classic work by Arthur M. Okun, *Equality and Efficiency: The Big Tradeoff* (Brookings, 2015).

15 For an excellent overview of the main empirical data and policies to deal with inequality in the US and other high-income economies, see *How to Fix Economic Inequality? An Overview of Policies for the United States and Other High-Income Economies* (Peterson Institute for International Economics, 2020), https://www.piie.com/microsites/how-fix-economic-inequality

16 Thomas Piketty, *Capital in the Twenty-First Century* (Harvard University Press, 2014).

17 In an interview given by Warren Buffett to *The New York Times* on 26 November 2006, https://www.nytimes.com/2006/11/26/business/yourmoney/26every.html

18 Marcel Fratzscher, *Verteilungskampf: Warum Deutschland Immer Ungleicher Wird* (Hanser, 2016). This is a richly documented book about the distribution battle in Germany. For non-German speakers, a shorter version can be found in Marcel Fratzscher, *The Germany Illusion: Between Economic Euphoria and Despair* (Oxford University Press, 2018).

19 See Jason Beckfield, *Unequal Europe: Regional Integration and the Rise of European Inequality* (Oxford University Press, 2019).

20 See Ivan Krastev and Stephen Holmes, *The Light That Failed* (London: Penguin, 2019), 37. During the pandemic, some of those who had left returned home. But will they stay?

21 A much-quoted phrase: see for example an interview by Ivan Krastev, 'We do not dream of the future anymore, we're scared of it', *Russia in Global Affairs*, 28

March 2019, https://eng.globalaffairs.ru/articles/we-do-not-dream-of-the-futu re-anymore-were-scared-of-it

22 Andrés Rodríguez-Pose, 'The revenge of the places that don't matter', *VoxEU*, 6 February 2018, https://voxeu.org/article/revenge-places-dont-matter

23 Luigi Zingales, 'The EU must be forged in this crisis or it will die', *Financial Times*, 5 April 2020, https://www.ft.com/content/8f554b7a-74d1-11ea-90ce -5fb6c07a27f2. See also the book he co-authored with the former chief economist of the IMF and governor of the Reserve Bank of India: Raghuram G. Rajan and Luigi Zingales, *Saving Capitalism from the Capitalists* (Princeton University Press, 2004).

24 Tabby Kinder and Emma Agyenmang, 'It's a matter of fairness: squeezing more tax from multinationals', *Financial Times*, 8 July 2020, https://www.ft.com/co ntent/40cffe27-4126-43f7-9c0e-a7a24b44b9bc

25 Paolo Gentiloni, 'An EU tax crackdown is essential for sustainable growth', *Financial Times*, 15 July 2020, https://www.ft.com/content/92081b99-86 a1-4c8f-b10a-39939b40bc09. Gentiloni is the European commissioner for economic affairs and former prime minister of Italy. See also OECD, *Tax Challenges Arising from Digitalisation* (OECD, 2020), https://doi.org/10.1787 /0e3cc2d4-en

26 See, for example, 'Warren Buffett: tax the rich', *Buffett Watch*, 28 June 2007, https://www.cnbc.com/2007/06/28/warren-buffett-tax-the-rich.html

27 Jesse Eisinger, Jeff Ernsthausen and Paul Kiel, 'The secret IRS files: trove of never-before-seen records reveal how the wealthiest avoid income tax', *Pro Publica*, 8 June 2021, https://www.propublica.org/article/the-secret-irs-files-tr ove-of-never-before-seen-records-reveal-how-the-wealthiest-avoid-income-tax ?code=jtk419-ja-fl-v2&emci=8b2578b1-42eb-eb11-a7ad-501ac57b8fa7&emd i=3a01e1cf-bcef-eb11-a7ad-501ac57b8fa7&ceid=1002614

28 Milanovic, *Capitalism, Alone*, 164.

29 Intelligence and Security Committee of Parliament Press Notice, https://isc. independent.gov.uk/wp-content/uploads/2021/01/20200721_Russia_Press_ Notice.pdf

30 See OECD, *Tax Challenges Arising from Digitalisation*.

31 Manifesto for the democratization of Europe: http://tdem.eu/en/manifesto. Most of the ideas are further elaborated in Piketty, *Capital and Ideology*, ch. 17.

32 James Tobin, 'A proposal for international monetary reform', *Eastern Economic Journal*, 4/3 (1978), 153–9, https://college.holycross.edu/eej/Volume4/V4N3 _4P153_159.pdf

33 Clemens Fuest and Jean Pisani-Ferry, 'Financing the European Union: new

context, new responses', *Bruegel Policy Contribution*, 16, September 2020, https://www.bruegel.org/2020/09/financing-the-european-union-new-context-new-responses

34 See Daron Acemoglou and James A. Robinson, *Why Nations Fail: The Origins of Power, Prosperity, and Poverty* (Random House, 2013).

35 Minouche Shafik, *What We Owe Each Other: A New Social Contract* (Bodley Head, 2021).

36 See also Xavier Prats-Monné, 'Education and the European social contract', in Helen Wallace, Nikos Koutsiaras and George Pagoulatos (eds.), *Europe's Transformations: Essays in Honour of Loukas Tsoukalis* (Oxford University Press, 2021).

37 Sandbu, *The Economics of Belonging*, 116.

Chapter 7

1 Shoshana Zuboff, *The Age of Surveillance Capitalism: The Fight for a Human Future at the New Frontier of Power* (Profile, 2019).

2 Ben Winck, 'The US tech sector is now worth more than the entire European stock market, Bank of America says', *Markets Insider*, 28 August 2020, https://markets.businessinsider.com/news/stocks/us-tech-stocks-worth-more-europe an-stock-market-apple-microsoft-2020-8-1029545001

3 *Unlocking Digital Competition: Report of the Digital Competition Expert Panel* (OGL, March 2019). It was a UK expert panel. https://assets.publishing.serv ice.gov.uk/government/uploads/system/uploads/attachment_data/file/785547 /unlocking_digital_competition_furman_review_web.pdf

4 Ulrike Franke and José Ignacio Torreblanca, 'Geo-tech politics: why technology shapes European power', *ECFR Policy Brief*, 15 July 2021, https://ecfr.eu/ publication/geo-tech-politics-why-technology-shapes-european-power

5 In the original version, Jean-Jacques Servan-Schreiber, *Le défi américain*, (Denoël, 1967).

6 'Big Tech faces its Standard Oil moment', *Financial Times*, 11 December 2020, https://www.ft.com/content/34a352a6-85d1-480f-9132-71c6416f101b. See also Nicholas Petit, *Big Tech and Digital Economy: The Moligopoly Scenario* (Oxford University Press, 2019).

7 This is the central argument in Thomas Philippon's book, *The Great Reversal: How America Gave Up on Free Markets* (Harvard University Press, 2019).

8 I have borrowed the image of Europe as a frustrated referee in digital games from Carla Hobbs (ed.), 'Europe's digital sovereignty: from rulemaker to superpower in the age of US–China rivalry', *ECFR*, July 2020, https://ecfr.eu/

publication/europe_digital_sovereignty_rulemaker_superpower_age_us_china_ rivalry

9   See, for example, Mathieu Duchâtel and François Godement, 'Europe and 5G: the Huawei case', *Institut Montaigne*, June 2019, https://www.institutmontai gne.org/ressources/pdfs/publications/europe-and-5g-huawei-case-part-2-cover .pdf ; Lindsay Maizland and Andrew Chatzky, 'Huawei: China's controversial tech giant', *Council on Foreign Relations*, 6 August 2020, https://www.cfr.org/ba ckgrounder/huawei-chinas-controversial-tech-giant

10 European Commission, 'Rethinking strategic autonomy in the digital age' (European Political Strategy Centre, 2019), 4, https://op.europa.eu/en/public ation-detail/-/publication/889dd7b7-0cde-11ea-8c1f-01aa75ed71a1/language -en/format-PDF/source-118064052

11 *The Power Atlas: Seven Battlegrounds of a Networked World* (ECFR/Mercator, 2021), 5.

12 See also Mark Leonard, *The Age of Unpeace: How Connectivity Causes Conflict* (Penguin, 2021).

13 See also Michael A. Landesmann and Roman Stöllinger, 'The European Union's industrial policy', in A. Oqubay et al. (eds.), *The Oxford Handbook on Industrial Policy* (Oxford University Press, 2020).

14 See Mariana Mazzucato, *Mission Economy: A Moonshot Guide to Changing Capitalism* (Allen Lane, 2021).

15 Richard Baldwin and Javier Lopez-Gonzalez, 'Supply-chain trade: a portrait of global patterns and several testable hypotheses', *The World Economy*, 2015, 38/11, 1682–1721.

16 Mark Leonard et al., 'Redefining Europe's economic sovereignty', *ECFR*, June 2019, 2 and 10, https://ecfr.eu/publication/redefining_europes_economic_ sovereignty

17 Leonard et al., 'Redefining Europe's economic sovereignty', 2.

18 IPCC, *Global Warming of 1.5 °C* (2018), https://www.ipcc.ch/sr15; and IPCC, *Climate Change 2021: The Physical Science Basis*, https://www.ipcc.ch/report /ar6/wg1/downloads/report/IPCC_AR6_WGI_SPM_final.pdf. See also the article by leading scientists summarizing the problem in non-technical language: Inês Azevedo et al., 'The paths to net zero', *Foreign Affairs*, 99/3, 2020, 18–27, https://www.foreignaffairs.com/articles/2020-04-13/paths-net-zero

19 See, for example, Jeffrey D. Sachs, 'Fixing climate finance', *Project Syndicate*, 15 November 2021. https://www.project-syndicate.org/commentary/fixing-climate-finance-requires-global-rules-by-jeffrey-d-sachs-2021-11

20 See Ian Manners, 'Normative power Europe: a contradiction in terms?', *Journal of Common Market Studies*, 40/2, June 2002, 235–58.

21 The full quote from Samuel Beckett's 1983 story *Worstward Ho* is: 'Ever tried. Ever failed. No matter. Try again. Fail again. Fail better.'

22 Martin Jänicke and Rüdiger K. W. Wurzel, 'Leadership and lesson-drawing in the European Union's multilevel climate governance system', *Environmental Politics*, 28/1 (2019), 22–42, https://www.tandfonline.com/doi/full/10.1080 /09644016.2019.1522019. See also Robert Falkner and Barry Buzan (eds.), *Great Powers, Climate Change, and Global Environmental Responsibilities* (Oxford University Press, 2021); Harriet Bulkeley and Peter Newell, *Governing Climate Change* (Routledge, 2015).

23 For a comprehensive review of the EU ETS scheme, see *A Literature-Based Assessment of the EU ETS* (European University Institute, 2019).

24 See Clemens Fuest and Jean Pisani-Ferry, 'A primer on developing European public goods', Ifo Institute, *EconPol Policy Report*, 16 (2019), https://www.ifo .de/en/publikationen/2019/working-paper/primer-developing-european-publ ic-goods

25 A few economists have already ventured far beyond mainstream economics, grappling with revolutionary concepts such as happiness economics. See for example Richard Layard and George Ward, *Can We Be Happier? Evidence and Ethics* (Pelican, 2020).

26 William Nordhaus, 'The Climate Club: how to fix a failing global effort', *Foreign Affairs*, 2020, 99/3, https://www.foreignaffairs.com/articles/united-states/2020-04-10/climate-club. See also William Nordhaus, *The Climate Casino: Risk, Uncertainty, and Economics for a Warming World* (Yale University Press, 2013); Martin Menner, Götz Reichert and Jan S. Vosswinkel, 'Climate clubs: chances and pitfalls', *Centrum für Europäische Politik*, November 2021, https:// www.cep.eu/fileadmin/user_upload/cep.eu/Studien/cepStudie_Klimaclub/cep Study_Climate_Clubs_Chances_and_Pitfalls_17.11.2021.pdf

27 See also Mark Leonard et al., 'The geopolitics of the European Green Deal', *Bruegel Policy Contribution*, 2021, 4/21, https://www.bruegel.org/2021/02/the -geopolitics-of-the-european-green-deal

Chapter 8

1 World Bank data.

2 See Frédéric Bozo, Andreas Rödder and Mary Elise Sarotte (eds.), *German Reunification: A Multinational History* (Routledge, 2017).

3 For a critical analysis of US foreign policy in the era of liberal hegemony, see Stephen Walt, *The Hell of Good Intentions* (Picador, 2018); John S. Mearsheimer, *The Great Delusion: Liberal Dreams and International Realities* (Yale University

Press, 2018); and Jeffrey D. Sachs, *A New Foreign Policy: Beyond American Exceptionalism* (Columbia University Press, 2018). For a more benign view, see Richard Haass, *A World in Disarray; American Foreign Policy and the Crisis of the Old Order* (Penguin, 2017).

4 'The White Man's Burden: The United States and the Philippine Islands' (1899) is a famous poem by Rudyard Kipling in which he exhorted the American reader to take on the responsibility of empire while warning about the personal costs this would entail. See also Niall Ferguson, *Colossus: The Rise and Fall of the American Empire* (Penguin, 2004).

5 Charles Krauthammer, 'The unipolar moment', *Foreign Affairs*, 70/1 (1990), 23–33, http://users.metu.edu.tr/utuba/Krauthammer.pdf

6 Ivan Krastev, 'The missionary who has to become a monastery' (Centre for Liberal Strategies, 2019), https://www.robertboschacademy.de/sites/default/fil es/documents/2020-09/Policy-Paper-Hypocrisy-2019-Final.pdf

7 See George Papakonstantinou and Jean Pisani-Ferry, 'New rules for a new world: a survival kit', *EUI School of Transnational Governance*, 9/2021, May 2021, https://op.europa.eu/el/publication-detail/-/publication/ac278123-b787 -11eb-8aca-01aa75ed71a1/language-en

8 See also Nathalie Tocci, 'The quest for European autonomy', in Helen Wallace, Nikos Koutsiaras and George Pagoulatos (eds.), *Europe's Transformations: Essays in Honour of Loukas Tsoukalis* (Oxford University Press, 2021).

9 André Sapir (ed.), *Fragmented Power: Europe and the Global Economy* (Bruegel, 2007), https://www.bruegel.org/wp-content/uploads/imported/publications /Fragmented_Power_Andre_Sapir.pdf

10 *A Strategic Compass for Security and Defence* (EEAS, 2022). https://www.eeas .europa.eu/eeas/strategic-compass-security-and-defence-1_en. See also Enrico Letta, 'The European Union as a global power?', in Wallace et al., *Europe's Transformations*; and Zaki Laïdi, 'Is Europe ready for power politics?', *EUI Working Papers*, 42 (2019). https://cadmus.eui.eu/bitstream/handle/1814/633 13/RSCAS%202019_42.pdf?sequence=1&isAllowed=y

11 See the carefully documented work of M. E. Sarotte, *Not an Inch: America, Russia, and the Making of the Post-Cold War Stalemate* (Yale University Press, 2021).

12 William J. Burns, *The Back Channel: A Memoir of American Diplomacy and the Case for Its Renewal* (New York: Random House, 2020), 109. For interesting insights into Russian thinking, see also Dmitri Trenin, *Russia* (Polity, 2019).

13 Mark B. Smith, *The Russia Anxiety: And How History Can Resolve It* (Allen Lane, 2019), 386.

14 *Siloviki* is a Russian term referring to members of the security forces who have been occupying many positions of power in the Putin regime.

15 John J. Mearsheimer, 'Why the Ukraine crisis is the West's fault', *Foreign Affairs*, 93/5, 2014, 77–89, https://www.foreignaffairs.com/articles/russia-fsu/2014-08-18/why-ukraine-crisis-west-s-fault

16 Antony J. Blinken, *Ally Versus Ally: America, Europe, and the Siberian Pipeline Crisis* (Praeger, 1987), 4.

17 Valentina Pop, 'Lithuania urges muscular EU security policy in face of Belarus threat', *Financial Times*, 10 June 2021, https://www.ft.com/content/907aa102-47fe-400f-bf01-3c8bfbb5191b

18 The results from polls conducted across Europe independently by two different organizations, the US Pew Research Center and the European Council on Foreign Relations (ECFR), showed repeatedly that positive views about the US under President Trump had indeed reached rock bottom.

19 Robert Kagan, 'A superpower like it or not: why Americans must accept their global role', *Foreign Affairs*, 100/2 (2021), 28–38, 36, https://www.foreignaffairs.com/articles/united-states/2021-02-16/superpower-it-or-not

20 See, for example, the statement signed by big names in top US academic institutions: 'Statement of concern: the threats to American democracy and the need for national voting and election administration standards', *New America*, 1 June 2021, https://www.newamerica.org/political-reform/statements/statement-of-concern

21 See Charles A. Kupchan, *Isolationism: A History of America's Effort to Shield Itself from the World* (Oxford University Press, 2020).

22 *The Good, the Bad and the Ugly* is the title of a classic 'spaghetti Western' film directed by Sergio Leone first released in 1966.

23 Ivan Krastev and Mark Leonard, 'The crisis of American power: how Europeans see Biden's America', *European Council on Foreign Relations*, Policy Brief, 19 January 2021.

24 Among EU members, Austria, Cyprus, Finland, Ireland, Malta and Sweden are not members of NATO. However, as a result of Russia's invasion of Ukraine, Finland and Sweden have applied to join.

25 See Jolyon Howorth, 'Europe and Biden: towards a new transatlantic pact?', *Wilfried Martens Centre for European Studies*, January 2021, https://www.martenscentre.eu/wp-content/uploads/2021/01/CES_POLICY-BRIEF_Biden-V3.pdf. See also Douglas Lute and Nicholas Burns, 'NATO at seventy: an alliance in crisis', *Belfer Center, Harvard Kennedy School*, February 2019, https://www.belfercenter.org/sites/default/files/files/publication/NATOatSeventy.pdf

26 Military expenditure database of the Stockholm International Peace Research Institute (SIPRI).

27 Max Bergmann, James Lamond and Siena Cicarelli, 'The case for EU defense:

a new way for trans-Atlantic security relations', *Center for American Progress*, 1 June 2021, https://www.americanprogress.org/issues/security/reports/2021/06 /01/500099/case-eu-defense

28 *Shared Vision, Common Action: A Stronger Europe – A Global Strategy for the European Union's Foreign and Security Policy* (EEAS, 2016), https://eeas.europa .eu/archives/docs/top_stories/pdf/eugs_review_web.pdf

29 See Sven Biscop, 'European defence and PESCO: don't waste the chance', *EUIDEA Policy Paper*, 1/2020, https://euidea.eu/2020/05/05/european-defen ce-and-pesco-dont-waste-the-chance

30 See also Tobias Bunde, 'Defending European integration by (symbolically) integrating European defence? Germany and its ambivalent role in European security and defence policy', *Journal of European Integration*, 43/2 (2021), 245–61, https://www.researchgate.net/publication/349514694_Defending_Eu ropean_integration_by_symbolically_integrating_European_defence_Germa ny_and_its_ambivalent_role_in_European_security_and_defence_policy

31 See for example Barry R. Posen, 'Europe can defend itself', *Survival*, 62/6, 2020, 7–34, https://doi.org/10.1080/00396338.2020.1851080; Stephen G. Brooks and Hugo Meijer, 'Europe cannot defend itself: the challenge of pooling military power', *Survival*, 63/1, 2021, 33–40, https://doi.org/10.1080/00396338.2021 .1881251

32 For an insightful and balanced analysis, see Grzegorz Kolodko, *China and the Future of Globalization: The Political Economy of China's Rise* (I.B. Tauris, 2020). See also Branko Milanovic, *Capitalism, Alone: The Future of the System That Rules the World* (Harvard University Press, 2019).

33 See Isabella M. Weber, *How China Escaped Shock Therapy: The Market Reform Debate* (Routledge, 2021).

34 See Hal Brands, 'The emerging Biden doctrine: democracy, autocracy, and the defining clash of our time', *Foreign Affairs*, June 2021, https://www.foreignaff airs.com/articles/united-states/2021-06-29/emerging-biden-doctrine. For a US realist perspective, see John S. Mearsheimer, 'The inevitable rivalry: America, China, and the tragedy of Great-Power politics', *Foreign Affairs*, 100/6, 2021, 48–58, https://www.foreignaffairs.com/articles/china/2021-10-19/inevitable- rivalry-cold-war. For a different and very critical view of US policy towards China, see Kishore Mahbubani, *Has China Won? The Chinese Challenge to American Primacy* (Hachette, 2020).

35 Graham Allison, *Destined for War: Can America and China Escape Thucydides's Trap?* (Houghton Mifflin Harcourt, 2017).

36 Kolodko, *China and the Future of Globalization*, 152–6.

37 Jelena Džankić, Soeren Keil and Marco Kmezić (eds.), *The Europeanisation*

of the Western Balkans: The Failure of EU Conditionality (Palgrave Macmillan, 2019).

38 Marc Pierini and Francesco Siccardi, 'Why the EU and the United States should rethink their Turkey policies in 2021', *Carnegie Europe*, 21 January 2021, https://carnegieeurope.eu/2021/01/21/why-eu-and-united-states-should -rethink-their-turkey-policies-in-2021-pub-83662

39 See Andrew Geddes and Peter Scholten, *The Politics of Migration and Immigration in Europe*, 2nd edition (Sage, 2016); Hugo Brady, 'Openness versus helplessness: Europe's 2015–2017 border crisis', *Groupe d'Études Géopolitiques*, 28 June 2021, https://geopolitique.eu/en/2021/06/28/openness-versus-helples sness-europes-2015-2017-border-crisis/?mc_cid=39b02c7c73&mc_eid=b5f27 eb8ef

40 Angeliki Dimitriadi, 'If you can dream it, you can do it? Early thoughts on the New Pact on Migration, and the impact on frontline states', *ELIAMEP Policy Brief*, 132/2020, https://www.eliamep.gr/wp-content/uploads/2020/09/Policy -brief-132-FINAL.pdf

41 For a good survey of EU–Africa relations, see Toni Haastrup, Luis Mah and Niall Dugan (eds.), *The Routledge Handbook of EU–Africa Relations* (Routledge, 2020).

Chapter 9

1 The most influential for years were so-called neo-functionalist theories starting with Ernst B. Haas, *The Uniting of Europe* (Stevens, 1958). They were developed mostly by US political scientists.

2 Mauro Cappelletti, Monica Seccombe and Joseph H. H. Weiler, 'Integration through law: Europe and the American federal experience', in M. Cappelletti et al. (eds.), *Integration through Law* (De Gruyter, 2013), https://www.degruyt er.com/document/doi/10.1515/9783110921540.3/html

3 Claudio M. Radaelli, *Technocracy in the European Union* (Routledge, 1999).

4 Cas Mudde, 'Populism in Europe: an illiberal democratic response to undemo-cratic liberalism – the *Government and Opposition*/Leonard Schapiro Lecture 2019', *Government and Opposition*, 56 (2021), 577–97, 577, https://www.ca mbridge.org/core/journals/government-and-opposition/article/populism-in-eu rope-an-illiberal-democratic-response-to-undemocratic-liberalism-the-govern ment-and-oppositionleonard-schapiro-lecture-2019/C624D1A36A87374340 85C127BE310016. See also Nadia Urbinati, *Me the People: How Populism Transforms Democracy* (Harvard University Press, 2019).

5 See also Yves Mény, 'Liberal democracy and its discontent', in Helen Wallace,

Nikos Koutsiaras and George Pagoulatos (eds.), *Europe's Transformations: Essays in Honour of Loukas Tsoukalis* (Oxford University Press, 2021).

6 Liesbet Hooghe and Gary Marks, 'A postfunctionalist theory of European integration: from permissive consensus to constraining dissensus', *British Journal of Political Science*, 39/1 (2008), 1–23.

7 This is admittedly a very simplified summary of theories of liberal intergovernmentalism that stress the role of national governments in European integration. See the seminal work by Andrew Moravcsik, *The Choice for Europe: Social Purpose and State Power from Messina to Maastricht* (Cornell University Press, 1998). See also Andrew Moravcsik and Frank Schimmelfennig, 'Liberal intergovernmentalism', in Antje Wiener, Tanja A. Börzel and Thomas Risse (eds.), *European Integration Theory*, 3rd edition (Oxford University Press, 2019).

8 Jürgen Habermas, 'Democracy, solidarity and the European crisis', lecture delivered in Leuven University on 26 April 2013, https://www.pro-europa.eu/europe/jurgen-habermas-democracy-solidarity-and-the-european-crisis

9 Dani Rodrik, *The Globalization Paradox: Why Global Markets, States and Democracy Can't Coexist* (Oxford University Press, 2011).

10 Kalypso Nicolaïdis, 'European democracy and its crisis', *Journal of Common Market Studies*, 51/2 (2013), 351–69.

11 See Paul Lendvai, *Orbán: Hungary's New Strongman* (Oxford University Press, 2018). And for a very different perspective in defence of Fidesz and Hungarian nationhood against 'left-liberal hegemony' exercised through European institutions, see George Schöpflin, 'What if?', *Hungarian Review*, 9/6 (2018).

12 According to the 'Global Freedom Score' compiled by Freedom House for 2020, https://freedomhouse.org/countries/freedom-world/scores

13 See Yascha Mounk, 'Democracy in Poland is in mortal danger', *The Atlantic*, 9 October 2019, https://www.theatlantic.com/ideas/archive/2019/10/poland-could-lose-its-democracy/599590. It got much worse after he wrote the article.

14 Daniel Kelemen, 'The European Union's authoritarian equilibrium', *Journal of European Public Policy*, 27/3 (2020), 481–99, https://www.tandfonline.com/doi/abs/10.1080/13501763.2020.1712455

15 Jacques Rupnik, 'The east–west divide revisited 30 years on', in Helen Wallace, Nikos Koutsiaras and George Pagoulatos (eds.), *Europe's Transformations: Essays in Honour of Loukas Tsoukalis* (Oxford University Press, 2021).

16 See Janis A. Emmanouilidis, 'Differentiated EUrope 2035: elaboration and evaluation of five potential scenarios', *EUIDEA Policy Papers*, September 2021, https://www.iai.it/en/pubblicazioni/differentiated-europe-2035-elaboration-and-evaluation-five-potential-scenarios

17 See also Herman Van Rompuy, 'Are we still allowed to dream?', in Wallace et al., *Europe's Transformations*.

18 See Frank Schimmelfennig and Thomas Winzen, *Ever Looser Union? Differentiated European Integration* (Oxford University Press, 2020).

19 See, for example, Federico Fabbrini, 'Reforming the EU outside the EU? The Conference on the Future of Europe and its options', *European Papers*, 2020, 5/2, 963–82, https://www.europeanpapers.eu/en/e-journal/reforming-eu-outside-eu-conference-future-europe. See also Sergio Fabbrini, *Europe's Future: Decoupling and Reforming* (Cambridge University Press, 2019). And for French readers, a road map for the creation of a European political union by a former member of the legal service of the Council of the EU: Christos Mavrakos, 'Une feuille de route en vue de la création d'une Union politique européenne (UPE): six étapes à suivre pour y parvenir', *ELIAMEP Policy Paper*, 2019, No. 29, https://www.eliamep.gr/wp-content/uploads/2019/11/Policy-Paper-No-29-Mavrakos-final-1.pdf

Chapter 10

1 Hedley Bull, *The Anarchical Society: A Study of Order in World Politics* (Macmillan, 1977). The author was one of the leading theorists of international relations and my mentor in my early Oxford days.

2 Christopher Hill, 'The capability–expectations gap, or conceptualizing Europe's international role', *Journal of Common Market Studies*, 31/3, 1993, 305–28.

Index

Page numbers in *italics* denote a figure.

European integration (*cont.*)
  lopsided 23–6
  parting of ways between
    globalization and 61
  and rule of law in member countries
    195–8
  winners and losers issue 24
European Investment Bank (EIB) 146
European Parliament *see* EP
European People's Party 196
European Public Prosecutor's Office
  (EPPO) 98
European Security Council proposal
  168
European Stability Mechanism (ESM)
  60, 91, 200–1
Euroscepticism, growth of 185
Eurozone 31, 70, 86–7, 91, 202, 214
  budget proposal 120–1
  and democratic accountability 99
  inflation 94
  managing of euro crisis 200–1
  north–south division inside the 90
exchange rates 82, 85–6
  search for stability 82–3
Eyskens, Mark 167

Facebook 129
'factory economies' 137
fake news 128
far-right parties 37, 38, 39, 41, 187
farmers 124
Fidesz Party (Hungary) 193, 196, 197
financial crisis 22, 30–1, 38, 69, 80,
    92, 105, 108, 112, 113, 213
  see also euro crisis
financial sector, growth of 108
Financial Times 132, 162
Finland 66–7
Fiscal Compact 200–1
Five Presidents report (2013) 80–1
5G 128, 134, 173
foreign direct investment 152

foreign investment, incoming 136–8
  joint screening legislation (2020) 138
former Soviet republics 28, 35, 36,
    154, 158, 220
'Fortress Europe' 48
Four Presidents report (2012) 80–1
France 46–8, 66, 72, 112
  central role of in European
    integration 63–4
  and defence 168–9
  and EMU 19, 21
  and euro crisis 31
  gilets jaunes protest 141–2
  and Iraq war 35
  Macron defeats Le Pen in
    presidential election (2022) 47–8
  Macron's ideas on Europe 48
  referendum on constitutional treaty
    and rejection of (2005) 29, 191,
    192
  relations and cooperation with
    Germany 63, 64–5, 93, 99, 102–3
Fratzscher, Marcel 60
free movement of people 38, 54,
    113–14, 117, 211, 212
free trade 25, 56, 123, 217
Freedom House 194
Fridays for Future movement 141
Friedman, Milton 57, 95
Friedman, Thomas 69, 109
Frontex 180
'frugals' 66
Fukuyama, Francis 26

Gaia-X 135
gangster capitalism 27
gas prices, rise in 145
GDP
  EU-27 world share of 152
  government spending share of 110
  leaving EU entails drop in 104
General Data Protection Regulation
  (GDPR) (2018) 132

IMF (International Monetary Fund)
33–4, 97, 98, 103
immigration crisis (2015) 22, 37–41
Merkel's strategy 40–1
similarities with euro crisis 41
immigration/immigrants 48, 108,
179–81, 220
anti-immigration parties 179–80
European attempts to discourage
large inflows 180
and 'Fortress Europe' 48
and people smuggling 179
remittances sent home 114
resistance to 114
and Ukraine War 181
industrial policy 136, 138
inequality(ies) 56–7, 105–6, 108–15,
125, 208, 213
elephant curve of 105–7, *106*
and European integration 112–15
factors explaining 107–9
growth in 59, 61, 126
as ideological and political 110
technological change and rise in
109, 129
US and income/wealth 111
wealth distribution 111
inflation 98
rise in 57
integration, internal cumulative logic
of 183
interdependence
economic 101, 123, 126, 139, 150,
156, 159, 161, 217
global 174, 216, 217
intergovernmental agreements 199,
200–1
outside the EU legal framework
199
Intergovernmental Panel on Climate
Change (IPCC) 140
International Monetary Fund *see* IMF
internet, birth of 133

Iran nuclear deal 74
Iraq war (2003) 34–5, 73
Ireland 32, 56, 87
and ECB 94
and taxation 119
and treaty revision referendums 192
Italy 50, 51–2, 65
and coronavirus pandemic 65
and ECB 94
and European recovery programme
52
and Euroscepticism 65

Japan 173
and public debt 98
Johnson, Boris 45
Juncker, Jean-Claude 33, 167
Just Transition Fund 147

Kaczyński, Jarosław 194
Kagan, Robert 164
Kazakhstan 28
Kennan, George 157–8
Kennedy School of Harvard University
46
Keynes, John Maynard 11, 85–6
Keynesian liquidity trap 97
Keynesianism 57
Kissinger, Henry 36
Klaus, Václav 27
Knapp, Wilfrid 11
Kohl, Helmut 19, 20, 83
Kosovo 177
Krastev, Ivan 113, 155, 194
Kuka 136
Kyoto Protocol (1997) 142, 143

labour markets 57–8
and gig economy 57
Labour Party (Britain) 24–5
Lakner, Christoph 105
Latvia 113
Le Pen, Marine 47, 195